THE COMPLETE BOOK
OF HOME REMODELING,
IMPROVEMENT, AND REPAIR

THE COMPLETE BOOK
OF HOME REMODELING,
IMPROVEMENT, AND REPAIR:

A Handbook for the Owner
Who Wants to Do It Right—
but Not Do It Himself

---

by A. M. Watkins

AVENEL BOOKS • NEW YORK

This book is for MARY ELLEN, and in general to all those who own houses but sometimes wish they didn't.

Contents

What This Book Is About

This is a guide and reference book for the more than 33 million American families who own their own houses but still have housing problems. It is for the homeowner—not the do-it-yourself handyman—who is confronted with one or more of three widespread housing problems:

First is the squeeze on living space. You need more room for your household activities, for the children, or for other pressing reasons. Or you merely crave a basement playroom, new porch, or new outdoor patio. How do you go about it logically and sensibly? Or should you buy a larger house?

Second is the need for remodeling and modernization. The kitchen or bathroom (or both) cries out for a new lease on life—modernization. You may merely wish to break through a wall to make the house more livable, move a door, or add new features like a handsome picture window, an attic fan, or even air conditioning. What planning principles and tricks of the trade should you know to get a successful job at a fair price?

Third is the recurring problem of maintenance and repairs. The heating, wiring, or plumbing is run-down and can't be put off any longer. We wish such problems would go away but it seems as if there is always something urgent to be done—a new paint job, a new roof (signaled by leaks), a remedy for a wet basement, or termites which portend real trouble (though not always, as reported in Chapter 23). Such problems usually confront us as emergencies (naturally) and more than ever we need immediate guidance. This book within reach, like Dr. Spock's for mothers, is designed to provide informed guidance when you must know about such things fast, as well as when you plan to remodel or modernize.

A Sampling of the Contents

A few examples will illustrate the viewpoint and content of this book:

Does it pay to remodel your present house or should you buy another house?

Is your house fundamentally suited for remodeling? What basic architectural rules should you use to determine how and where new rooms should be added?

What are the key facts to consider, depending on the project, when you plan a new kitchen or bathroom, finish off the attic or bathroom, or add a new wing?

What is one of the best and least expensive ways of improving the design and livability of almost any house, quickly and easily? (See Chapter 13.)

What are the most common causes of high upkeep and maintenance expense in houses? How can you check them once and for all?

What should you know about choosing high-quality building materials and products (without paying luxury prices), such as wall and floor materials, heating, wiring, exterior paints, roofing, and insulation?

When are brand-name products a reliable guide to quality and when are they not?

How do you find reliable contractors and repairmen? What essential points should be written into every contract?

What are the most widespread home-improvement rackets to avoid?

The answers to these and a host of other questions are answered in detail in the following chapters.

The Purpose of This Book

This book, in brief, is for men and women who are enthusiastically interested in houses and want to know what makes a successful house. Its aim is to help you plan and execute home improvements, avoid the common (and often painful) pitfalls, and help you discriminate between the impulsive change of plan, which may sound marvelous in concept but doesn't work out in practice, and the remodeling plan which will really turn out to be a genuine success. You need not absorb a lot of technical data. The knowledge required (and presented here) is basically nontechnical and much effort has been made to present it in clear and understandable words.

This book is also for those who may not be particularly interested in houses per se, but want and often need quick nontechnical facts about specific parts of their houses when suddenly confronted with the need for urgent remedial work or repairs. It is for people who desire to talk knowingly and with confidence to contractors and home repairmen so that they can understand them and, equally important, so they can understand you.

Though this book is expressly not for the do-it-yourself handyman, there is nonetheless much useful information here, too, if you tackle your own work yourself. You will not find step-by-step rules for using power tools and building a new room by hand. But you will find essential facts about the proper design and execution of such projects, plus such things as how to choose the best-quality materials at the lowest prices consistent with long-term satisfaction.

Contracting Your Work vs. Doing It Yourself

A few things should be said about the virtues of contracting your own work versus doing it yourself. Unless you are handy with tools and enjoy such work, it's usually best to stick to your own profession (or hobby) and farm out the work on your house.

The savings envisioned on do-it-yourself jobs are often an illusion. What you may save on labor is offset several times over by emotional wear and tear and maddening delays (largely because of inexperience). There is also the decided likelihood that the amateur will botch up a job simply because of limited knowledge.

To do your own work you will need a full quota of tools, which costs money. An expensive tool is often required for one kind of job and is never needed again. You are generally charged top prices for lumber and other materials. The professional contractor not only buys at contractors' discounts but he also knows when low-cost lumber is perfectly satisfactory for a given job, whereas the unsuspecting homeowner is sold a high-priced bill of goods over the counter.

It is far more satisfactory and far less time-consuming when you know exactly what results you desire and then hire it out to be done. You leave the cutting, sawing, and mitering to skilled workmen. Be firm about the quality of the products used and the results desired. Leave the details to the specialists.

Do-it-yourself work can indeed be highly satisfying if you like such work, if it is your hobby, or if the money saved on labor means a great deal to you. If so, by all means go ahead. The easiest jobs are the simple manual jobs that require few tools, such as building shelves, painting, or putting down insulation between ceiling joists. Sometimes, of course, we are compelled to do our own work simply because we want to have it done exactly right. We'd gladly pay the going price for a dependable workman, but try and find one.

On the other hand, there are certain jobs that no one but an expert should tackle. The amateur treads on dangerous ground when he takes on such work as wiring, plumbing, tinkering with the heating system, breaking through a wall, and sometimes even when putting down a new kitchen countertop. Such work can be decidedly hazardous, if not so intricate that a small oversight can lead to outright calamity. This does not mean that you should refrain from changing a faucet washer (but know in advance that the exposed faucet neck should be properly protected before you apply the wrench). It means that a good pro generally can save you much time and trouble, leaving you free to do other things (or just sit out back enjoying yourself while the work is underway).

The Author's Credentials

"Upon what meat doth this our Caesar feed . . . ?" I am a graduate engineer and professional writer with experience in the building field. I have been an associate editor of *House & Home* and *Architectural Forum* magazines, and am author of the book, *Building or Buying the High-Quality House at the Lowest Cost,* and the booklet, "How to Judge a House." I have written numerous articles about housing and houses for such magazines as *American Home, Better Homes & Gardens, Harper's, House & Garden, Redbook,* and others. I am also a homeowner with first-hand experience (much of it frustrating in the beginning in remodeling and repairing my own houses).

Much of this book therefore reflects what I have learned from personal experience, on top of much research into the various phases of home improvement and remodeling, including interviews and discussions with remodeling contractors, builders, architects, engineers, and home-product manufacturers.

But unfortunately no one can tell you the best products to buy when new rooms are built, when a house is painted, or when you buy a new furnace, new kitchen fixtures, bathroom products, and so on. Too many technical considerations constantly intrude. There is no one pat answer for every such question.

Great effort is made, however, to steer you toward the special qualities and characteristics to seek out in particular products and materials. And rather than pussyfoot, leaving the reader dangling on half-answers, I have chosen whenever possible to make specific recommendations about products, based on a consensus of opinion gathered for this book, coupled with my personal conclusions. Specific recommendations on products can be made because the publisher and I will not have to contend with horrified advertisers (usually those whose products are deficient in quality).

The contents of this book reflect the author's opinion throughout for the same reasons given by Somerset Maugham in *The Summing Up.* If he seems to express himself dogmatically, he said, "it is only because I find it very boring to qualify every phrase with an 'I think or to my mind.' Everything I say is merely an opinion of my own . . . there is only one thing about which I am certain, and this is that there is very little about which one can be certain."

The nature of some of this book is basically technical, of course, and requires technical substantiation. There is such substantiation throughout, I assure you, even if every subject is not documented by reams of supporting technical facts. In many cases the pros and cons of a subject are presented squarely on all sides and followed by a concluding opinion of what I think is clearly the best recommendation.

A few other points: To simplify things for the reader, the book is divided into separate sections dealing with the broad phases of remodeling and home improvement. It is plainly not necessary to read the various sections consecutively, though this may be useful. At the end of the book a summary check list is included for quick reference before you go ahead on a particular job or just before you buy a major part for your house.

By necessity, the subject of some chapters overlaps material presented in other chapters. Certain facts, for instance, on having a warm, new room coincide with essential information in the chapters on heating and insulation. Rather than repeat whole sections again, you are therefore referred to the chapter with the background facts. Occasional repetition does occur in some chapters in order to make the chapters as self-sufficient as possible. Essential facts are also repeated here and there to avoid too much cross-referencing for the reader.

ACKNOWLEDGMENTS

Some of the material in this book is excerpted in part or uses basic research from published magazine articles by the author. I wish to thank the following magazines for permission to use such material:

The American Home for material in "The Ten Biggest Home Improvement Rackets," and in the "Bathroom" chapter; *Better Homes & Gardens* for excerpts in "Central Air Conditioning" and "Insulation"; *Home Modernizing* for material in "Converting a Porch to a Year-round Room," and to *Redbook* for material in "Avoiding Home Repair Bills."

Credit is given to *New Homes Guide* and *House Beautiful's Building Manual* for occasional use of research material used in articles by the author originally published by each.

Small portions of this book were published (in another form) in a book written by the author, *Building or Buying the High-Quality House at the Lowest Cost,* and in a booklet "How to Judge a House," also by the author.

The author is also grateful for helpful advice and suggestions from Doubleday editors Sam Vaughan, Jake Page, and Denise Rathbun, and also to their assistants Anne Hutchens and Nancy Dravneek.

Part 1

WHEN IS REMODELING WORTHWHILE —FOR YOUR PRESENT HOUSE —OR ONE YOU MAY BUY?

Should you invest a lot of money into improving your present house, or is it better to buy another, more suitable house? What would complete remodeling cost? Which improvements increase the resale value of your house? Which do not pay out?

Another alternative, considered a challenge if not an adventure by many people, is buying a big, old house at a bargain price and turning it into a silk purse. Though Mr. Blandings tried it, he made an expensive mistake (to put it kindly). How do you determine if a big old house is truly a bargain? (For that matter, many of the same guides for judging the remodeling potential of an old house for sale can be used for judging the potential of your present house.) These are a few of the important questions that confront every family bent on remodeling and are discussed in this first section.

Inherent charm and character of old houses are reasons for staying put if you live in one, or buying and remodeling one, rather than a new house. Such houses are usually located in an established neighborhood with trees, lawn, and stable taxes. But check for the nine most common flaws encountered in old houses, described in text.

National Lumber Mfrs. Assn.

Chapter 1

Should You Buy and Remodel
Another House?

Your present house is inadequate. The children demand more space. Your mother moves in, or your house is no longer adequate for your social activities, or you simply want more elbow room. A host of reasons can put pressure on obtaining more living space or simply improving the efficiency of existing space. Should you pour money into improvements or buy another house?

The Advantages of Remodeling

The biggest single reason for remodeling a house is its location. Most of us have deep roots in our neighborhoods—friends, children's playmates, ties to schools, churches, social groups, and established relationships with merchants (and also perhaps to home-improvement contractors). Buying another house generally means cutting old ties and starting off anew, which can be a severe wrench to parents and children alike (unless with a stroke of luck you discover the ideal house nearby).

Often overlooked is the cost of moving, which can be steep—as much as a couple of thousand dollars above and over the buying price of another house. On top of the movers' bill, this includes expenses for closing costs, the inevitable decorating expenses (new curtains, painting), furniture, and, especially for a new house, landscaping.

A new house nearly always means additional expenses for screens, and storm windows, extra kitchen cabinets, more storage, and a painful assortment of other bills that easily can add up to $500 or $1000 before you're done. Your commuting-to-work costs and taxes may be higher, plus very likely a higher interest rate on the new mortgage than on your present mortgage. This is why the cost of moving, and tackling the immediate needs of a new house can add up to at least $1000 and sometimes as much as $2000 over the cost of the house. The same money by itself probably could pay for considerable improvement of your present house.

This Victorian house, built in 1896, was bought by author despite need for repairs. It offered much space—1750 square feet of living area, including five rooms upstairs, for approximately $10,000 under the price of a new house of comparable size.

Cost of Buying Another House vs. *Remodeling Cost*

The economics of buying versus remodeling obviously will vary from family to family. Here are the various expenses to figure:

1. Total cost of buying another house
Price of new house $——

Closing costs: title search and insurance, mortgage fees (usually ½ to 1 per cent of mortgage amount), state and federal transfer taxes, lawyer's fees, appraisal charge, survey, recording deed. Figure from $350 up to $750, more for large, expensive houses.   ——

Packing and moving expenses   ——

New decorating needs (essential lamps, rugs, curtains, special paint, new furniture, odds and ends)   ——

Landscaping   ——

Other costs related to buying and living in a new house
For example, will you need a second car? _____

A. Total cost of a new house $_____

B. Minus price obtainable for your present house
(Be realistic—most houses do not bring as much as we
would like)   —_____

C. Net outlay for a new house $_____

    2. Total cost of remodeling and improving your present
house
Estimated total cost of remodeling construction and materials $_____
Financing and credit charges if remodeling is financed
(This varies according to the kind of loan. Figure at least
10 to 12 per cent simple annual interest for a regular home
improvement loan, noted in Chapter 32; about 6 per cent
if you refinance your present mortgage or obtain a second
mortgage)   _____
Closing costs and fees, if mortgage refinancing is obtained   _____

D. Total cost of remodeling and staying with your present
house $_____

E. Difference in cost between buying a new house and remodeling your present house
    Net cost of new house, Line C above $_____
    Cost of remodeling, Line D above   —_____
Difference in cost between buying and remodeling $_____
    (If cost of remodeling exceeds cost of buying, subtract
    Line C from Line D)

A few notes: To avoid complications, the above tabulation omits such
things as commuting costs, and the difference between interest charges
on your present mortgage and a new mortgage. Also consider the cost of
upkeep and maintenance for a new house compared with an existing
house. Don't be misled here. It may surprise you, but the cost of upkeep
and repairs for new houses often runs higher than for old houses. According to one telling survey, new-house owners spend an average of
$335 a year for maintenance and repairs, versus $150 a year by the
owners of older houses. Buying a new house does not necessarily solve all
one's problems.

Flat-roof house of 1000 square feet (before photo) was doubled in size by raising the roof and inserting four bedrooms and a bath upstairs at a cost of approximately $10,000. Removal of closets for first-floor bedrooms provided space for stairway. Two first-floor bedrooms were combined and turned into a spacious family room.
House Beautiful's Building Manual.

Disadvantages of Remodeling

Your present neighborhood may be losing appeal. A move may be motivated by better schools in another area. The neighborhood may be going downhill and it's time to get out; lacking strict residential zoning protection, your house may be hemmed in more and more by stores, gas stations, and even factories. Or a proposed new superhighway may slice through the neighborhood like a scythe.

On top of this, large-scale remodeling is no picnic. It often involves delays and much concern. You will live amid a stream of workmen coming in and out for what seems like years. It takes patience and endurance. If temperamentally unsuited for it, you may do better to sell out and get another house. And of course your house may be so old and structurally rundown that it is unsuitable for remodeling. The structure must be sound to begin with.

How Much Remodeling Is Practical?

Assume you wish to remodel. Will you get your money back if you decide to sell the house later?

For years real estate people have cautioned against putting so much money into a house that it becomes overpriced for its neighborhood. In other words, don't expect to get $30,000 for a house where the best houses in the area are worth no more than $25,000. A house worth $21,000 in the same neighborhood can not stand more than $4000 worth of improvements. No matter how much more money is spent on improving the house, if sold later it is not likely to bring more than $25,000.

Some experts offer a flat rule of thumb: Don't improve a house by more than 30 per cent of its current value. Otherwise you pass the point of diminishing returns. You will not get your money back if you decide later to sell.

Good Exceptions to the Rule

For one thing, many of us like our house and neighborhood and intend to stay put for a long time. We want a better house for our own pleasure and enjoyment. All right, we may not retrieve our entire investment if we sell someday. That will not bar us from enjoying a modern house up to the hilt while we're in it. Besides, depreciation is to be expected every year.

For another thing, the rule of diminishing returns applies mainly to older houses and uniform neighborhoods. It does not hold firm in other parts of a town and in many housing developments built since the end of World War II. Nearly everybody in such places has remodeled. Most of the houses around are worth considerably more money than their original cost.

A classic example is Levittown, Long Island (which critics at one time blithely consigned to the slums of the future). Not only has Levittown blossomed with literally thousands of new trees (and made fools of the critics), but houses that originally sold there for $7500 and $8000 now sell for $10,000 to as much as $20,000 (!)—over double the original price in some cases.

What Should You Do?

If in doubt get suggestions from a few bankers and real estate brokers. Figure the total cost of the improvements desired. This behooves you to make a complete list of all improvements and repairs desired, not only for new living space but also for modernizing a kitchen or bath, and bringing up to date such things as the wiring and heating plant.

The decision may hinge on practical considerations and emotional reasons. If a man expects to be transferred in a few years, extensive remodeling is obviously unwise. On the other hand, if you plan to stay where you are, you really like your house and are attached to the neighborhood, remodeling is your best bet (even if you must put more money into it than a conservative would recommend).

Cut through the surface layers to your basic bedrock desires. Do you really want a new house and a fresh start or perhaps a step-up to a bigger, more impressive house? If that's what you *really* want, don't waste time and money on remodeling.

Or do you really like and enjoy your present house. Are you so strongly attached to your neighborhood that moving would be a severe wrench that you will always regret, and with only a little more room or extra facilities your present house would be perfectly satisfactory? Then remodeling can be a richly rewarding experience.

After all the hard pro and con facts have been weighed one against the other, how do you honestly *feel* about moving versus remodeling? This is largely an emotional decision, tempered by realities, to be sure. But it is usually the best indication of what to do.

What Improvements Most Increase House Value?

Improving a house is no guarantee that it will be worth more money even if you do not price it above the prevailing price level of the other houses around. Be aware of this. Some people are fired by the idea of expanding and modernizing a house in order to sell it later at a high price. At the very least, they expect to get every cent back spent on improvements. This is speculative business.

Some improvements decidedly increase house value, others do not. Adding space adds the greatest value to a house (provided it is well designed); e.g. a third or fourth bedroom, or a family room. A new kitchen and new bathrooms also add distinct value.

But don't expect to get back all the money spent on such improvements in a higher house price if you later sell. This seldom happens. Such improvements may serve only to firm up the market value of a house and that's all. Without them, your house otherwise may go begging later or sell at a deflated price. With them, you succeed only in putting a floor under the resale value of the house.

Which Do Not?

Certain kinds of improvements mean little to home buyers. These include such things as a basement recreation room, paneled den, a new patio (however glamorous), an outdoor barbecue pit, and, particularly notorious, a back-yard swimming pool (which scares off many buyers). Buyer psychology is a peculiar thing, real estate agents find. The typical prospect says, "That's a fine new recreation room, but I can buy a house down the road without one for $1000 less. (Later he may spend the equivalent time and money to finish off the basement there.)

In short, remodeling a house should be tackled for its own sake, for the benefits to you and your family. The increased value to you is the main consideration. The increased resale value of the house should be a secondary point. This view can also pay off if you must sell later. For well-chosen remodeling, done primarily to improve a house for your family, rather than with one eye on what an unknown future buyer may desire, is more likely to be a real triumph, and then indeed make your house substantially more appealing to other people.

What Does Remodeling Cost?

Here is a range of costs for the most popular home-improvement work. I emphasize strongly that these are *approximate* costs for typical houses in the $20,000–$30,000 price bracket. They are listed here to give you an idea of approximate costs. No two jobs are alike and your specific work could cost more or less than the average.

Modernized kitchen	From $2000 to $5000, depending on size and number of new cabinets and appliances

Modernized bathroom	$1250 to $2500, depending on size, kind and amount of tile and plumbing work
New, full bathroom	$1500 to $3500
New half-bath	$600 to $1250, provided partitioned space is available
New interior living space (converting attic, garage, or basement)	$750 to $2500, depending on size and new construction required
New exterior rooms added onto house	$6 to $10 a square foot, depending on heating and wiring required, excluding kitchen and bathrooms
Exterior painting	$400 to $1000 depending on house size and number of windows and doors
Interior painting	$350 to $1000 depending on number of rooms
New roofing	$20 to $30 per 100 square feet of roof for asphalt shingles
Wall and attic insulation	$300 to $700, depending on house size
New warm-air heating furnace	$400 to $1000
Hot water heating boiler	$500 to $1250
Complete new heating system	$1500 to $3500 depending on house size and kind of heating
Water heater	$125 to $225
Typical plumbing repairs	$250 to $600
New carport	$500 to $1000
Garage	$1000 to $1500
Fireplace	$500 to $1250 depending on type, location, and amount of "cutting-in" work
Screened porch	$750 to $1500
Patio	$175 to $300 for 10×20-foot concrete slab only

Chapter 2

Buying and Remodeling
a Large, Old House

The biggest single appeal of a large old house is *space*. Many older houses have 50 to 100 per cent more space than new houses at the same price. As a rule, this means houses built before World War II.

More and more old houses are going begging in today's market. After being put up for sale at wildly high prices with no takers, they often can be had for considerably less money. The market abounds with potential bargains but you must seek them out with care. The older the house, the more likely the need for expensive repairs and improvements. What may seem like a bargain at first can turn out to be a hellish white elephant.

An old house is a bargain only if it is fundamentally sound. Its structure and utilities should be checked thoroughly by an expert. Don't take the casual word of a real estate agent or even that of a friend. Too much money is at stake.*

An old house is truly a good buy only if its price *plus the cost of necessary improvements* does not exceed the price of a new house of comparable size. This key fact will tell you if you have really sniffed out a bargain. A rough estimate can be made from the cost figures in the last chapter, but firm bids for the essential improvements needed should be obtained before you buy the house.

---

* Best expert for checking a house is a good builder, architect, or remodeling contractor (preferably one whom you will call on to do the remodeling). If you live in Chicago, Detroit, Indianapolis, northern New Jersey, or within 75 miles of New York City, call Home Inspection Consultants, Inc. (listed in the phone book). This is a firm of professional engineers that inspects houses for prospective buyers for $35 to $50, depending on house price, 1/10 of 1 per cent of house price for houses priced at $50,000 or higher. It expects to expand to other cities in the future. You could also read the chapters on "Buying an Old House" and "Who Can Check a House For You?" in *Building or Buying the High-Quality House at the Lowest Cost* (Doubleday, $4.95).

New house prices today range from about $12 per square foot of living area (excluding garage and basement) up to about $20 a square foot, somewhat more for custom-built houses. The exact price depends on local building costs. A good old house may be had for less than $8 to $10 per square foot. The trick, of course, is to be sure that the gap in the price is not quickly breached and exceeded by the additional cost of essential improvements.

Other Old-House Advantages

An old house is ensconced in an established neighborhood and often has trees and charm. You may even find one in your present neighborhood. It may even be sitting on highly expensive land that would otherwise cost you dearly if bought as a vacant lot.

The dirty work of modernizing can be done before you move in, an inestimable advantage. Workmen will not be underfoot, and they can get their work done faster and more efficiently when not coping with people living in the house at the same time.

The cost of remodeling sometimes can be financed along with the

Remodeled house in Portland, Oregon, was formerly an old farmhouse, "before" photograph. The handsome results are shown in the "after" photograph. Bay window in old dining room was replaced with sliding glass doors and opens on a new porch deck of Douglas fir. House was fundamentally sound and bought for $9500. An additional $10,000 was spent on remodeling, including extensive interior changes, new kitchen and bathroom, as well as new exterior wall siding installed over old wood shingles. Remodeling design by Ron Barrows and Dick Miller.

Photos courtesy Western Pine Assn. Charles R. Pearson.

house cost itself under one mortgage. Say an old house is priced at $18,000 and $10,000 worth of improvements are needed. Your total $28,000 cost could then be financed with one mortgage as if you were buying a $28,000 house.

But first you must get firm estimates on the necessary improvements, and then an appraisal of the future value of the house *after remodeling*. Naturally the mortgage lender needs assurance that the improvements will make the house worth $28,000 or he will not risk a loan. Such financing involves planning and special arrangements, and you have to talk with bankers and/or savings and loan officials.

Buying an Old House

The rest of this chapter is chiefly for readers who are seriously shopping for an old house. Others can skip it.

Primary considerations with an old house you may buy are its basic design, room layout, and suitability for your family. Rules for judging the floor plan are the same as those for judging the remodeling potential of an existing house (following chapter).

Is the house located in a good neighborhood? This is of high importance. The neighborhood should not be going downhill and it should be zoned strictly for residential use. Check this at the town or village hall.

Does the house appeal to *you?* This is a personal thing. Do you really like the house with no doubts about it? The danger here is being soaked a wildly high price just for charm, particularly with the large number of old wrecks on the market priced sky high solely because of an idyllic brook running through the property. There is little charm and less profit if the place has to be completely rebuilt.

The Ten Most Common Flaws in an Old House

Most old houses have 1. *old-fashioned kitchens* and 2. *inadequate bathrooms*. These are the two leading deficiencies likely to be encountered and often the most expensive to correct. Figure accordingly—as much as $5000 to $6000 of modernizing expense right in the beginning, unless you can accept the existing kitchen and bathroom facilities. Don't talk yourself into this too easily. A woman spends much time in her kitchen and the whole family makes demands on a single bathroom—often at one time.

Moreover, various other repairs are generally needed. Arthur Tauscher, president of Home Inspection Consultants, Inc., recorded the construction flaws encountered in a random sampling of 1000 houses over ten years old that his firm had inspected for prospective buyers. The two most fre-

Even the most run-down houses can be successfully modernized if the structure is fundamentally sound, as shown here. A 100-year-old derelict Wisconsin farmhouse was transformed into a handsome dwelling. Old-fashioned porch was enclosed to gain space for kitchen and living room. Front door was moved to permit better interior furniture placement and windows were rearranged and new ones added.

quent ones were overloaded wiring (in 84 per cent of the houses) and termites or wood rot (in 58 per cent).

Based on such findings, the following is a summary of the most common flaws to look for in an old house you may buy and how to detect each. Not all old houses, however, are rife with flaws. By and large, only two or three of the following common flaws may be present in an older house, and they may not be severe in houses less than ten years old.

3. *Inadequate wiring.* This is the most widespread construction flaw. The older the house, the poorer the wiring is likely to be unless a previous owner has rewired. There should be a 3-wire, 240-volt, 100-ampere capacity main electric board, more for large houses or if there is an electric range or electric heat. You can usually see three wires from the electric pole to the house. If only two are visible, it is an obsolete 120-volt service. Be sure you're looking at the overhead electric wires to the meter, not the telephone wires. The amperage capacity is normally noted on the main electric board. (There is also an ampere number on the meter, which is something else again.)

Look for plenty of electric outlets, switches, and lighting fixtures throughout the house. Normally look for at least one electric outlet in each wall of every room, two or more in long walls, at least two or three outlets concentrated above the kitchen countertop work space for appliances, a wall switch for every ceiling light fixture and (for ideal wiring but seldom seen) a light control switch at each door in rooms with two or more doors.

4. *Termite damage and wood rot.* These occur mostly in houses more than five to ten years old, and are hard to detect unless you are an expert. Have a termite expert check the house before you buy. FHA and VA officials generally require this before they will approve a mortgage on an old house. Its importance cannot be overemphasized. Wood rot can be searched out at the same time.

5. *Rundown heating.* This depends largely on house age and the type of heating. Many houses over 25 years old were built with a coal heating plant which may have been converted to oil or gas. If the original hot-water or steam heat is still in a house 25 years or older, how much longer it will last is questionable. Look on the boiler name plate to see if it is cast iron or steel. (No name plate is an indication of a low-quality heater). The cast-iron kind is likely to last longer. Look inside for signs of cracking, and around the exterior base for rust and general deterioration. If the heater is a large, old, hot-air gravity furnace with no fan, it too is likely to expire at any time.

A heating plant in a house only 10 or 15 years old also can be troublesome. Sometimes the unit is too small for the house. The best way to check this is to visit the house on a cold day, if possible. Have the system turned on and the thermostat up to 80 degrees. How long does it take for heat to reach each room after starting? A warm-air system should provide heat within 10 or 15 minutes, a hot-water or steam system within a half hour. Also listen for noisy operations.

Does the heater burn gas, oil, or coal? Gas burners last the longest and are generally best of all, provided local gas rates are not high. If in doubt about an oil burner, a serviceman should give it a combustion test. (He checks the exhaust gases leaving the heater. They should not exceed 600 degrees F. after 20 to 30 minutes; the CO_2 content of the flue gas should be between 8½ and 14 per cent. Among other things, the burner flame should be bright yellow with orange tips and *no smoke*.) Look and sniff around the bottom of the oil tank and on the floor below the tank for signs of oil. If there are signs, the tank probably leaks and you will need a new one.

"Radiant heat" (usually through pipes laid in the concrete slab floor) should be approached warily. Defects are difficult to correct. Though a good system when properly installed, many of them were not put in as well as they should have been, particularly in development houses. It is less likely to be troublesome when encountered in a custom-built house. It should have indoor-outdoor temperature controls (a small temperature sensing device on an outside wall wired to the inside controls).

As for coal heat, experts say that it is risky to convert a coal unit to automatic gas or oil if the equipment is more than 15 to 20 years old. If it is older and you prefer gas or oil, figure on replacing the entire heating unit, not merely converting it to gas or oil.

Take the name and phone number of the heating dealer who services the system. This is usually noted on a card near the heating unit. Ask him about the system. What kind of repairs are needed? How long will the system last? He may or may not come clean with you, but what you may learn is worth the effort.

6. *Sagging structure.* The foundation may have settled and wrenched the house out of joint, or beams may have sagged as a result of wood rot. Look carefully at the squareness of the exterior walls, for level windows and doors, and a level first floor. Stand about two feet back from each corner of the house and sight laterally straight down the walls for trueness. A major bulge or protuberance with bent or broken wall siding spells trouble. A few inches out of plumb is usually of small importance. Inside the house, the condition of basement beams and supporting columns is particularly important. Notice also if all doors line up squarely with their frames.

Nearly all houses settle a little so don't panic if the structure is not perfectly true. On the other hand, severely cracked walls, windows and doors out of joint, and sloping floors should be thoroughly investigated.

Sometimes an old house may need only one or two new supporting posts and beams underneath at a cost of a few hundred dollars. But a major structural failing can mean extensive rebuilding at a cost of several thousand dollars. Get accurate bids beforehand on the cost of shoring up the house.

7. *Poor plumbing.* Common troubles are weak water pressure due to clogged or corroded pipes, and a bad septic-tank system. Bad plumbing is mostly a problem in houses with iron or steel pipes that are 25 years old or older. Copper, brass, and bronze pipes last much longer but were not introduced until about 1940. A magnet can tell if the pipes are iron or steel. They will attract the magnet, but copper, brass, or bronze will not. Test for water pressure by turning on the top-floor bathroom faucets. Turn on the bathtub and sink faucets, and flush the toilet at the same time. If the water slows down to a bare trickle you can expect plumbing woes. The pressure in the street mains, however, may be low and then a booster pump will be needed. A call to the water company should tell you if the street pressure is adequate.

Is there a septic tank, a cesspool, or a city sewer? If no street sewer, be wary even if the house is comparatively new. Overloaded septic tanks and cesspools are major problems in many areas. Septic-tank problems are also more likely in a house with an automatic washing machine and several children. When was the septic tank or cesspool last cleaned? Cleaning is normally needed every three or four years. Who did the cleaning? Call him and ask about the condition of the tank. A good source of information on septic-tank problems is the public health department. They can tell you if such problems are prevalent locally. Septic-tank repairs may run from $100 to $1000.

8. *Roof and gutters.* What kind of roof and how old is it? An asphalt shingle or built-up roof on a flat or low slope often needs repairs or replacement if it is more than 10 to 15 years old. Walk around the house, and standing back, inspect roof and gutters. A good roof will be even and uniform. A worn roof will contain broken, warped, or bent shingles, giving a ragged appearance.

To inspect a flat or nearly flat asphalt roof, go up on the roof. Look for bare spots in the mineral surfacing, separations, breaks in the felt, and rusty flashing around the roof edges and around the chimney. Note the condition of the horizontal gutters, especially if they are wood. Are they clogged with leaves, or clean and well maintained? The best time to check for roof leaks and bad gutters is during a heavy rain (even if you get a little wet). Check inside the attic for water stains and discolorations, the ceiling below for stains and cracks.

9. *Inadequate insulation.* Almost all houses built before 1945 were built with no insulation. Many houses built from World War II up to

around 1955 were built with attic insulation but little or no wall insulation. Most houses built since 1955 got both wall and ceiling insulation, though not necessarily enough. Regardless of age, most houses with brick or stone walls have little or no wall insulation.

Nonetheless, insulation has been added to many houses after building. Attic insulation often can be seen between attic floor joists. (Insulation should not be under the roof between the sloping roof rafters of the attic; it does little good there.) Ask if wall insulation has been blown into the walls. During cold weather you can get an indication of the insulation inside by holding your hand against the inside surface of an exterior wall. Then hold your hand against an interior partition. The exterior walls should not feel much colder than the inside wall. If they do, much heat is leaking out; there is little or no insulation.

10. *The faucet water heater.* Is it a separate water heater and tank? Or an indirect, coil water heater that is part of the hot-water heating boiler? If it is a separate tank heater, check the name plate for capacity and type, and judge it according to the standards in Chapter 24. Open the little door at the base of the tank where the pilot light and burner mechanism are; with a flashlight look for signs of rust or leaks in there. These are the first signs of trouble brewing.

The condition of a coil water heater (built into the regular, hot-water house-heating boiler) is hard to ascertain unless you are an expert. The most common complaint about them is insufficient hot water. If possible, see if its heating capacity is given in gallons, of hot water supplied per minute (gpm), and rate it according to the standards in Chapter 24.

How Flaws Vary with Location

The location of a house, its climate zone, or a special condition peculiar to your area can be the tip-off to certain flaws.

Wet basements are widespread in areas with damp soil such as Long Island and much of New Jersey. Cracked or settled foundations are a special problem in marshy places, as around New Orleans in houses close to the levees. They are also a problem in houses built on filled or reclaimed land that was once marshy.

Septic-tank and cesspool troubles are prevalent with damp, low-lying ground or hard clay soil, as along the Atlantic seaboard from Long Island south to Florida. Rusty water pipes are troublesome in cities like Philadelphia with hard and corrosive water. On the other hand, run-down water heaters are most likely in areas with soft water that is murder on water heaters (as noted in Chapter 24).

Roofs are most likely to need frequent repair or replacement in the hot South and Southwest due to the intense sun; the sun is savagely hard

on a roof in hot Texas, New Mexico, and Arizona. Deficient aircondi-
tioning systems are more likely in the South, where the first ones were
installed and where they labor hardest. Conversely, run-down heating
systems are more likely in the coldest parts of the North. To check on
local problems when you're moving into a new part of the country, call a
few local repairmen, banks specializing in short-term home-improvement
loans, or the local FHA or VA office.

Other Checks for an Old House

Outside. Is the exterior paint in good condition? Most houses require
new paint every three to five years. If the paint is failing, the kind of failure is highly important. Paint normally chalks as it ages, leaving a dull
powdery surface. It should not blister or peel (flaking). This is a sign of
more serious trouble, especially if it shows on a recently painted house.

If there is an outside chimney, is it snug against the house wall? Or is a
crack developing between the chimney and house? Chimney separation
often means serious structural trouble.

A crawl-space under the house should be inspected. Crawl in with a
flashlight. Is it dry? Is the wood sub-structure free of rot and condensation?
What about termites? There should be insulation under the house floor
or around the inside walls of a closed-off crawl-space *and* a vapor-barrier
material over the crawl-space earth. The underside of porches and outside
stairs should be inspected in the same way.

Inside, the living quarters. Does the kitchen conform to the work-triangle principle? (See Chapter 12.) Is there adequate space for modernizing,
if necessary? For adding new equipment such as a dishwasher? Inspect
metal cabinets for rust and corrosion; wood ones for warping; both kinds
for ease of operation. Check the sink for chipped enamel, rust stains,
and scratches. Try the faucets for quick hot water and good pressure.
Look under the sink, a crucial place, for signs of water leaks, rust, and rot.
Is there a kitchen exhaust fan and is it properly located (in the ceiling or
high on the wall over the range).

Open and close all windows and doors. Look for ease of opening and
closing, and for weather stripping around window and door frames.

Small wall cracks generally are inevitable, especially in plaster walls.
Serious cracks are deep ones that start at the corner of a room, or are
deep gashes at the joint where the ceiling and wall meet.

The fireplace. You should see light when you look up the chimney from
the fireplace (with the damper open, of course). Every fireplace should
have a workable damper. Every chimney should be lined with flue tile;
i.e. you should not see the bricks. Absence of chimney lining can be
serious but is correctable. How well the fireplace works usually can be

judged merely by burning paper in it. If smoke pours back into the room, the fireplace may be defective.

Bathrooms. Are the fixtures of adequate design and in good condition? Is the bathtub under a window? It's best when it isn't. Check the joining of the tub with the floor and wall for a good waterproof seam. What about the condition of wall and floor tile? An interior bathroom without windows should have an exhaust fan connected to a convenient but safe switch. Decided drawbacks are an old-fashioned bathtub with legs, no tile floor, no wall tile around the bathtub and shower.

The attic. Is it easily accessible by means of stairs or a pull-down staircase ladder? If you can reach it only by setting up a ladder, this will be a nuisance, particularly if the attic is used for storage. Are there attic air vents (the bigger the better)? Check for attic insulation while you're there. In winter, check the insulation for dryness. If it feels moist to the touch, attic ventilation is inadequate.

Look for moisture condensation and/or wood rot. If present, these usually can be corrected by increasing attic ventilation, but make sure that the condition has not advanced so far that the beams are seriously weakened. Are there signs of roof leaks, such as stains or discolorations? A clue to good, over-all construction quality, incidentally, is a chimney that is totally self-supporting and independent of house framing. A chimney may be framed into the house, but attic floor joists and beams should not be tied directly into the brickwork; the house should not lean on the chimney.

Miscellaneous. Is redecorating or new paint needed? Are there screens and storm windows and doors, or will you have to buy them? Do appliances come with the house? How old are they? Are they in good condition? Will your car fit in the garage? What about the condition of driveway and sidewalks?

Before starting out to judge an old house, arm yourself with a few tools: a clipboard, paper and pencil for taking notes; a 50-foot tape; flashlight to look into dark corners; knife or ice pick to detect termites and wood rot; magnet to determine whether pipes are iron or not; a level to check structural trueness; a screwdriver, pliers; four-foot ladder; and coveralls for crawling under porches and into crawl spaces. Too much? Embarrassing? Not for the largest single purchase most of us ever make.

One Other Indication of Likely Repairs

Nobody knows for sure what the most common repairs and remodeling jobs are in houses. Accurate national statistics do not exist. FHA figures, however, from its home-improvement program, are an indication of the most likely repairs and improvements you may encounter when.

you buy an old house, as well as the most common repairs to expect in your present house. Here is what they are from a recent year though, unaccountably, rewiring is omitted from their summary):

Type of improvement	Percentage of families that did it
Additions and alterations, (new rooms, garages, carports, etc.)	20.7%
Insulation	17.0%
Exterior paint, siding	12.5%
Heating	11.0%
Interior paint, other finishing	9.5%
Plumbing	8.3%
Roofing	5.3%
Miscellaneous	15.2%

The above percentages are in terms of the *number* of families that did the above work (with FHA loans). They are not in terms of the amount of money, all told, spent for the respective kinds of work done. This last is a different matter. Insulation, for example, accounts for the second largest kind of remodeling done with FHA loans, but it is farther down the list in total money spent. The figures are for single-family houses, which account for about 90 per cent of all FHA improvement loans.

Part 2

THE FUNDAMENTALS OF HOME-IMPROVEMENT DESIGN AND CONSTRUCTION

Unfortunately, every change does not improve a house. A good many merely complicate household activities and leave the house misshapen. The wrong space is added in the wrong place. What might seem like a marvelous idea, theoretically, turns out impractical. Being human, all of us are susceptible to mistakes, particularly when as amateurs we tread new paths that architects and contractors have long known as professionals.

Remodeling requires experts. Yet many of us who would never dream of building a new house without consultation seem to figure that another rule applies when we decide to alter or change our present home.

To help you get over the first obstacles, this section therefore deals with fundamental facts about house design and construction as related to remodeling. An understanding of what makes a house tick—its basic layout and design—is essential first of all. This means architecture (which has to do with far more than mere appearance and style).

Often the best advice is to hire an architect for major alterations and additions. This can be considerably less expensive than you think. There are also such things to know as when and where it pays to add new space, when not to, which walls can be easily removed, and the perennial problems raised by zoning ordinances and building codes.

Chapter 3

Good Planning:
How to Diagnose Remodeling Needs
and Prescribe the Best Solutions
for Your Family

Before rushing headlong into tearing down walls, it pays to know a little about basic house design—the principles of a good floor plan, room layout, house-site relationship, and good orientation (exposure) in relation to the sun.

Do you achieve maximum use and pleasure from your *existing* space? Or are some rooms constantly overloaded while other space goes neglected? In many situations, of course, *all* the space is overloaded.

A common flaw in old houses is that they face the street. There is a front porch, living room, dining room, and kitchen, in that order, from front to rear. As one architect has said, the front porch was fine "when the street was a kind of communal meeting place, but today our streets are gasoline alleys." With the new appeal of outdoor living and rear gardens, the same house has ceased to be satisfactory.

Interior remodeling can turn the entire house toward the rear to face a private outdoor patio or garden. You turn your back to street traffic and noise. A picture window could be installed in the rear to let in the outdoors. Sliding glass doors for easy access to a rear patio are another good idea.

Another common and deceptively irritating drawback is a kitchen isolated at the rear of the house. A rear kitchen no longer makes sense for several reasons. It was relegated to the back of the house when we had cooks and servants. Today we are our own servants, yet stuck with an obsolete, remote kitchen location. A woman in a rear kitchen—where she is trapped much of the time—has to traipse from one end of the house to the other every time the doorbell rings, and make the same long walk the other way on returning from a shopping trip laden with groceries. These examples are good reasons for a kitchen near the family entrance. They also emphasize that a house is for living.

An understanding of the following principles can help you diagnose the drawbacks of a house and also help avoid errors when new space is added to the house. Space should be added in the proper place for your family's living habits, not just where it is convenient to add for a remodeling contractor.

Do You Have Good "Zoning?"

Houses have three main zones: living, sleeping, and working. Each zone should be separate from others, yet each properly related to the others, the street, the sun, and the outdoors.

Are the bedrooms separated from the noise of work and play? Can you entertain guests without waking the children? A buffer zone, not just a mere partition, should shield bedrooms from the rest of the house. This can be a hall, bathroom, or adroitly placed closets.

Can unfinished laundry be left as is without being in view of a chance visitor? It depends on the zoning.

The two-story house is an example of natural zoning between the second floor bedrooms and the rest of the house on the first floor (but it has disadvantages, too, such as the time and energy expended going up and down the stairs). Even better, if not an ideal example of good zoning, is a house laid out like an H or a U, the living and sleeping zones at opposite ends of the house, neatly connected across the middle by the kitchen and utility work zone—and all on one level. Though theoretically ideal, this is expensive to build because of the large wall and roof area. Careful design can give much the same results in a more compact plan. Good zoning also goes hand-in-hand with room arrangement and good circulation (which refers to the movement of the occupants within the house).

Six Tests for Good Circulation

What is a good floor plan? The few main routes in a house used over and over again are the key. You can spot them by six tests:

1. *Does the family entrance lead directly from garage or driveway to kitchen?* This is all-important. The main entrance for a family is usually through the kitchen. Hence the garage and driveway should be near the kitchen for quick entry and swift grocery unloading. The garage-to-kitchen route should be sheltered from rain. Travel through the kitchen plainly should not run smack through the kitchen work area (where food is prepared).

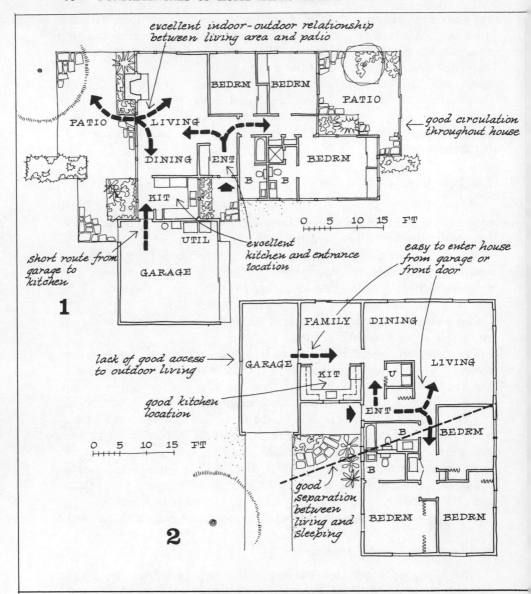

Diagrams illustrate good and bad points of typical house plans. They emphasize the importance of good circulation within a house, and good zoning between the living, working, and sleeping areas. Same points apply to all houses and are important to know when remodeling.

2. *Is the kitchen centrally located?* The kitchen should be a command post, not a foxhole. From the kitchen a woman should have control over the entire house. She should be near the front door and family entrance.

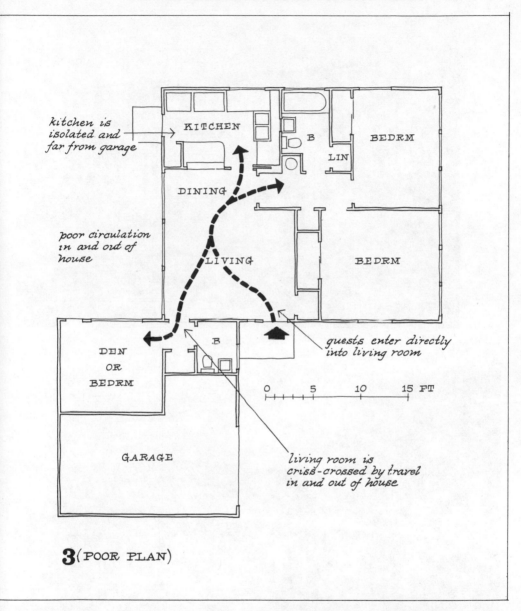

kitchen is
isolated and
far from garage

KITCHEN

B

BEDRM

LIN

DINING

poor circulation
in and out of
house

LIVING

BEDRM

DEN
OR
BEDRM

B

guests enter directly
into living room

0   5   10   15 FT

living room is
criss-crossed by travel
in and out of house

GARAGE

3(POOR PLAN)

She should be able to watch children playing outside, and also be near the dining room, living room, and outside patio. The remote, isolated kitchen is a widespread curse. It probably leads to more wear and tear on people, particularly mothers of small children, than any other planning defect.

3. *Does the front door (main entrance) lead directly to the center of the house?* Guests enter here. A center hall or foyer will help greatly. It

Fifty-year-old, four-car garage in Minneapolis was bought by architect Hugh G. S. Peacock and converted into an elegant townhouse. Retaining the classic lines, he replaced the garage doors with handsome glass windows and doors, and turned the car apron into a terrace. New interior has large living-dining area and kitchen.
©1962 The Curtis Publishing Co., courtesy The American Home. Warren Reynolds.

will shield people inside from casual visitors as well as from the inrush of wind, snow, and rain. The main entrance should be close to the driveway and street. A clothes closet near the front door is essential.

4. *Is the living room shielded from cross-traffic?* It should not be a main highway for people going in and out of the house. It should be a dead end so you can read, talk, watch TV, or entertain guests in peace without kids running through every few minutes, or vice versa.

5. *Is there good room-to-room circulation?* Can you go from any room to any other room without passing through a third room (except the dining room)? From any entrance to any room without walking through a second room? The main bathroom in particular should be accessible from any room and not require passage through another room. (Flouting this rule alone has blackballed houses from FHA mortgage approval.) And beware of bedrooms in series which require passing through one to reach another.

6. *Is there a good indoor-outdoor relationship?* Is it easy to reach the patio, terrace, or outdoor play area from the house? Normally this calls for a door in or near the living room to outdoors, or a side or rear door to avoid walking through the kitchen (which is likely to be cluttered with dishes when you're entertaining).

Lot and Site Considerations: Which Direction to Expand?

A review of your lot's characteristics can throw new light on remodeling plans. For example, merely by moving the front-door location from the front to side sometimes can open up new opportunities for revitalizing the entire house with a minimum of new construction.

Divide the land around your house into three zones: public, service, and private. The public zone is the front lawn in public view. The service zone includes sidewalks, driveways, clothes-drying, and trash storage. The private zone is for patio, play, and garden. Sheer logic calls for giving over as little of your land as possible for public and service use and retaining a maximum for private use.

Ideally, a house should be set forward on its lot toward the street, with small public and service areas in front and on the side. The back of the house is opened up for maximum private use. This means a minimum of front lawn to be mowed, short approach driveway and walks, reduced snow shoveling, and if new utility pipes and wires are needed from street to house, they will be short and economical.

Sometimes the same happy results can be achieved by going only halfway—orienting the house to one side or the other, not necessarily to the rear. It may be a solution if you have a wide lot with little depth. In all cases, of course, you should look for privacy between you and your closest neighbors.

Orientation in Relation to the Sun and Wind

Does bright sunshine pour delightfully into your bedroom when you awaken in the morning? Does cheerful sunlight flood the kitchen and dining room at breakfast time? Or does it seem that you always have to turn on lights during the day?

The orientation of a house and the rooms within—their exposure to the sun—makes the difference. You may be unable to do much about the

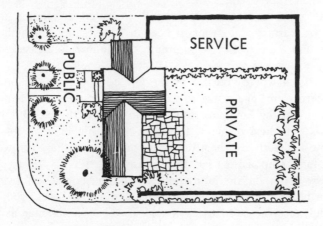

Good exterior planning is facilitated when you visualize your lot being divided into three zones: public, private, and service. Here the house faces rear for maximum use of its lot and maximum privacy.

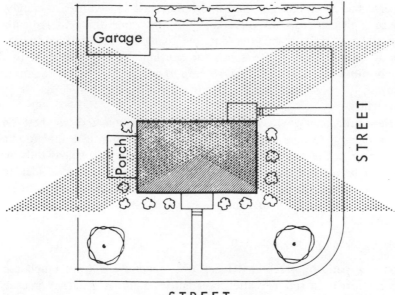

This example of poor site planning causes inconvenience every day. Lot is cut up illogically, causing disorder, wasted land, long driveway and walks, and no privacy.

whole house, short of turning it around on a giant turntable. Neverthe-less, new living space can be greatly enhanced with proper orientation. For that matter, simply changing a few windows or adding one can swiftly transform a small gloomy room into an incredibly pleasant and "large" space. (See Chapter 13.)

In addition, when rooms are properly oriented in relation to the sun, they will be warmer and easier to heat in winter, fuel bills will drop sub-stantially, and there will be a minimum of window condensation. In sum-mer the same rooms will be 5 to 10 degrees cooler.

Regardless of where you live in the United States or any other part of the Northern Hemisphere, the sun in winter is in the south almost all day long. It rises in the Southeast and sets in the Southwest. But in summer the sun rises in the Northeast, travels a much higher arc across the sky, being almost directly overhead at noon, and sets in the Northwest. A few scientific facts emphasize what this means:

1. Every room on the south side of a house receives five times as much sun heat in winter as in summer. 2. East and west rooms, on the other hand, receive six times as much sun heat in summer as in winter. 3. Rooms and windows facing north receive no sunshine at all in winter, and only a little in summer; the farther south you are, the more sun shed on the north side in summer.

In general, therefore, a house should face broadside to the south to receive the most sunshine in winter, the least in summer. Actually, the house itself can face any direction. The important thing to remember is that the big windows of your daytime living areas (kitchen, dining, and family rooms) should face south for sunshine and natural light to flood in. A south orientation is not so important for the living room, unless you use it a good deal during the day; a good many people use it mostly at night.

New bedrooms obviously have less need for sun and are best on the north or east. On the east, you may welcome that bright sun flooding in first thing in the morning. Bedrooms on the west can get awfully hot in summer by the time you are ready for bed. Thus, it is a good idea to put a new carport or garage on the west as a sun shield in summer or on the north as a wind shield in winter.

Sun vs. a Cool Breeze

A new patio or porch that faces west generally will get much too hot for comfort on a summer afternoon and evening. It generally goes better on the south, east, or north, providing, of course, it is still conveniently near your main living area. A south or southwest exposure can be excel-lent for a terrace or patio if it is protected from the west sun in summer and northwest winds in winter. A few protective trees or a simple fence on the west side can do this. Then you may have a marvelous sun trap in late fall and early spring for sunning yourself at times when it would otherwise be idiotic to relax outdoors.

The prevailing breezes also bear on the best location for patio or porch. A call to the nearest airport will tell you their usual direction. Of course, the requirements for catching the breeze may clash with the need for good sun protection; then a compromise is in order. By and large, the sun is your bigger foe and protection from it ranks first.

Large windows facing south also mean less glass exposed to cold north winds in winter. Additional winter protection can be had with a wind-break of evergreen trees on the north, as is frequently seen near farm-houses in the wind-scourged Great Plains. (The evergreen windbreaks planted throughout the Great Plains—one of F. D. Roosevelt's little-publicized New Deal conservation projects—turned out far more success-fully than even its most ardent advocates had expected.) If you live in the South, a south orientation may be less desirable. You may do better if a house faces north with the patio on the north or northeast. And here, by all means, avoid a southwest or west orientation.

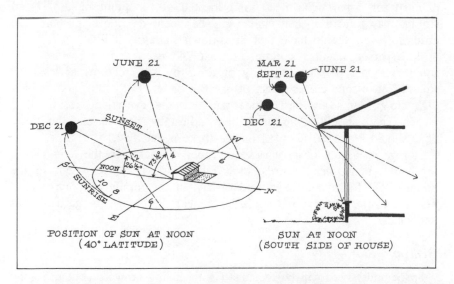

POSITION OF SUN AT NOON   SUN AT NOON
(40° LATITUDE)   (SOUTH SIDE OF HOUSE)

The amount of sunshine and light your rooms receive and how comfortable you will be inside depend greatly on house exposure to the sun. But the sun's overhead loca-tion changes from summer to winter. In general, large windows should face south so they can be easily shaded in summer by wide-brim roof overhangs (or comparable exterior shading devices). But in winter (December 21 arc) sunshine will flood in through the same windows under the overhangs, as the sun is lower in the sky. Dia-gram also shows why sunshine will enter a house in winter only through windows with a southeast to southwest exposure.

Now every room need not face south. The *principles* of good orientation are what to remember. You may be confronted by a clash between the needs of good orientation and remodeling a house in relation to the street. To make matters worse, you may be torn between these considerations and a third one—locating new rooms so that they take advantage of a splendid outside view. It's a dilemma. Something must give.

Unfortunately, the best solution will be a compromise depending on the house and the needs you consider foremost. Not everybody can look out on a distant mountaintop. It's fine if you can swing it. If not, or if you live on flat land, a nearby flower garden or lawn can be quite satisfactory. Every house need not face Mecca.

What About Storage Space?

A remarkable number of overlooked nooks and crannies exist for storage in even the smallest house. But first break down your over-all storage requirements into two parts: Live storage for the things used from day to day and dead storage for such things as trunks, screens, sleds, and garden equipment, which are used only part of the time.

Live storage requires chests, drawers, closets, and shelves, sized and planned for a particular need, and located at the point of use. Dead storage may call for special facilities; a basement or attic helps here. An attic, however, should have that drop-down staircase at least.

Each person requires a closet at least 24″ deep and 48″ wide, or 8 square feet per person. A family of three or four requires at least 40 square feet of total closet space; 60 is even better. Full-width and ceiling-high closet doors are best, since you can see everything inside at a glance. There should be an inside light, adjustable shelves, and the closet floor should be raised about 2 inches to keep out dust.

Storage needs obviously vary from room to room: In the living room for books, magazines, records, card tables, and fireplace wood; in the dining room for linen, silver, and dishes; in the family or playroom to hide the clutter of toys; and space in or near the garage for garden tools and bikes.

Bedroom Storage

Space under beds can be reclaimed with sliding drawers (but use good rollers). They are best for semidead storage (items not required every day); e.g., for blankets, out-of-season clothing, and even linens.

If you currently use bedside tables, consider replacing them with a headboard over the bed for books and magazines, or shelves on each side. The old pull-down Murphy bed may be a good idea for new additions or guest rooms where space is limited and the bed isn't needed every night.

Maximum convenience and storage is obtained by use of ceiling-high folding doors. Note double shelves at top of closet and raised floor at bottom.

Float Away Door Co.

Built-in Storage

This is sometimes cheaper than furniture and serves a double purpose, especially for new additions. Frank Lloyd Wright was the acknowledged master of it in his houses. He would line the walls with built-in seats and couches, fitted with cushions, with the space underneath used for drawers and cabinets (which also cut down house-cleaning problems).

In addition, the space under a built-in window seat can double as a chest for children's toys. The dead space inside of interior walls can be reclaimed by built-in shelves and small cabinets. Simply break open the wall and install them. Storage walls are superb for this. They are special ceiling-high wall cabinets with shelves and drawers which also serve as a partition between two rooms. They are not yet in general use, however, so you have to shop for them, or have them built.

A host of factory-made storage units are now available for a variety of uses. You don't have to call in a carpenter every time. They can be chosen and grouped in different combinations, not only for storage walls, but also for dividers, headboard arrangements, and handsome living- and dining-room cabinets with table-top counters. Plastic drawers are also becoming popular because of their light weight, versatility, and rugged construction. They don't expand and contract with weather changes.

Recommended Storage Standards, According to Southwest Research Institute

1. A coat closet near the main entrance.
2. Storage in the living room for books, records, card tables, fire-place wood.
3. Adequate kitchen cabinets (specified in Chapter 4).
4. Storage near the dining room for linen, silver, and dishes.
5. A place for ironing board, soap, laundry necessities in the utility area.
6. Built-in bathroom storage for towels, soap, and toilet paper, as well as a medicine cabinet and laundry hamper.

Much built-in storage is obtained by means of a storage wall (left) which also serves as a room partition. Wall is only head high, permitting continuous ceiling line to adjacent room and giving a feeling of airiness and great space.

Ben Schnall.

7. A big enough closet in each bedroom (minimum sizes noted earlier).
8. A convenient place for trunks, boxes, sleds, screens, and similar things.
9. A place near the outdoors for lawn mower, garden tools, and summer furniture.
10. Total floor area of all general storage, excluding closets already noted: Under 30 square feet is poor, over 50 is good.

Exterior storage island also serves as a divider for this double carport. Storage like this is particularly appreciated when you do not have a basement. This unit is made of western red-cedar boards and reversed battens to match the house.

West Coast Lumbermen's Assn.

Chapter 4

Should You Hire an Architect?

It is a notable fact that nearly every glamorous remodeling story published in magazines is the handwork of an architect or professional designer. Such jobs did not succeed by chance. A good rule, therefore, is: Hire an architect for a major addition or alteration.

The good architect knows how to add the most usable space at the least cost, how to revise the house to give maximum livability, which walls can be safely torn down, what solutions offer handsome results. He also knows how to juggle the various ingredients for good orientation, site planning, and efficient room layout.

An architect also knows the local codes and zoning ordinances. He can steer you to good contractors, advise you about the contract, and help you avoid legal snarls and potential pitfalls.

But when it gets down to paying for an architect—anything from about $150, say, for consultation and rough plans, up to $500 or more for complete architectural service—most of us balk. We can save this particular expense, we think. This can be the height of penny-wise and pound-foolish "planning." You otherwise will probably pay a contractor for the plans needed for major work so you might as well have it done by a planning expert.

You don't need an architect when you merely make repairs or add modern equipment, such as rewiring, plumbing, heating, and cooling and so on. You are safe with a good contractor. The same holds true, as a rule, when you remodel a kitchen (though not always), or bathroom, or make a minor, inside wall alteration.

You get into the architect's realm when you want to create new space instead of simply altering existing space. His forte is original design, particularly when complete planning is required.

Thus, it's best to call on an architect when you add new space to a house, whether it be a whole new wing or just a room or two. The architect's touch can help you avoid a "remodeled look," and if necessary by designing balancing improvements in other parts of the house so that the sum of the whole adds up to one coherent design, not two separate structures, painfully stuck on to each other.

Architect's Fees

Fees vary according to the amount of work required. To keep the cost down, blueprints may be all you need. Rough drawings and consultation can be done for as little as $150 to $200, based on $15 to $20 an hour, and depending on the amount of planning detail desired. The price goes up another step if you want complete specifications on all materials to be used. It is highest—from 12 to 15 per cent of over-all cost—if the architect provides day-to-day supervision and must take constant changes and revisions.

Use an architect who is experienced with remodeling work and likes it. A seasoned young architect with an architectural firm often is glad to take on remodeling jobs on his own time, for additional experience perhaps, or for the love of the work until he can branch out on his own.

The names of architects who do remodeling can be obtained from the nearest chapter of the American Institute of Architects (AIA). Contractors and builders also should be able to recommend a few (though some builders and some contractors, not knowing the difference between good and bad design, will pooh-pooh the idea).

There are also architects to avoid. Some have a reputation for extravagance. Thus, the same care should be exercised in choosing an architect as for choosing a contractor or repairman. Ask for the names of other people he has done work for, see them and find out how well they fared. It's as simple as that.

On hiring an architect you sit down with him and tell him in detail what you want. Prepare a list for him in advance of everything you wish. If possible, give him the blueprints of your house, too, as this can save you and him much time and trouble.

He draws up preliminary sketches and plans for your approval, then gives you finished plans and specifications. Minor corrections are made, if necessary. Then the plans and specs are given to contractors for bids. If a certain specification is unduly expensive, a contractor will often tell you so and perhaps recommend an alternative. The total bids may be too high for your bank account. (But don't necessarily blame the architect, since every square foot of space you want costs that much more money.) In either case, a three-way conference with architect, contractor, and yourself usually can thrash out compromises. Then you are in the clear and the job should roll smoothly.

One last caution: Avoid changes during construction as these can cost you dearly. Try and think out everything you need while the job is in the

Handsome window wall opens up to patio and excellent countryside view, also makes the room feel quite spacious. This neat design shows the obvious touch of an adept architect. Thermopane insulating glass is used to prevent window condensation and helps keep the room warm in winter.

Libby-Owens-Ford. Warren Reynolds.

planning stage. Changing your mind after the contractor has started work has the effect of throwing a monkey wrench into his schedule, regardless of how slight the change may seem to you.

Sometimes he can accommodate you at little or no extra expense. But more often than not it throws his whole job out of gear and he has no alternative but to charge you accordingly. This is why advance planning is so important and why every effort should be made to get the plans absolutely complete before work is started.

Chapter 5

Ten Fundamental Tips
on Adding New Living Space

1. Use existing space.

The quickest, easiest, and least expensive way of adding new living space to a house obviously is by finishing off unused existing space like an attic or garage. The basic floor, walls, and roof are already installed.

Use your imagination. If the attic is too shallow for headroom, perhaps the entire roof can be lifted. This can be easier than it sounds. You may have a one-story house with a flat roof. A new second story often can be added above for less cost than the same amount of new space added at ground level.

The same principle applies when new space is added horizontally to a house. If you can close in a corner of the existing structure, for example, only two new walls may be required rather than three. Or add on to the existing house where little-used existing space can be given full-time use in the new addition.

You simply add space adjacent to a large foyer, hall, or an oversized room where the existing space could be better utilized as part of your new rooms and thereby reduce the amount of new construction required. You may change the whole character or function of the old space entirely, but so what? The test is whether it will serve you better.

2. Obtain a complete plan in advance.

One of the most widespread disappointments with remodeling occurs after a new addition or new garage is attached to a house. A happy family treks outside to savor the grand, new addition for the first time, but what they see may be a heartbreaking calamity—the new addition appears stuck out from the house like a sore thumb. Its style, architecture, and roof lines clash with the original structure.

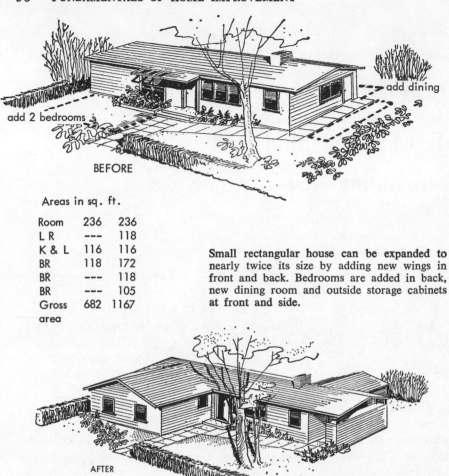

add dining

add 2 bedrooms

BEFORE

AFTER

Areas in sq. ft.

Room	236	236
L R	---	118
K & L	116	116
BR	118	172
BR	---	118
BR	---	105
Gross area	682	1167

Small rectangular house can be expanded to nearly twice its size by adding new wings in front and back. Bedrooms are added in back, new dining room and outside storage cabinets at front and side.

This sad view is much less likely if a complete plan of the work is prepared in advance. This is essential not only for additions but also for many other remodeling jobs. If you do not use an architect, a good contractor will automatically prepare professional drawings before he starts work. You can see at a glance if the new extension blends with the house, and particularly whether the new roof will conform with the old. If things look awry, that is the time to make design changes. Some contractors build a sound structure but have little sense of style.

Another idea: Take pictures of your house, blow them up, and sketch in changes you plan. Use a grease pencil, which is easily erased, and excpriment as much as you wish. How do the changes look? Ideas will come to you simply by doing this. The cost is small and it can be well worth the effort.

3. *Make new roof, windows, and doors conform with the old ones.*

In addition to the style and architecture of a new addition being compatible with your existing house, it's usually best when the new roof is a straight-line extension of the old roof. This gives unity and cohesion to the finished product. The over-all house also will look larger than it would with the new roof at a different level from the old.

New windows and doors should line up with the tops and bottoms of the old windows. If smaller new windows are used, they should line up with either the top or the bottom of old windows and preferably at the same time with the middle horizontal bar of old windows, i.e., be half the height of old windows.

One problem, generally insoluble, is achieving a perfect match between the roof shingles and exterior wall material on a new addition with the existing roof and walls. A good man will tell you this. He will frankly say that he will try for "the closest possible match."

Old roof shingles and walls fade and bleach with time. Even if you receive the identical products and color, their newness will make them look different. Furthermore, roof shingles and wall materials undergo changes from year to year. The manufacturer's dye may differ slightly from before; a perfect match with his former product is literally impossible. Unfortunately, little can be done about this, so when it happens, brace yourself and don't be inconsolable. The new addition will gradually start to catch up with the old as fading and bleaching take their toll.

4. *Determine location of buried utility lines.*

Before work is started on a new addition, determine the location of water pipes and wires buried outside. It can be an expensive surprise if, say, the septic tank is later discovered directly under a new room. It will have to be relocated at no small cost. These things are usually but not always shown on the original plans of a house. Sometimes, however, they were buried at a different location than originally shown without the plans being changed. For this reason it's best to locate all utilities with absolute certainty.

5. *Don't freeze bedroom location.*

This deserves special mention because a new bedroom or two is generally and automatically added to the bedroom wing of a house even though another location may be better and less expensive. Don't blind yourself to other locations, especially for a new master bedroom. This may be better located on the other side of the house from children's bedrooms, particularly when children are beyond the infant stage. Architects often do this in custom houses to assure privacy for both parents and children alike. If you have infants, an intercom system can be put in to hear them at night.

For that matter, a new family room or just another room may be your chief need and an existing bedroom may be the ideal location for it. Take advantage of its location and add a new master bedroom instead, perhaps with its own study and bath; it can be attached off the bedroom wing or on the other side of the kitchen.

6. *Make sure new work is permitted by local zoning rules.*

Zoning rules generally call for a minimum of space left clear on all sides of a house to the property lines. Setback requirements limit how close you may build to the street. They also may require off-street parking for at least one car in addition to a garage or carport. Carports may be barred altogether.

Some towns disallow one-story or split-level construction or dictate the kind of architectural style permitted. Others are zoned strictly for one-family houses and an inspector will scrutinize any alteration that looks as if it could be rented out as an apartment. This generally bars a second kitchen, for example, and casts suspicion on any new room with a sink, running water, and gas or electricity for a range.

Thus new work should not be started until you are sure it is permitted by local fiat. Consult local officials. If in doubt, obtain a copy of the local zoning rules and building codes from your municipality. If your plan is disallowed you can appeal to the local zoning board for a "variance." Reasonable requests are often granted. You are allowed to vary from the rules. You will have to appear at a hearing and it's a good idea to enlist the support of neighbors in advance or at least sound them out for potential opposition.

7. *Obtain a building permit.*

A building permit is required for most major alteration jobs, and nearly all new construction. Obtaining a building permit requires filing an application accompanied by a construction plan. The contractor normally handles this for you unless you serve as your own contractor, in which case, of course, you must do it. Allow at least a week for processing.

Not all remodeling, however, requires a permit. Finishing off a basement or attic, redoing a kitchen or bath, new roofing, or even a new heating plant, are examples of work that usually do not require a permit. In general, any work that entails a change or addition to the basic structure of the house does require a permit.

Such things as new plumbing, wiring, heating, and a new fireplace may not require a permit, but nonetheless they must conform with the local building code for each, and often must be done by licensed contractors. The purpose of a building code is to assure safe, sanitary, and fireproof construction (although many old-fashioned codes are restrictive to an extreme degree).

8. *Refer to the original plans of your house.*

The original plans can be invaluable. If you don't have a set, try to get them from the builder of the house. Another source is your local building department, which may have plans on file for all but the most ancient houses.

The original plans can provide a vital insight into the construction details, the thickness of walls, the size and location of the main beams, as well as showing walls which may be *verboten* because they contain pipes or ducts that would cost wild sums to alter (as noted below). This kind of knowledge can help a contractor immensely. He isn't forced to guess and bid in the dark on new work, and therefore need not hike his price as a safeguard against unpredictable construction problems.

9. *Know which old walls can be altered or moved.*

Some walls can be easily torn down or moved, others not. It depends primarily on whether the wall is a load-bearing or non-load-bearing wall.

The load-bearing kind helps support part of the house above. Sometimes called a structural wall, it can not be arbitrarily moved without risking a collapse. It can be eliminated, however, when it is replaced at the ceiling by a supporting beam as long as the wall itself. This takes on the wall's structural function. It is more expensive than moving or altering a non-load-bearing wall. A non-load wall normally can be eliminated entirely. An exception, mentioned earlier, is one with ducts or pipes.

You can tell a load-bearing wall because it generally runs parallel to the longest outside walls of the house and at right angles to the floor and ceiling joists. A look in the attic or at the floor joists at the basement ceiling will tell you which way the joists run. Any wall in the house that runs at right angles to these joists is nearly always a load-bearing wall. This applies to interior partition walls as well as exterior walls. Conversely, an interior wall that runs parallel to the joists is generally a non-load-bearing wall; it can be easily altered or removed.

The kind of house you have will also indicate the kind of walls. In a rectangular house with a gabled roof, the long exterior walls support the roof, and the interior load-bearing walls run parallel to them and support the ceiling. Remodeling costs will be lower when these walls are left alone. The shorter exterior walls at the ends of the house together with the interior partitions parallel to them are usually non-load-bearing walls. They generally can be altered or removed at the least expense. This means that the most economical expansion of a gabled-roof house is adding on to one or the other gable ends; i.e., extending the length of the house.

All four exterior walls of a house with a hipped roof are load-bearing; they support the roof. Any interior wall parallel to the longer exterior walls is load-bearing. Any wall parallel to the two short outside walls is nonload-bearing. Adding a wing to any side of a hipped-roof house therefore will require some reframing of the existing house.

A wall that harbors pipes or ducts inside—a carpenter's nightmare—may be so expensive to alter that it's best to leave such walls alone. You can sometimes locate the apparatus without a Geiger Counter by a look at the basement ceiling to see where pipes and ducts start upstairs. They are found in walls close to radiators and warm-air heating vents.

Electric wires in a wall, on the other hand, ordinarily can be rerouted at small expense. When exterior walls are torn down, salvage the doors and windows and as much of the rest as possible for the new addition.

10. Save money by subcontracting work yourself (though not always recommended).

Sometimes hundreds of dollars can be saved by doing your own subcontracting. A good example is a magazine editor I know who saved $500 on a bathroom remodeling job. He had a $2400 over-all bid from a "one-stop" contractor to handle the whole job, provide new fixtures, plumbing, glass shower stall, ceramic wall tile, plus other such things as new electric fixtures, painting, and the necessary carpentry work. To save money, the editor decided to subcontract each part of the job by himself. He hired the plumber, tile man, electrician, carpenter, and scheduled the work of each. The bills for each added up to $1900.

In other words, you take over the chief contractor's responsibilities. You will expend as much (perhaps more) time and effort arranging for and scheduling the various tradesman's work. You save what he would otherwise have to charge you for his time, office overhead and other related expenses. This may run from 20 to 30 per cent of the total cost. You can save it for other kinds of work, not just bathroom remodeling.

But be forewarned. You should be temperamentally suited to making many phone calls and to riding herd on a parade of workmen. You should be fairly familiar with the work of each trade involved. This is where the knowledge and experience of a good over-all contractor can be well worth what you pay him to handle the complete job.

In fact, it is best not to do your own subcontracting on a major remodeling job unless you *are* a contractor. Remodeling is a tough business that takes an immense amount of special knowledge and experience. It is, after all, akin to custom-building. Even the most knowledgeable layman is seldom equipped to do it. Moreover, when you deal directly with certain subcontractors they are likely to quote you higher prices than they would otherwise quote a regular contractor.

Although sometimes it may pay to subcontract the work for a kitchen or bathroom, finishing off an attic or basement, or any other job that requires fewer than three or four trades, extending a house or adding a new wing is a different matter. As many as ten to fifteen different trades will be involved and you can easily overlook an essential one, or bring them on the job in the wrong sequence, or pick a fly-by-night worker.

Part 3

WHAT KIND OF NEW
LIVING SPACE?

This section deals with the most common kinds of new living space needed in houses. It presents basic design information about finishing off an attic, basement, or garage, adding or closing in a porch or patio, and obtaining a new family room.

In each case there are inherent pitfalls which can lead to serious drawbacks unless the proper precautions are taken in advance. There are also certain advantages related to a particular space, which can and should be exploited.

Not included in this section, however, is information on construction materials. Facts about choosing high-quality flooring, wall, and ceiling materials, along with other kinds of products, are given in Part 6.

Chapter 6

Converting an Attic
into a Good Room

A primary requirement for economical attic conversion is enough head-room to start with. There should be enough roof slope to give at least 7 feet of height, free and clear, to the finished ceiling. Less than 7 feet of clear ceiling height at the side walls can be tolerable, of course, (this allows for a sloping roof) but there should be enough headroom here for sitting down without bumping your head.

Window Dormers

Attic conversions generally require the installation of a dormer addition—not just a single-window dormer but a wide shed dormer that will extend the length of the finished room or almost so. Single-window dormers do not add enough headroom and light to pay their way. A shed dormer, of course, is simply a means of raising the roof of one side of the attic.

The most common mistake with a new dormer is not extending it out far enough to the exterior wall of the house. It should extend out to within at least 18 inches of the exterior wall, and preferably to the wall itself if you can afford a few more dollars. The depth of a dormer has a direct effect on the finished ceiling height inside the room. Unless it extends out to within 18 inches of the exterior wall, you could be short-changed on interior headroom. This is a key point to check when bids are obtained for attic remodeling. What seems like a bargain price often is the result of cutting back on dormer extension. The customer doesn't realize the loss until too late. You can be sure of what you are getting by obtaining a plan in advance that shows the exact dimensions of the finished room including an elevation view with ceiling-height dimensions.

When the roof is broken for a dormer extension, salvage all the good, old shingles that you can. Mixed in with the new ones for the dormer roof they can provide a closer matching of the new roof to the rest of the house roof.

Sometimes the entire roof or at least half of it can be raised bodily. It depends on the house. The simpler the roof, the easier and less expensive it is. The expense involved may be well worth the cost of obtaining as much as an extra floor of living space.

Sometimes, however, the local building code puts severe restrictions on attic modernization. A key requirement is that the attic floor beams must be strong enough to support new rooms. In general, 2×6 beams are the minimum size required, depending on the house and the span of the beams. Sometimes they must be 2×8s.

Yet many houses are built with smaller 2×4 beams which can doom the whole project. But don't give up without a fight even if your floor beams are not strong enough. A smart architect or contractor may come to the rescue with a comparatively inexpensive means of beefing them up, with a steel girder, for example, and you're in the clear. Some codes also lay down rules on the minimum ceiling height required.

Dormers vs. *Windows and Skylights*

Dormers are not always essential. If you have enough headroom to start with, gable-end windows and roof skylights can provide as much air and light at less expense. Opening up one or both gable ends of the attic with a large glass window and letting sunlight flood in can make an astonishing difference in the feeling of space obtained. All or most of it could be a single sheet of fixed glass to cut costs. Ventilation can be provided with a second, smaller window that opens. One of the new flat or bubble skylights built into the roof (described in Chapter 15) can let air and light into the center of the space.

A warning about windows and skylights: Too much glass exposed to direct sunshine can make the new space insufferably hot, not only in

Sloped-roof skylight is a neat economical way of letting air and light into an attic room, rather than adding a more expensive dormer window.

Ventarama Skylight Corp.

summer but in spring and fall too. Thus a large gable window facing south or west is not recommended unless it can be shaded on the outside. Apply the principles of good orientation and window placement given in Chapters 3 and 13.

Space, Room Division, and Stairs

The stairway location is decisive. A central stairway is normally required to attain two separate rooms in the attic. A stairway at either end almost always dictates one room only.

A feeling of space and openness can be had by the use of head-high partitions, storage walls, and closets. All partitions need not extend full up to the ceiling. Leave a clear space of at least a foot open above the partitions so that the ceiling will be open and the room will seem larger and pleasanter than if cut up by full partitions.

Chimney, vent pipe, and heating-duct obstructions are real problems. Moving a brick chimney is usually out of the question because of the expense. A chimney is usually boxed-in, that is, finished over on remodeling to match the walls. At the same time it can be neatly combined with a closet. But it can pay to investigate the possibility of moving a vent pipe or ducts.

For safety, the stairway should be 3 feet wide and rise at a 30- to 35-degree angle, no more. Tread width plus riser should add up to about 17 inches. Thus, 7-inch risers between steps call for a 10-inch-deep tread. Railings are best about 32 inches above the stair treads.

If a new bathroom is installed in the attic, piping costs can be reduced by locating it above a downstairs bathroom. The important element here is a location that permits new piping vertically upward from the existing pipes, plus convenient access to an existing plumbing vent stack (the large pipe rising through the roof for release of sewer fumes and gases, discussed in Chapter 12).

Heating and Cooling Comfort

Most attics are cold in winter and torrid in summer. This calls for *thick* insulation all around the walls and ceiling of a new attic room. Its importance cannot be overemphasized, regardless of your climate zone. Use full-thick (3-inch) insulation for the walls, and as much as 6 inches over the ceiling to keep out roof heat in summer. Good ventilation is achieved with adequate window openings. Ventilation the year around is also essential under the roof and all around the outside of the finished living space; i.e., ventilation to keep the structure dry is essential under the roof in winter as well as a help in cooling during the summer.

Providing heat in winter may not be difficult because of the natural rise of warm air from the rooms below, but you can't count on this. Some provisions for heat is generally required. If new attic space is well insulated, the chances are that the main house heater will have sufficient extra capacity for the new space. But new heating ducts or radiators obviously will be needed.

An alternative is the use of a separate gas or electric heater, which may be less expensive than tying in with the house heating system. A gas heater will require an exhaust vent to the outside plus an intake air vent to the room to assure adequate air at all times for its combustion.

Heat may be less important if you live in a warm or mild climate and the space is well insulated. Then, a few floor vents could be installed to encourage natural entry of warm air from the floor below. But this also opens up paths for noise travel in and out of the new rooms, and a loss of privacy. Noise can be reduced if the vents and their short duct connections have a couple of right-angle bends and are also lined with acoustical tile. This is a simple job that can be done for $15 to $25 by a good carpenter.

More details on heating, insulation, and wiring are given in the respective chapters on these subjects. And as already noted, facts about choosing materials, window design, and so on are given in the sections on each.

Chapter 7

What Makes a Successful
Basement Room?

What is the best use for a basement? It depends, first, on your greatest need. With children, a downstairs playroom is a help (if only for retaining your sanity upstairs). It is a natural spot for a workshop (though a ground-level garage puts necessary tools closer to their point of use for odd jobs upstairs).

It can be a laundry or utility space if necessary (though here again a first-floor location will save much stair-climbing inconvenience). It can be an entertainment and party room, a good many people say, but this puts special emphasis on making it a cheerful and pleasant place. For that matter, a basement also can be transformed into a truly pleasant living space of almost any kind if adequate windows can be installed and if it is naturally dry.

Much can be learned about making a basement pleasant by observing the finished basement areas in the homes of friends. When is such space successful? The acid test is how often it is used *voluntarily* for the purpose intended. Do children head downstairs to play without being told to do so? Are successful parties held in the basement? Or do people tend to stay upstairs, shunning the expensive, new, basement party room? Does the family naturally drift down to it?

Planning and Design

This depends, obviously, on the kind of basement space you want. Decide what you want and draw a floor plan. Work with an accurate scale diagram of your existing basement, including the location of stairs, heating equipment, and interior walls.

Keep the plan as open as possible. Close off only those areas that require privacy or are unsightly. Make the stairway look airy and light by leaving the space under it open and running your floor covering into that

Remodeled basement of Tacoma, Washington, house includes this all-purpose room. Light colors and white ceiling make it seem larger and more spacious than it actually is. Separate darkroom, storage and freezer room are blocked off by wall at left.

Douglas Fir Plywood Assn.

Basement playroom is cheerful and comfortable chiefly because of light-colored western pine, light tile floor and ceiling. Space under stairs harbors hide-away television set; it also could be a closet.

Western Pine Assn. Serating.

area. That is, unless you're pressed for storage space and the same space is a natural for it, or for a built-in TV set or record player.

The ceiling can be dropped, if necessary, to close in pipes, wires, and other unsightly obstructions. Gas and electric meters can be enclosed within cabinets, with hinged doors to permit them to be read.

Paneling is often the desired cover for walls. There is a great variety of different kinds and a broad range of prices. Hardwood paneling is generally less expensive than other kinds and has rugged wearing characteristics. It comes ready to paint or with finished grainy surfaces, or with a hard plastic finish.

There is also veneered plywood, available in a wide range of finishes and designs, and becoming more and more economical. You can get it with a factory finish or in unfinished grades. Often the factory-finished kind is a better buy, though a little more expensive in first cost than the unfinished kind. Figure your cost for finishing materials, brushes, etc., and you may be ahead of the game by choosing the pre-finished paneling. (Also see section on paneling, Chapter 16.)

You could also use gypsum wallboard (dry-wall) which is about the cheapest wall cover of all. You will have to paint it though, and figure this cost on top of the material cost.

One kind of wall cover not to use in the basement is any material that will be damaged by moisture or water. This includes some hardboards, fiberboard, and some plywoods and solid wood panels which may be particularly sensitive to water. Check on this before buying.

Lighting

Lighting can make the difference between a really successful basement space and a dimly lit bust. You'll generally need plenty of lighting, not just a fixture or two. Special recessed fixtures can be installed in the ceiling. A variety of styles and types are available with fluorescent and incandescent bulbs. At the same time, strive for a bright, well-lit space by using light-colored or white walls and ceiling. The lighter the surrounding surfaces, the more light reflected and the less light absorbed, thus a higher over-all light level.

New Windows

Just because basement walls are of solid brick or masonry is no reason to rule out new windows. Punching a hole in such a wall for a window is generally easier than it may sound and eminently logical. Obviously there should be enough exposed wall above ground level for the window. With the usual 2 to 3 feet of basement wall rising above ground level, a ribbon of wide horizontal windows can be installed with remarkable success.

Deeper windows can be installed wherever the ground may slope away from the basement walls by 4 or 5 feet. If the ground slopes off sharply from one end of the house, there may be enough exposed wall for a large picture window. This can work wonders for a basement, almost single-handedly transforming it into a full-fledged room.

If very little basement wall is above ground, attack the problem the other way—by excavation. In effect, the wall is raised above ground level. With suitable terrain a private sunken garden can be located outside. At the very least, a small excavation can provide a well for a single window.

A more ambitious scheme is extending part of a basement wall, and only the basement wall itself, several feet out past the house walls. This need be only an 8- or 10-foot portion of basement wall, which is roofed over with a glass skylight or greenhouse glass. Not only will sun and light flood into the entire basement, but with a southern exposure the portion under the glass can make an excellent sunning spot virtually the year around.

Other Suggestions

A really warm basement floor can be had by building up a new wooden floor several inches above the cement floor. A vapor barrier (of heavy 55-pound roll-roofing building paper or plastic sheet at least 4 mills thick) plus an inch of insulation should be installed under the raised floor.

Every basement should have a 36-inch wide door directly to outdoors for carrying large things in and out.

The basement stairway should become an inviting approach to downstairs. Vertical rails are mandatory along its length, particularly for safety with children and old folks.

The basement should be inspected for termites and wood rot *before* it is finished off. Termite people will do this for a small charge. Otherwise you risk the hidden spread of incipient termites and rot to your new walls as well as to the basic house structure. (See Chapter 23 for preventing termites.)

Achieving a Dry Basement

All bets are off if your basement is chronically wet. Converting a wet basement into a livable space is foolhardy unless the wetness problem is cured first.

Even a minor water-seepage problem can cause much wood-rot damage. Eliminating dampness and water requires, first, tracking it down to its source.

Water entry is often the result of poor ground-water drainage away from the house. The water sinks into the earth and then pushes through the walls. Waterproofing the inside of the walls is only a halfway remedy even with the best paints. First precaution is to be sure that the ground outside slopes away from the house on all sides so that rain water is shed away from the foundation walls.

Make sure that the vertical drain pipes from roof gutters down to the ground are not clogged. This is a frequent trouble and the water breaks through and into the basement. Roof drains ("leaders") that spill their water directly onto the ground should be directed away from the house; a concrete splash block should be put below them so that the water does not sink directly into the earth.

Sometimes a tile pipe drain is required in the ground all around the house exterior. This is about the only cure for a chronic wet basement condition. Unfortunately, a trench must be dug all around the foundation walls and the tile pipe laid in it. The pipe is put down at a depth equal to the basement-floor level. Its purpose is to catch ground water, before it presses into the basement, and carry it away. The exterior wall surfaces also could be waterproofed with a good waterproofing material sold in paint and hardware stores. And obviously all cracks and holes in the basement floor and walls should be filled in.

Sometimes the basement floor is a surprising source of dampness. Moisture from the ground below will rise in the form of vapor, straight up through ordinary concrete. Lay a sheet of waterproof building paper or heavy aluminum foil directly over a portion of the floor and weight it down. After a few days pick up the paper to see if its underside is damp. If it is, the floor vapor can be kept down by sealing the floor with a good coat of vapor-barrier masonry paint. Another solution is to cover the floor with waterproof building paper (the 55-pound kind at least), and then build a new floor above it.

Dehumidifiers

If moisture is a persistent problem, an electric dehumidifier may be your only solution. It removes moisture from the air and will keep the basement dry provided your problem is not acute. A dehumidifier will remove from about 10 to perhaps 25 pints of water a day, depending on the type and brand. (This isn't much when you realize that an ordinary window air conditioner will wring out 100 to 200 pints of moisture every 24 hours.)

Choose a dehumidifier with an automatic humidistat control so it will not run all the time. The control automatically turns the unit on or off as required, according to a preset humidity level. The water wrung from the air settles in a pan or tank integral with the unit. You empty it by hand, unless you can locate it above a floor drain, or have a pipe drain attached.

Unfortunately, there are no rules for choosing the size and capacity needed. Obviously, the larger your basement, and the greater your moisture problem, the larger the dehumidifier required. Check manufacturer's ratings, especially the water-removal capacity, one against the other, and also discuss it with a good dealer. Since brand quality changes continually, look up dehumidifier ratings in *Consumer Reports* magazine. In general, prices run from about $75 to $125.

Sump Pump

A sump pump is the solution when you have a really bad water condition in the basement and there's no way to get rid of it save pumping it out. Don't fight it, just get rid of it. You dig a small hole in the basement, near the main source of water, line the hole with cement, and have an electric sump pump installed in the hole. Normally, the job can be done for $50 to $75.

Chapter 8

Other Rooms, Other Needs—
Family Room, Living Room, Bedrooms,
Laundry

A New Family Room

A so-called family room is needed by virtually every family but nobody knows exactly how to define it. This depends on your family. Indeed, you may have one and not know it.

It is also called a "rec" room, a game room, Florida room, or even a "lanai." The early colonists called it a keeping room. In the 1920s it was called the "whoopee room," generally a finished room, usually in the basement, for adult parties (and dancing the Charleston) and a daytime space for children's play.

Its keynote is informality. Ideally, it is a household's center of gravity for a variety of family activities that relieve your formal living room of noise, clutter, and toys. It is for informal everyday living and entertaining, for watching TV, sewing, listening to records, reading, children's play, card games, hobbies, coffee with neighbors, or just plain informal talk and conversation. In short, it neatly handles those overflow activities that often occur by default in a crowded kitchen or formal living room, neither of these rooms being satisfactory as a genuine family room.

The First Requirement

The trouble is that some family rooms are a hopeless bust, while others are a great success (sometimes by accident). The key to success is deciding in advance precisely why you need a family room. This depends on your family and it is not so much what new activites you intend to use it for, but what your family likes to do now that could be carried out more enjoyably in a family room.

What will your family room be used for? Do you have children who need a play area (because they are either underfoot in the kitchen now or messing up the living room)? Do friends, neighbors, and relatives drop in frequently? Do you play bridge regularly, listen to records, or just need an informal room to relax in for the whole family with the living room unsuitable for such uses?

Make a list of what *your* family likes to do, the activities you think could be centered in a family room. This is your first requirement.

For that matter, the list may show that you really don't need to spend money for a new family room. A few changes in your dining room or living room may make one of these sufficiently versatile to take up the slack when for deceptive reasons these rooms are not now carrying their share of the load.

New corner fireplace is the focal point of this new family room. It was formerly a garage! Warm pecky-cypress paneling makes a good backdrop for the antiques.
©1960, *The Curtis Publishing Co., courtesy of The American Home. Kranzten Studio, Inc.*

Family room was made large and spacious by floor-to-ceiling glass opening on an inviting private patio. *Western Pine Assn. John Hartley.*

Small living room is bright, cheerful, and large as a result of floor-to-ceiling glass. *Ben Schnall.*

This happened, for example, quite by accident in my own house with a large dining room that was largely neglected except at dinnertime. We impulsively put a couch in the dining room and the transformation was remarkable. It is now the natural spot for reading the paper and after-meal coffee, while often at the same time the children (age five, two-and-a-half and one) confine their play there, apparently finding it a secure place with parents unobtrusively present. They no longer leave their toys and debris strung around the adjacent living room. We didn't need to build a new room.

Location Is Crucial

The best location is adjacent to the kitchen with easy access to outdoors. There are good reasons for this. A mother can keep an eye on children, be readily available in a crisis, and in addition, children, especially young ones, like to know that a parent is nearby. Being close to the kitchen also simplifies the serving of food and refreshments that would otherwise require a trek through the house for delivery.

A location on the opposite side of the kitchen from the living room can be particularly effective. The kitchen serves as a buffer between adults in the living room and the noise of children in the family room; at the same time the kitchen can serve both rooms.

Do you have the space now? Look around your present kitchen. Can you convert a dining room, carport, garage, breezeway, porch, or even a patio into a family room?

But remember that a family room should be airy, bright, and exposed to plenty of daylight. This calls for at least one southern exposure, anywhere from the southeast to southwest side of the house, especially in a northern climate. A southern exposure is less important in a warm climate. On the other hand, access to an outdoor patio or play area is virtually essential in a warm climate so that the family room can be a natural link between indoor and outdoor living.

The lowest level of a split-level house may be a good location. In a cold climate, however, this space is often so cold and poorly heated that it is off limits in winter. Adding insulation and improving the heat are usually required.

As a rule, avoid a basement location because it is inconvenient, because it lacks plenty of light and air, and as noted in the previous chapter, because you may find everybody back upstairs after the novelty wears off. A basement playroom may be superb for the roughhousing of older children who do not need supervision, or for a workshop, say. But its basic nature rules against the cheerful informality and convenience required of a good family room.

Size, Decoration, and Construction

A good size for a family room is about 14×20 feet. Minimum size recommended is about 12×14.

Choose light and gay colors to make the room feel large and cheerful. Cool shades of blues and greens are good in a warm climate. Warm colors like reds, browns, yellows, and oranges are better in a cold climate, particularly to make up for limited sunshine during winter. Wall and floor materials should be chosen for ruggedness, low upkeep, and easy cleaning. (See Chapter 16.) They'll take a constant beating. An acoustical tile ceiling is good for putting a damper on noise. It is not recommended, however, if you intend to listen to records, particularly hi-fi, because of its muting effect on music.

Plan for plenty of built-in storage. Make a list of everything you intend to store there and then build the appropriate shelves, cabinets, and drawers. Free-standing storage partitions are excellent for separating the room into zones, as well as providing built-in storage. Another good idea is a window seat with a hinged top. Toys can be tossed into it at night or when a quick clean-up is necessary before guests arrive. Put the top down for extra seating capacity and instant neatness.

Other Ideas

A nearby bathroom for washing up can be a boon. If you already have one conveniently near, fine. Adding one can be expensive, of course. If you will need a bathroom anyway but cannot afford it now, plan for it when the family room is being built and have the necessary plumbing lines installed so that the bathroom can be completed later at minimum expense.

A fireplace is a good idea and can be had comparatively inexpensively with one of the neat little prefabricated fireplaces now on the market.

Don't forget a place to eat. If there isn't space for a regular table, consider a pulldown table or counter, hinged to a wall. It can also serve double duty as a desk, card table, or game surface.

But don't load down the room with every conceivable feature you can think of. Think out in advance exactly what you want and omit everything else. A pool table may be great for Jackie Gleason's home, but not for yours.

New Living Rooms

When you contemplate a new living room analyze the good and bad features of your present one. Do you use it fully? Or do you find that it is hardly ever used, except perhaps when you have company? Why is it used or not used much? This is the crucial question. It may have an isolated location, stuck in the front of the house while your family gravitates to the rear and the back yard.

Does it feel bright or pleasant with plenty of window light and air? Or is it dark and gloomy because of few windows and poor light? Summarize its good and bad features so the good can be repeated and the bad omitted.

Add-A-Room package comes with 4-foot-wide panels that are quickly erected over a concrete or wood floor. Besides sliding glass panels, solid insulated panels are also available. Room size varies from 8×12, up to 12×20 feet, depending on number of panels used. Room can be assembled by two men over a weekend. Prices start at approximately $875, plus installation. Package was developed by Alcoa, is sold by Montgomery Ward. This is obviously the efficient way to build, and other comparable room packages are expected to be introduced in the future.

Aluminum Company of America.

What about location and traffic circulation? As noted in Chapter 3, a living room should be free of cross-traffic from one part of the house to another. It should be a dead end and not a major thoroughfare. Is it convenient to the dining room and kitchen so that there can be a smooth flow and relationship among these three rooms?

Is it big enough? Are there good places for furniture and storage? Will it be bright and cheerful with plenty of light and air? Size depends much on personal requirements and you can get an idea of its adequacy from the size of your old living room. A feeling of roominess and large size can be had with a high ceiling or a sloped cathedral ceiling, plus the judicious use of large windows (but not the usual foolhardy, front picture window). A large glass area should look out on a private garden, patio, or pleasant view.

A living room should have at least two exposures, and its design should permit your furniture to face the three main focal points at once—fireplace, TV set, and outside view. It's a great nuisance when furniture has

Entrance hall in Bellevue, Washington, house was transformed into an attractive foyer by new stairs, new door, and relocated window. Lack of balustrade gives feeling of airiness (but is obviously not sensible with small children).

to be switched around every time you watch TV, enjoy the fire, or merely sit pleasantly with guests, looking out the window.

New Bedrooms

The same analysis of present bedrooms and the same tests for size, furniture placement, and a bright cheerful countenance apply to new bedrooms as well as to a new living room.

Bedrooms for adults should be large enough to hold a desk and chairs as well as bedroom furniture. A child's bedroom needs space for study and play. Windows should be large enough to let in ample light and air.

Windows in at least two different walls formerly were mandatory for cross ventilation, but are less important now because of air conditioning.

A common drawback is the use of high, ribbon bedroom windows for privacy. People feel just as compelled to draw curtains or shades over them as over large windows. They are also particularly imprisoning in children's bedrooms, hard to see through, and hard to get out of in case of a fire.

The Laundry

Like other rooms, the location of the laundry is important. Where is it? Ideally, it should be near the kitchen and the bathroom where it will save many steps for a woman. A location near the bathroom eliminates steps in gathering soiled clothes and putting away clean ones. It also eliminates the need for clothes chutes, and requires little additional plumbing cost.

In a two-story house, a first-floor location gets the nod over a basement location. It makes laundering much simpler and a woman is not burdened with the chore of getting a clothesbasket up and down the basement stairs. Putting the laundry in the kitchen has become a popular idea. But it draws fire from women who dislike the idea of soiled clothing in an area where food is prepared.

A hall location is also increasingly popular but too often it is small, cramped, and lacks adequate light and ventilation. The total amount of

Built-in laundry is neatly closed in when not in use, and space serves as pleasant, all-round utility room. *Joseph W. Molitor.*

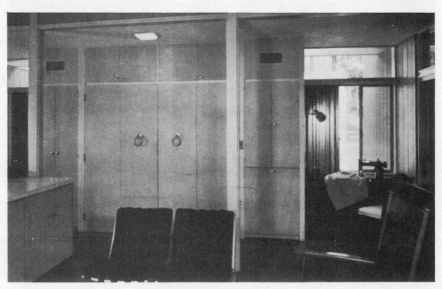

space needed for a laundry depends on your equipment. The smallest space recommended with an automatic washer, drier, and ironing-board area is about 6×12 feet.

There should be a cabinet or shelves for storage of soap, detergents, iron, and so on, counter space for sorting, and a space for a clothes rack, no longer so important for drying but a convenience when ironing.

Equipment Sequence

The equipment should be arranged for all movements in one direction toward where clothes are dried; from hamper, to sorting counter, to sink if necessary, washer, drier, and ironing counter. The normal sequence for a right-handed person is right to left, which means the drier should be on the left of the washer when they are side by side. This puts special emphasis on having the doors of the washer and drier open in the right direction. For the recommended right-to-left washer-drier location, the washer door should be hinged at the right or at the bottom; the drier door at the left or at bottom. The opposite is required for a left-handed woman.

The drier should be located near an outside wall to permit easy venting to outdoors. A vent is essential, for without one much moisture, heat, and lint will be blasted into the house. Some driers, however, have drain-pipe attachments for carrying away their exhaust; they do not need an air vent.

An excellent laundry planning booklet is available for 15¢ from the University of Illinois' Small Homes Council, Urbana, Illinois.

Chapter 9

Converting a Garage
or Carport, or Building
a New One

Probably no other enclosed space under a roof offers the wealth of opportunities for an inexpensive addition than a ground-level garage attached to your house. Construction costs are sharply reduced since the basic floor, walls, and roof are already in place. This assumes, of course, that new shelter for the family carries higher priority than for the family car, and that a new place for the car is possible.

What kind of space do you need? A garage can be turned into a family room, bedroom or two, guest room, playroom, a versatile covered patio or porch in summer, or even a new and better location for kitchen, dining room, or living room.

Its location usually dictates its best use. Close to the kitchen, it can be a natural for a family or playroom, or even a new master bedroom or study. Bordering on the side or rear of the house, it almost always can be used as an adjunct to an outdoor patio or play area.

Indeed, one of the newest and most logical garage ideas is opening it up with windows, screens, and sometimes sliding glass doors so it becomes a cool and sheltered retreat in summer for children's play or adult relaxation and the outdoor area just outside turned into a private patio. The same idea, of course, is eminently practical for a carport. Come winter, summer furniture is stored away and the space turned back to shelter for the car.

Privacy from the street and neighboring houses is essential. It is usually easy to achieve merely by leaving the front door of the garage closed in summer, and breaking through a rear or side wall so that the new space for living opens up on a private outdoor area. At the very most, a discreet fence can be erected to screen a new carport living area or patio-garage from the street.

Regardless of what you do to a garage, new windows are inevitably needed and the garage door opening may be a problem. New windows are usually easy to install but they should conform in style with the rest of the house windows and also line up with adjacent windows in the house. If the door opening faces a potentially good view, not just the street, it can take a large window or sliding glass doors with the apron outside turned into a private patio.

Carport was converted to double-duty garage by installing overhead doors at both ends. In summer, garage serves as family/play area with attached patio, with front door closed for privacy.

Kranzten Studio.

The garage floor, usually lower than the rest of the house, can and most often should be raised to the same level as the house floor to avoid the hazard of steps. Often the ceiling is sloped high to its peak and leaving it open will give you the expanse of an open-beam, vaulted ceiling in the new room, a much nicer idea than putting in the usual flat (and uninspired) ceiling.

What about the car? If new shelter is required, it is almost always cheaper to build a new carport or garage for it than add a new room to the house. But before any work is launched, check your building and zoning codes for setback and driveway restrictions. This is extremely important because space for off-street parking may be required by law, in addition to the space needed for the new carport or garage.

Building a New Carport or Garage

The location may take a little juggling, depending on your requirements. It should be located close to the kitchen for convenience and speedy grocery unloading. On the other hand, the closer it is to the street, the lower the driveway cost. These two requirements may or may not clash. The garage need not be attached to the house. By setting it off 10 to 20 feet from the house it can sandwich a patio or breezeway between it and the house.

In a cold climate, try to locate it, if possible, on the north side of the house where it will shield the house from cold north winds in winter. Next best bet in the North is a location on the west to shield you from hot summer sun in summer. A west exposure is obviously best in the South for protecting you from the sun during the hottest time of day.

What Size?

A one-car garage or carport should be 10×20 feet at least, inside dimensions. For two cars, minimum inside dimensions are 18 feet 4 inches ×20 feet. You may want to expand it slightly for elbow room with a large station wagon or Cadillac. You may be inclined to shrink the size to save money if you have a small car, but this may be unwise; it can put a hitch into selling the house. Naturally, ample extra space should be allowed if you want a laundry area or workshop, say, built into the garage.

An extra 2 feet of width or length can provide for many built-in storage cabinets or shelves. Enclosed storage cabinets are an excellent idea, especially when they serve as one wall of a carport, for outdoor furniture, garden tools, lawn mower, toys, and bicycles. And the floor of a carport should be pitched, preferably toward the driveway and street, for natural rain-water drainage.

Chapter 10

Porches and Patios; and Converting a Porch into a Year-Round Room

The location of a new porch or patio is of primary importance: Its location should provide a natural link between the house and the outdoors.

A location on the side or back of the house with a private view is obviously better than one facing the street. If located close to the kitchen or dining room, either a porch or patio can be a convenient and delightful place for summer meals as well as a retreat from summer heat. At the same location it can be a play area for children.

Consider the exposure of porch or patio to sun and winds, as mentioned earlier. With a southern exposure and turning its back to cold northern winds, a porch or patio can be a delightful spot in fall and winter. This is especially true for the patio designed to catch the sun during these seasons but roofed over to keep it cool in summer.

If summer cooling is your chief consideration, a porch should be located so it will receive the prevailing summer breeze where you live. The direction of the breeze can be obtained from the nearest weather bureau office or airport. (In a hot and humid climate, however, even the best, new screened porch does not offer much relief from muggy humidity; the same money spent on central air conditioning could well mean richer benefits all summer long.)

Privacy Is Essential

Will you have privacy? If you feel exposed to passing traffic or neighbors, you will not enjoy the place as much as you'd like. This is particularly important when you spend much time in summer dining outside, entertaining, or just relaxing in welcome coolness. It even can be close to

A successful patio requires convenient access to and from the house, as shown here. Note sliding glass doors and no steps.   *Western Pine Assn.*

the street or the next house but privacy can be built-in by adroit location of a wall or fence to screen you from view.

You will want a light or two and a couple of electric outlets. At least one outlet should be connected to heavy-duty wiring capable of handling a coffee maker, electric frying pan (for morning pancakes outside), or other cooking appliances (see Chapter 22 for wiring specifications).

Use rugged waterproof materials, not only for resistance to rain (and snow too in the North even with an enclosed, screened porch), but also so that you can hose down the walls and floor. This calls for a slight slope in the floor and drainage openings around the floor to let water drain away. Screen the openings so bugs cannot enter.

This outdoor patio is a natural adjunct to the living room. Patio is covered by an extension of the house roof.   *Techbuilt.*

A new patio can be built for as little as $200 to $300 (without roof). Cost of a new screened porch starting from scratch and roofed over generally runs from $750 up to about $1500, depending on its size and how much existing house wall it can borrow.

Transition Porch

If a new porch is to be a transition step, later to be made into a fully enclosed year-round room, the walls, floor, and roof should be insulated when they are built. Use plenty of insulation; its cost is a lot cheaper if it is installed while the structure is being built, compared with adding insulation afterward. Make provisions for heating for the same reason, as the heating pipes or ducts will also cost less if installed during initial construction; the radiators can be added later.

Design the screen openings for the kind of windows you will want. Windows can be installed later with a minimum of expense. This and other ideas for a transition porch are perhaps best illustrated by an actual example which also illustrates how a present porch can be converted into a year-round room.

Converting a Porch into a Year-round Room

Many families, to be sure, want a porch that is a porch and it doesn't make sense to give up a cool summer porch for a regular year-round room. The airy benefits in summer are much too desirable to lose. You can have your cake and eat it too if the new room is properly designed to retain its coolness for continued summer use as before, and simultaneously be a truly warm and comfortable room in winter.

I was torn by exactly this problem with a screened porch on a small house we once lived in. It was a delightfully cool retreat in summer with a lovely view of a small lake. At the same time, new year-round living space was urgently needed (because of a baby) and the porch was the logical place for obtaining it at the least expense. It seemed logical to convert the porch into a warm winter room and design it so it could be turned back into a cool porch in summer.

Before: Porch in suburban New York house had concrete floor, low walls, and ribbon screening, was useable in summer only.

After: Splendid view of lake and airy feeling was retained for year-round enjoyment by means of sliding glass windows with matched screens and storm windows. Room is amazingly warm in winter despite all the glass and a north exposure because of baseboard radiators (arrows), and floor, walls, and ceiling being insulated to the hilt. Comparable heating warmth can be obtained with series of warm-air heating outlets in the floor or baseboard under the windows.
Alexandre Georges.

Starting point was a small screened porch only 9×12 feet in size. It had three exposed walls and was attached to the house at its fourth wall. It had a cold, concrete floor built over the ground and continuous screening around the three exposed walls.

After mulling over a variety of ideas, I decided to replace the screening with a ribbon of glass windows. Horizontal, sliding wood windows were chosen because they came with matched screens and storm windows, and highly important, the window glass units could be removed easily in summer leaving only the screens. It was the the ideal solution and worked perfectly when hot weather came. (In fact, only a few of the windows, not all, had to be removed in summer to let in enough breeze for cooling.)

Replacing all the screening with glass gave another big advantage. That much glass made the small 9×12 room seem much larger than it actually was. Even on the coldest and gloomiest days of winter, the large expanse of glass made the room remarkably pleasant because of the view and the feeling of great space. In summer, too much glass exposed to hot sun can turn a room into a hothouse. But in this case, the porch exposure was chiefly north and east and it did not receive that much sun in summer.

Keeping Warm in Winter

Of all things, the new room also turned out to be the warmest, most comfortable room in the house in winter, though this took a little doing. The original porch had been built a few years before. I had full-thick

insulation installed in the new walls and roof at that time, figuring it would pay off later. The combination of a lot of window glass, plus a cold concrete floor and a cold northern exposure obviously demanded special attention to insulation and heating. Three things were done:

First, rigid insulation board was installed all around the exposed perimeter of the floor slab. This is an absolute necessity for concrete floors in the North. Second, a built-up wood floor, including a layer of insulation board, was installed over the concrete. Third, hot-water-heating baseboard radiators were installed around the three exposed walls of the room. A hot-water-heating boiler was used to heat the rest of the house and the new radiators were simply connected to it. (I wasn't sure that the existing house heater had spare capacity for the new room—another reason for keeping down the new room heat requirements with maximum insulation.)

All of these things may sound unnecessarily expensive but their cost is low. Without any one of them the room could easily have been too cold for comfort in winter. There were also the storm windows to reduce heat loss through the glass. But storm windows were not required on all the windows for the room to be remarkably warm in winter; cold downdrafts from the glass were virtually eliminated by the rising heat from the baseboard radiators. At the height of winter, storm windows were essential on two sides of the room to shield it from icy cold winds bearing down on the house from across the lake. They were not required on the third side.

A Common Mistake Made

A separate heating control should have been provided for the new room. Because it wasn't, the room *overheated* when it was flooded with early morning sunshine in spring and fall. Its radiators were controlled by the single house thermostat in the living room. If this thermostat was turned down, the rest of the house (not well insulated) got too cold. I had discussed the need for a second thermostat (zone control) beforehand with two different heating contractors. Both dismissed the idea, saying it was unnecssary.

Total Cost

The cost of remodeling the porch came to $100 over the original estimates, a total cost of $865. The extra cost was due to two new doors, which required much extra installation labor because they were ordered too large by mistake. Both the inside and outside doorways had to be enlarged for the new doors. It was an expensive personal oversight that I paid for.

What a difference outside improvements can make, as shown by these before and after photos. This is a typical development house in Levittown, N.Y. Private outdoor patio, rich landscaping, and new carport were added by owners, turning a bare lot into lush private grounds.

Ben Schnall.

We also forgot that doors require hardware—doorknobs and latches—and overlooked this cost. I subcontracted each part of the work myself, and the cost (in 1958) added up as follows:

Cost of ready-made windows and doors, including storm sash and screens	$325.00
Vinyl-asbestos floor tile and mastic	21.00
Electric wiring (four outlets)	24.00
Edge insulation, mastic, and related materials (labor by owner)	12.00
Heating (materials and labor)	170.00
Carpentry labor for floor, windows and doors, and floor tile	313.00
Total	$865.00

Part 4

KITCHENS AND BATHROOMS

There is much more to a good kitchen than shiny appliances and roomy cabinets. Is it planned for efficient and convenient food preparation? Are there adequate countertop areas and ample, well-designed storage? What about the quality of the kitchen sink, faucets, and countertop material, as well as appliance quality? Will it be a pleasant and cheerful place to work in with plenty of air and light?

Even the most glamorous kitchens pictured in advertisements are often deceptive and poorly planned (often because a good many are fake arrangements set up in a lavish photographer's studio). The ingredients for a good kitchen break down into several major elements.

Knowing a few basic planning principles is also important for good bathroom design. A good bathroom also requires good quality fixtures, though you need not choose the fanciest, most expensive fixtures. This and other facets of bathrooms are discussed here too.

Compact kitchen in California house is bright and cheerful because of open planning
and overhead skylight bubble. Note ledge behind kitchen counter which shields the
clutter of dishes at mealtimes from people in adjacent room.

Courtesy Skydome Skylights. Ernest Braun.

Chapter 11

What Makes a Good Kitchen?

The three most essential features are proper appliance location (in relation to each other), adequate countertop space in between, and plenty of planned storage for necessities at or near their point of use. It is not quite as simple as that, however, partly because of the expense involved, and also because limited size and awkward shape of a kitchen space may make for difficult planning.

A couple I knew had such a problem. They ended up with a near-perfect new kitchen, later published in a national magazine. But this was only after they called in an architect and discarded five trial plans in a row before they hit on the sixth and final layout.

You need not hire an architect, but you should know the essential points of good planning. But before going into the layout of the kitchen components, an appraisal of kitchen location and exposure is in order.

Is the Kitchen Centrally Located?

The importance of a central location has been noted earlier and should be repeated. The ideal location is one that is near the garage, near the family entrance to the house, near an outdoor patio or living area, and not far from the front door. The kitchen is a woman's activity center and in it she should be close to the center of all family activities.

If your present kitchen is isolated at a rear corner of the house, say, perhaps it can be moved to a better location. Main expense here will be new plumbing, but this need not be unduly expensive compared with the inevitable cost of changing pipes around at the present location. Wiring and lighting is another expense, but this cost will not vary much with location.

Good Kitchen Exposure

Is your present kitchen and dining room bright, pleasant, and flooded with sunlight during the day, especially in the morning? Or is it cast in shadows most of the day and perhaps later cursed with heat and glare? It depends on its exposure.

The best exposure for kitchen and dining room is generally a southeast exposure. This will give you bright morning sunshine the year around. A kitchen facing the south gets less morning sun, especially in summer, but more afternoon sun. A kitchen on the east gets sun only in the morning. A kitchen on the north gets little morning sun except in summer (which may be fine if you live in the South) and it is exposed to cold winds in winter.

A kitchen on the west or southwest is probably worst of all; it gets the most sun heat in the late afternoon, which can make it insufferably hot.

Neat corridor kitchen has excellent layout, plenty of countertop space and storage cabinets of wood. One drawback, however, is lack of small eye "screen" at end of counter to hide pots, pans, and other cooking utensils from eyes of diners. *Mutschler Kitchens.*

Conventional storage cabinets are not always needed. Here is convenient, built-in shelf storage within arm reach over counter, each designed for particular items to be stored. Also note row of built-in staple cabinets directly over rear counter.
Monsanto Chemical Co. Robert C. Cleveland.

Turning a poor exposure into a good one may be managed merely by moving a window, adding a new window, perhaps adding a skylight in the ceiling, or shading a big window exposed to hot sun.

Is Your Kitchen Large Enough for Remodeling?

According to a pioneering study at Cornell University, the minimum kitchen *work area* should be 96 square feet (12×8 feet or the equivalent). This is the minimum area needed to start with, excluding dining space. According to the Small Homes Council of the University of Illinois, the smallest work area for a U-kitchen arrangement is 8×10 feet. With a separate oven and dishwasher, the minimum should be 112 square feet (8×14 feet for example). These are *minimum* rules; try for more.

The All-important Work-Triangle Principle

Even the most glamorous kitchen installed by the usual kitchen remodeler can be a disaster because of shameful appliance scrambling (usually by men). They ignore the fundamental design principle—locating the refrigerator, sink, and range in that order from right to left (in reverse order, perhaps, if you're left-handed). This gives you the much publicized "work triangle," designed to save steps and conform to the natural sequence of food preparation, from refrigerator to sink-center to range. It is the starting point as well as the bedrock of a good kitchen plan.

According to the Cornell study, the refrigerator-to-sink-to-range should form a triangle of between 12 and 22 feet. The ideal for most women is 16 to 20 feet—about 5 feet from the center front of the refrigerator (or refrigerator-freezer) to center front of sink; about 5 feet from sink to center front of range; and about 7 feet from range back to the refrigerator.

The space near the refrigerator is often called the mix center. The refrigerator door should open toward the sink, and a handy countertop space at least 18 inches wide is needed next to the refrigerator for unloading food taken from the refrigerator.

The sink center, both a preparation and clean-up area, is the core of the kitchen and an active area. Dishwasher, garbage disposer, and main supply cabinets go here. Counter space at both sides of the sink is essential. The range or cooking center also requires counter space on both sides plus cabinets. Some people say the sink should be placed under a window, but this is not essential, especially if it disrupts the kitchen plan. A separate oven can be located in a less important area. It too should have counter space on one side at least (for hot dishes).

One more word about the work **triangle.** The ideal triangle is not

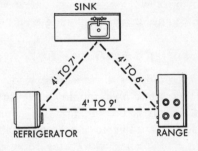

Essential kitchen requirement is an efficient work triangle formed by refrigerator, sink, and stove. Diagram gives shortest to longest leg dimensions recommended. It's best when no more than two of the three fixtures are on the same wall.

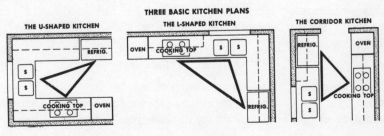

THREE BASIC KITCHEN PLANS

THE U-SHAPED KITCHEN   THE L-SHAPED KITCHEN   THE CORRIDOR KITCHEN

possible in every space. This need not bother you if you make an intelligent compromise. It's a case of knowing the rule before breaking it.

What Is the Best Kitchen Shape?

The work triangle can form one of four basic shapes: the U-kitchen, "L," corridor or pullman kind on two parallel walls, and the one-continuous-wall arrangement which is in effect a flattened-out triangle.

The U-shape gives the best traffic and work triangles. It is compact and efficient, with every appliance within a few steps of any other. It adapts well to an open-plan kitchen. The L-shape kitchen is efficient and adapts itself to almost any space. The corridor kitchen can be good if it is not a passageway for people walking from one part of the house to the other; it is also inhospitable by its nature, not good for a family that likes to sit and talk in the kitchen. The one-wall plan should be your last choice: i.e., when space is too narrow for one of the first three shapes, an efficient work pattern and ample counter space are difficult to achieve with it.

Three Most Common Kitchen Flaws

A Small Homes Council study of the kitchens in over 100 housing developments showed that the three most widespread flaws are not enough cabinet storage, insufficient countertop space, and no counter at all next to the range. Here are the SHC's minimum standards:

At least 8½ feet in length of base-cabinet storage; 11 to 13½ feet of length is ideal. This includes the cabinets under the sink and the storage portion of the range.

At least 5 to 8½ feet of wall cabinets.

At least 1½ feet of counter space on each side of the sink, on at least one side of the range, and on the open side of the refrigerator. The refrigerator door should open toward the sink.

New Method of Kitchen Planning

Here is how to plan a kitchen, based on a new concept developed by Professors William H. Kapple and Helen E. McCullough of the University of Illinois' Small Homes Council. By using this concept anyone can lay out a good kitchen. It employs the work-triangle principle in terms of the five essential work centers and the countertop space required for each. It puts great emphasis on adequate countertop space, which is a prime essential, and also because adequate storage space follows almost automatically in the space above and below adequate counters.

You begin by knowing the minimum recommendations for the five work centers, as follows:

1. Refrigerator with 18 inches of countertop space on the open-door side.

2. Mixing center: A 3½-foot counter next to the refrigerator, sink, or range.

3. Sink with 3 feet of countertop on the right, 2½ feet on the left (for dishwashing, food preparation involving water).

4. Range with 2 feet of heat-resistant surface on the left or right, preferably on the left.

5. Serving center: At least 2 feet of countertop preferably next to the range, or next to the refrigerator, second-best location.

Each of the above "work center" recommendations are based on each one standing alone by itself. In many cases several of them will be flush to each other against the same wall. Then adjacent countertop areas will be combined and less total countertop area is needed for the shared countertop surface than if each center were by itself.

Here is the rule to remember when two or more adjacent work centers are combined: The total shared countertop surface should be equal in size to the widest counter in the combined group plus one additional foot and that's all.

For example, say your refrigerator center and mixing center are flush to each other. The refrigerator center by itself requires 18 inches of countertop, the mixing center 3½ feet. When these two share the same combined counter, the combined total counter required is 4½ feet (the largest one being 3½ feet plus 1 foot).

If the same two work centers are also combined with the sink center, a total of 4½ feet of shared countertop surface is still all you need between the refrigerator and sink. The same rule applies, this figure being obtained from the 3½-foot mixing center (largest counter among the three grouped together) plus 1 foot.

In similar fashion, all five work centers would be combined if grouped together flush against one long continuous wall (one-wall kitchen). Then the total countertop surface would amount to 10 linear feet for all five combined work centers. This is considered the minimum countertop space for an efficient kitchen. Minimums mean just that. If you can, err on the side of generosity for a rewarding bonus in an important room.

Step-by-step Planning of a Kitchen

Planning a kitchen may sound complicated at first but it comes clear, and its logic and simplicity are astounding, as you try it. You start with the first part of the kitchen, the refrigerator, and go around the walls

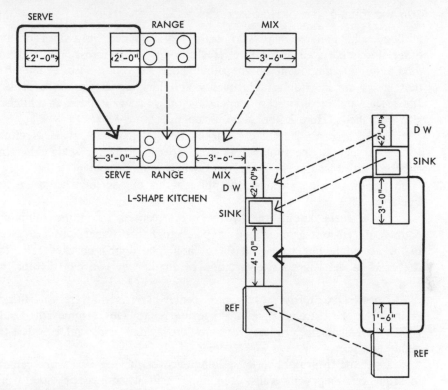

Diagrams show how to apply the University of Illinois' kitchen-design formula (explained in text) to the basic kitchen shapes when you plan a kitchen. When two or more separate counters are combined, total counter length for the combination is the sum of the widest one plus 1 foot. *House & Home,* © 1961 Time Inc.

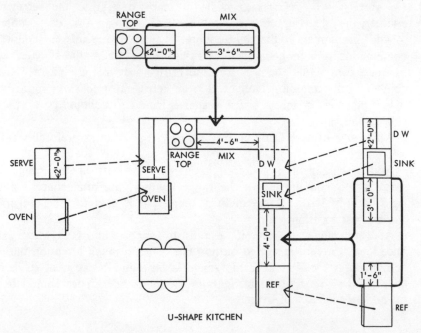

adding each appliance and work center in sequence. If a door or any other nonusable wall space interferes, simply jump across and add the next required component on the other side. As you proceed, remember that snags are inevitable, adjustments and juggling are to be expected. It's a trial and error process, depending on your wall space and kitchen size and shape. Here is the step-by-step process:

1. Make a scale diagram of your kitchen on paper. A scale of either ½ or ¾ inch to the foot works well. Special pads for scale diagrams can be had at stationery stores and will simplify the work. Try for a U-shape, or L-shape arrangement, though this of course depends on the kitchen.

2. Make scale cutouts of the five work centers using the minimum counter dimensions given above. Typical appliance dimensions are given in the accompanying table, but these should be double-checked later for the exact model you get. A variation of an inch or two can disrupt the best plan.

3. Locate the refrigerator work center (refrigerator plus 18-inch counter) at the extreme right, the starting point. This assumes the usual right-to-left sequence, unless you are left-handed and prefer a left-to-right sequence.

4. Continue from right to left adding each of the required work centers in sequence along your walls. Remember that when two or more work centers are combined in a continuous counter the total length of the shared counter is less than otherwise needed. Thus:

Add mixing center (3½-foot counter) to the left of the refrigerator (as you face the refrigerator). If this can go next to the refrigerator counter, the two counters are combined into a single 4½-foot counter.

Add sink center. If the right counter is flush to the missing counter, a combination 4½-foot long counter will serve for both. If your walls permit a continuous counter from the refrigerator to the sink, a 4½-foot counter is the minimum you need from refrigerator to sink; more could help if you have space. If a dishwasher is included it should be on the left side of the sink.

Add range center: Cooking range plus 2-foot counter preferably on the left side.

Add serving center, a 2-foot counter at the left of the range—last stop. If it is combined with the range counter, the total space for both need be only 3 feet. If it cannot go here, put it next to the refrigerator, second-best location.

Add separate wall oven, if desired: It can go almost anywhere, since once loaded it can be turned on and not demand much attention until the bell rings. A location near the range is best and because of its heat it should not go next to the refrigerator. Some counter space should be put on one side of a wall oven.

5. Consolidate your plan. If your kitchen lacks enough running wall surface to accommodate all the necessary centers, obviously something must give. It is best, however, not to trim a little here and a little there. Instead, group the work centers together with fewer separate units.

In addition, sometimes a door can be eliminated or moved. Perhaps a wall can be removed. Or a few feet may have to be added onto the kitchen by new construction. This should be your last alternative because of the expense. If no other out is possible, consider adding on new space to the kitchen by cantilever construction. The floor is extended out past the present exterior wall without a new foundation wall required below.

Does the over-all countertop length equal or exceed the required minimum of 10 feet? Check the size of the work triangle from refrigerator to sink to range to see that it falls between the recommended 12- to 22-foot over-all perimeter.

6. Locate storage cabinets in the best location under the counter and on the walls. Use the minimum standards already given. Obviously, cabinets should be located to store particular equipment and utensils nearest to where they are used. Cabinets for dishes and tableware are best at the serving center, nearest the dining room. Storage at the mixing center should provide for such things as bowls, sifters, grinders, mixers, plus flour, sugar, and spices. Sink storage should allow for dishwashing supplies, pots, strainers, brushes, knives, and vegetables that don't need refrigeration. Range storage should, of course, hold pots and pans.

Kitchen Planning Notes

The standard counter height is 36 inches. A few inches lower may be better if you are short. Standard depth is 24 inches. Although most appliances conform to these dimensions you need not be frozen to them. Some appliances also come in 30- to 34-inch heights. A baking and mixing counter is often lowered to 32 inches for convenience. You could install a pull-out shelf or tabletop at this height. Sometimes to conserve space, counter depth can be reduced to 22 or even 20 inches. This shortest depth is squeezing it a little but may be essential.

There should be at least 10 linear feet of base cabinets and 10 linear feet of wall cabinets. This counts "full-use" cabinets such as a cabinet under a counter. It does not include part-use cabinet space, such as below a sink, drawers in a free-standing range, corner cabinets, or wall cabinets above the range or refrigerator.

Corners are often a problem. Base cabinets should be added around a corner (giving a continuous countertop around the corner) only if you gain cabinet space by turning the corner. You should be able to add at

WIDTH REQUIREMENTS FOR STANDARD APPLIANCES

EQUIPMENT		WIDTH IN INCHES																	
		20"	21"	24"	26"	27"	28"	29"	30"	31"	32"	33"	34"	36"	39"	40"	41"	42"	48"
FREE-STANDING RANGES		E/G	G	E/G			G		E/G					E/G		E/G			
DROP-IN AND WALL-HUNG UNIT RANGES				E/G		E/G			E/G					E		E/G		E	E/(
BUILT-IN 4 BURNER RANGE TOPS				E/G		G			E/G					E/G				E	E/(
BUILT-IN OVENS				E/G								E/G							
DISHWASHERS				E					E										
SINKS																			
REFRIGERATOR FREEZERS	9 CU FT			E		E						E							
	10 CU FT				E		E	E				E							
	11 CU FT				G		E		E	E									
	12 CU FT						E		E	E	E/G		E						
	13 CU FT									E	E/G	E							
	14 CU FT								E	E	E/G	E							
	15 CU FT										E	E							
	16 CU FT								E		E/G	E							
	17 CU FT										E		E			E			
	18 CU FT										E								
	20 CU FT																		E

NOTE: E INDICATES ELECTRICAL MODEL. DATA FROM NATIONAL ELECTRICAL MANUFACTURERS ASSN.
G INDICATES GAS MODEL. DATA FROM GAS APPLIANCE MANUFACTURERS ASSN.

Chart gives common dimensions of appliances to use when you plan a kitchen before you have chosen the specific appliances you will use.

House & Home, © 1961 Time Inc.

least 3 feet of new cabinet space after turning the corner, measured at a right angle out from the *front* of the counter at the start of the corner. If 3 feet of new cabinets cannot be added, do not turn the corner. Instead, extend the countertop and cabinets to the wall and stop.

Peninsula and island cabinets are a good way to add base cabinets and extra countertop space. A peninsula cabinet sticks out at right angles from a wall cabinet toward the middle of the kitchen. It is worthwhile only if it can project out at least 3 feet. An island counter and cabinet stands by itself in the middle of the kitchen. It should be at least 4 feet from the range and at least 3 feet from the nearest base cabinet. A serving table or counter on wheels often can be just as good, particularly if you don't have the space for a permanent island.

Storage Tips

Extra storage capacity often can be found with a little imagination and a hard look at every corner and cranny of the kitchen. Much of the food, canned goods, and utensils kept in a kitchen can fit a space as little as 5 to 6 inches deep. So if necessary you can break into a wall and build recessed shelves in the unused space between the wall studs. Ideas like this can help you expand storage in your present kitchen as well as in a new one.

Other storage suggestions: Shallow cupboards 8 to 12 inches deep built in the unused wall space around doors and windows (good for hanging pots and pans); the unused space above and below a built-in oven; high shelves to the ceiling above existing cabinets for things used infrequently; a long shallow cabinet of perhaps 6 inches deep at the rear of a deep counter.

A few additional tips: Cabinets that face each other should be at least 5 feet apart. A dining table or snack bar should be at least 3½ feet from the nearest appliance or cabinet. Neither the refrigerator nor wall oven should be put in the middle of a continuous countertop run.

Choosing a Good Sink

Specify a sink of stainless steel or enameled cast iron. Stainless steel costs a little more but neither chip easily, both are easy to keep clean, and will last indefinitely. Stainless steel is the "prestige" kind nowadays. It will show water spots in hard-water areas, and you shouldn't take the word "stainless" absolutely literally; careless use can stain it.

Enameled cast iron requires scouring to kill black marks, its most annoying drawback. It looks fine but is often confused with the porcelain-on-steel sink, the cheapest, poorest kind, yet the most widely used because of low price. Porcelain-on-steel requires constant scrubbing, chips easily, and quickly loses its gloss. Avoid this kind. Try for a double-basin sink if you have the space, a boon for such things as draining dishes, though you may not want to sacrifice valuable counter work surface for it.

Choosing a Good Faucet Set

Most people today want a single-lever ("one-armed") faucet. Its convenience and ease of operation make the conventional double-control faucet as old-fashioned as a washboard. With a single-lever control, the right temperature and quantity of water is had with the touch of a finger. (You get water by pushing the handle forward like an airplane stick, the farther forward, the more water. Pushing the handle to one side or the other at the same time gives hotter or colder water. Scalding hot water is avoided by pushing the handle to the right setting before turning on the water.)

Nearly all single-lever faucet brands are of good-quality design. But if you get the usual double-control conventional faucet, be careful to get a good-quality kind; nearly every manufacturer makes cheap, shoddy kinds as well as better-quality sets. See the section on bathroom faucets in the next chapter for how to tell the difference.

Regardless of the kind of faucet you get, almost all manufacturers offer special optional features: A spray hose attachment for rinsing (but look for automatic operation by means of an on-off thumb lever); a soap dispenser which will cough-up soap on demand; and of all things, a separate dispenser for hand lotion or whatever else you might want dispensed at your fingertips. These features must be requested in advance so they will fit the trim you are getting.

Countertop Surfaces

New countertop surfaces may gleam handsomely, but how long will they stay that way? Are they easy to clean, stainproof and rotproof? It depends on the materials used. Here is a run-down of countertop materials in order of desirability.

A plastic laminate (Formica, Micarta, Panelite, for example) wipes clean with one swipe, will not stain, rot, or fade, and has good heat resistance to spilled boiling water. But hot pans can mar it and knives may cut it. It should last at least twenty years if it is the high-pressure kind (1/16 inch thick), not the low pressure kind (1/32 inch thick).

Sheet vinyl, lower in cost than a laminate, is easy to clean, and quiet with dishes. The chief limitation is poor resistance to heat. Hot pans will stick to it or melt it and boiling water can damage it.

Linoleum is colorful, attractive, and heat resistant but shows stains, scratches, and knife cuts. Because water can rot it, don't use it near the sink.

Stainless steel, increasing in popularity, is highly durable, stainproof, heatproof, easy to clean, and surprisingly resilient. But it is hard on knives (naturally), will show scratches, and is noisy.

There are also ceramic tile, marble, and wood. Chief features of the first two are good heat resistance and durability but both are hard on dishes. Tile will not stain but marble will. Both are easy to clean. Wood is best for a chopping center; it does not chip, crack, or dent, but does stain easily. It will show heat rings unless kept rubbed down with a good sealing agent (hot mineral oil).

The ideal kitchen therefore would have a combination of materials: tile, marble or stainless steel where hot pans are put down (range center); wood for your chopping and food preparation (mix center); plastic laminate or vinyl for good looks and easy cleaning elsewhere and particularly around the sink. This combination is expensive, but the best of all if you can afford it. The proper surface in the right place will not only mean low upkeep expense, less work and longer satisfaction, but is also a decided plus feature if you put the house up for sale after a few years. Then the kitchen will still look new.

Storage Cabinets

Choosing between wood and steel cabinets comes down to a matter of personal preference. Both are made in a variety of colors, styles, and quality. A few dollars more will give you a lustrous, easy-to-clean surface in either wood or steel.

Wood cabinets should be given a hard, sprayed-on, factory-paint finish, and you should insist on kiln-dried, treated wood or warping may be a problem. The best finish on steel, for low upkeep and long life, is a baked enamel finish applied in the factory. Steel cabinets should be made of bonderized, cold-rolled steel at least 22 gauge in thickness (the lower the gauge number, the thicker). The drawers of both kinds should move in and out smoothly and this requires metal slides and nylon rollers. Then any drawer can be pulled out all the way without sagging or sticking. Ask also for magnetic latches and adjustable shelves.

Good Lighting and Wiring

Good lighting calls for light shed over the sink and the main work surfaces, particularly deep under kitchen cabinets. A central kitchen light fixture is not enough. A woman standing at the sink, for example, ends up working in her own shadow. A light is needed over the sink. Extra illumination, often with short (but "warm") fluorescent bulbs, should light up countertop areas. There also should be at least two or three well-placed electric outlets along the wall behind the countertop area for plugging in small appliances.

Visualize where your small appliances will be used, the mixer, toaster, knife sharpener, and others. Electric outlets should be located in the wall nearby and above the countertop level. New wiring normally will be required, along with new outlets, particularly because such appliances generally require heavier wiring than required for ordinary lighting outlets.

The wiring and lighting alone for a kitchen may cost from $50 to $100, perhaps more if an elaborate job is necessary. See Chapter 22 for other wiring tips.

Removing Cooking Heat, Smoke, Grease, and Moisture

The best way to keep the kitchen well ventilated is with a good exhaust hood located directly over the range and exhausting to outdoors. The hood should cover all or most of the four burners. This normally calls for a hood about 30 inches deep from front to back and 3 to 4 feet wide. Some hoods are only 20 inches deep, which means reduced efficiency. Locate it no more than 26 inches above the range, if possible. A higher location means diminishing ability to catch rising fumes.

The larger the air-blowing capacity of the fan inside the hood, the better. The minimum requirement is at least 40 cubic feet per minute (cfm) of capacity for each linear foot of hood length. Thus, a 4-foot-long hood should have a fan with a capacity of at least 160 cfm (4 times 40). Minimum air capacity for a peninsula or island hood is 50 cfm per foot of length. The fan should come with an HVI (Home Ventilating Institute) certification tag. It's best not to accept a hood without this tag.

The larger and thicker the grease filter inside the hood, the better. Compare the size and thickness of one brand against another when you shop for a hood. The best filter would be one about 1 inch thick, but unfortunately ½ inch is the thickest available as this is written. Check that the filter can be easily removed for cleaning.

Noisy fan operation can be quite bothersome. The amount of noise varies according to the brand. Gauge the noise by having hoods turned on in a showroom before you buy. Most hoods come with a two-speed fan setting, a good feature to have. This permits you to cut down the speed (and noise) to a low setting during light cooking.

List prices for exhaust hoods generally range from about $45 to $75.

Exhaust Fans (No Hood)

An exhaust hood can get rid of as much as 85 per cent of your cooking fumes. An exhaust fan by itself is about 50 per cent efficient at best. But this depends on having it properly located, and getting a large enough fan for your kitchen.

The fan must be located over the range to do its job. This means in the wall behind the range and from 1 to 2 feet above the range surface, or in the ceiling directly over the range. Any other location is practically useless. A fan only a few feet to one side or the other of the range will catch no more than about 10 per cent of your cooking fumes; the rest of the air it exhausts is ordinary kitchen air.

The fan should have an air-handling capacity of at least 300 cfm, the minimum to accept. Its cfm capacity should be large enough to completely change the air in the kitchen every three to four minutes, thus provide at least 15 air changes an hour. Figure the total air volume of your kitchen in cubic feet and divide by 4 to determine the fan size required. A kitchen 12×15 feet with an 8-foot ceiling height therefore has 1440 cubic feet. This divided by four gives 380, the minimum fan size in cfm. A kitchen with 1200 cubic feet of volume or less should have a minimum 300 cfm fan. Like a good hood, a good exhaust fan should have an HVI certification tag.

Noisy operation is a widespread problem with exhaust fans as well as with exhaust hoods. Nearly all fans are noisy but some are noisier than others. The quietest fans are those with a low turning speed, which is measured in rpm (revolutions per minute) and usually noted on the fan name plate. The quietest fans are normally rated between 1400 and 1750 rpm. The noisiest ones turn over faster and as high as 3000 rpm, a speed to avoid.

A good trick for reducing fan noise is to locate the fan at the far end of its air-outlet duct, not at the beginning near the range. The grease filter, however, should be at the kitchen inlet side.

Ventilation can be a tough problem if your range is located against an interior wall. But it's not an insolvable problem. The fan could still be installed in the ceiling directly over the range with its exhaust duct *inside* the ceiling running between ceiling beams to the nearest exterior wall. This need not be very expensive to do, especially when carpenters are on the job for other work.

Ventless Hoods

The other alternative is the use of a ventless hood. Though they are less efficient than direct exhaust to outdoors, many people find them quite satisfactory.

Remember, though, that a ventless hood can remove only smoke and grease. It does not get rid of cooking heat and moisture, which are discharged back into the kitchen. So don't expect a ventless hood to cool the kitchen during hot weather.

The quality of a ventless hood depends most on its grease-filter efficiency and its fan air-handling cfm. The larger and thicker the filter, the better. As there are no industry standards available for judging filters, you have to compare the size and thickness of one brand against another. Also compare cfm ratings, the more air handled the better, and look for an HVI certification tag. The hood size, of course, is also important. It should be large enough to cover all or most of your burner surface. Ventless hoods range in price from about $75 up to $125.

Odor Removal

Some ventless hoods contain special filters to remove cooking odors. The only good odor-removal filter is the activated charcoal kind. It should contain from 2 to 3 pounds of activated charcoal. This will normally last about a year or two, and then the carbon must be replaced. There are also ventless hoods with other kinds of odor-removal filters, such as an ozone generator, which will not only do you little good, but too much ozone generated is a health hazard.

Considering cost, the price of a duct built into the ceiling with a conventional exhaust hood could well make the duct a better choice (especially since a duct gets your heat, smoke, and odors outside). In addition, noise can be reduced by locating the fan at the end of the duct, as just mentioned on the preceding page. Unfortunately, there are no other solutions to the heat and smoke problem, short of putting the stove on an outside wall or eliminating all cooking.

Operating Tips

If you install a hood, either the exhaust or ventless kind, or an exhaust fan, and it doesn't perform as well as you'd expect, investigate the movement of the air being drawn into the fan. The air should sweep across the range before being drawn up into the hood or fan. There should be no open windows or open doors close to the range. Then the fan will draw air in from this easy source; the air short-circuits the range and is pulled directly in by the fan, leaving your cooking fumes untouched.

Other tips on operation, as well as on choosing and installing kitchen hoods and fans, are given in a booklet, *Home Ventilation Guide,* available free from the Home Ventilating Institute, 1108 Standard Building, Cleveland 13, Ohio.

Appliances

New models and new features for old appliances are continually being introduced. It is bewildering to keep up with them. Do shop and do keep your eyes open for special features you will like. But also be on guard for the eye-catching "sales" feature designed chiefly to sell an appliance and actually of little or no worthwhile value to you once you start using it.

Carefully visualize how you will use each appliance and exactly how a special feature may or may not simplify things for you. It depends largely on your own particular cooking habits and whether or not *you* really want a special feature. Why pay extra for something that is pointless to have in your kitchen (even if it is ballyhooed in national advertising or on TV)? Is it truly functional for you, or is it a gimmick? By and large the simpler the device, the better.

Quality and serviceability, too, can vary greatly. But these are difficult to judge at first glance. Not only are certain brands better than others, but one manufacturer's different models can vary greatly in quality and usefulness. As we have mentioned elsewhere in this book, just about the best guide to quality is *Consumer Reports and Consumers' Research Bulletin* (but even they are not infallible).

Built-in appliances give a neat, unified appearance to a kitchen. A huge variety is available and new models are constantly being introduced. Built-in appliances, however, generally cost more than free-standing ones. They also may require more space than free-standing ones. With limited money, consider the use of free-standing refrigerators and ranges that have a built-in look. Of course, some of your present appliances can be incorporated in a new plan, with the layout adjusted to accommodate them.

Ranges

Should you get a gas or electric range? The choice is easy to make if there is a big difference in utility rates. Another consideration is whether you use gas or electricity for house heating and water heating. The same fuel also used for cooking can be more economical than otherwise, since the more fuel used for all purposes, the lower your unit cost for fuel.

All other factors being equal, choose the kind of range that appeals to *you*. Both gas and electric ranges are available in modern models that are convenient, fast, good-looking, accurate, easily cleaned, and remarkably automatic.

There are built-in ranges and free-standing ranges. The built-in kind usually looks better and fits naturally into a kitchen. Built-ins with separate cooking tops and ovens are particularly popular for remodeling. The oven section can be a single oven and broiler, a double oven, or an oven and independent broiler. It comes with no top or side panels and is installed in a custom cabinet or wall.

There are countertop ranges with pull-down burners. A pair of them could be combined with a pair of permanent burners, since two burners are all you need some of the time. The other two can be folded back out of the way, which frees range-top space for other use, then pulled down during heavy cooking demands.

A new kind of built-in is called the "drop-in" range, a one-piece range with counter-high surface burners and oven below. It drops into a counter and fits over a base cabinet about as high as a conventional, range storage drawer.

There is also a free-standing range called a "slide-in" which gives a built-in look with an inexpensive installation. It is squared to fit neatly between adjacent cabinets, at the end of a line of cabinets, or backed to a cabinet of the same size. Optional side panels are available. Chrome trim on the sides can overlap the adjacent counters to give you a continuous countertop and keep spilled crumbs from falling between the range and cabinets.

The "console" or "high-oven" range is still another kind with a neat contemporary look. It can be hung on a wall or set on a special base cabinet. An eye-level oven and broiler are above the surface burners, which usually slide out. Panels for the top and side are optional.

The size of your range may be crucial. Some models are only 20 inches wide but the oven will be small and the top cramped for space. Others range in size from 24 inches wide up to 40-inch wide units with two ovens. Built-in ranges generally require at least 24-inches of width, though many are wider. Since more space is needed for the cooking top, a built-in may be difficult to fit in when you have limited space.

Refrigerators and Freezers

Do you wish a combination refrigerator-freezer or a separate freezer? In both cases, you must evaluate your need for fresh food-storage space versus freezer space. Combinations are available with the freezer compartments at the top or bottom, and there are also new, wide models with a complete vertical freezer section, including its own door, next to its full-height refrigerator section.

If you have a separate freezer in the kitchen, the refrigerator will need freezing space only for ice cubes, and perhaps not even that. If the freezer is not located in the kitchen, you will probably want a larger freezer compartment in the refrigerator to hold such everyday food as frozen juice and vegetables.

You can get models with semiautomatic defrosting, automatic defrost, and those in which frost never forms. It depends on the price you pay. The least expensive refrigerators must be defrosted by hand.

Freezers generally require defrosting only a few times a year. Thus a combination model may have an automatic defrost system for the refrigerator, but manual for the freezer. The most advanced combinations and freezers in which frost never forms have the air inside circulated by fans. The forced-air circulation may mean an increased need to cover or wrap the foods inside the refrigerator (foods for the freezer obviously should be well wrapped in any case). But no freezer space is lost to frost build-up, packages stay dry and easy to remove, and their labels stay legible.

When buying a refrigerator be sure to specify the way the door should open for your kitchen. It should open toward a counter in the direction of the sink. Most units have a "right-hand" door, which means the hinges are at the right and the door opens on the left. You will want a left-hand door if your refrigerator-to-sink-to-range triangle is left to right (going clockwise). The same principle applies to combinations, of course, and also to a separate freezer, depending on where you locate it.

There are also built-in, wall-hung refrigerators which can put everything over a counter or cabinet within arm's reach, without stooping. Unloading is merely a matter of putting things down on the counter below with a minimum of effort. They are expensive, to be sure, about $500 to $600, but are worth considering if you can afford the money and want the utmost in convenience.

Dishwashers

The newest full-size dishwashers can do an excellent job, providing automatic washing and drying with hotter water than your hands can stand. They can be loaded in any order, at any time, thus keeping the kitchen free of clutter, and you turn the machine on when it has a full load.

Hand rinsing of dishes is eliminated before loading by getting a unit with an automatic prerinse cycle. All you do is discard food waste before loading. Many models contain booster heating coils to assure hot enough water. This is important because washing efficiency depends greatly on the use of hot, 160- to 180-degree water, which you may not have from your water heater, or for that matter not want it that hot for the rest of the house.

Another solution here is a two-way temperature valve available for water heaters. One side provides the very hot water required for the dishwasher, the other side provides lower-temperature hot water for other uses.

Many models offer a choice of features. "Rinse only" is handy when you wish to hold a few dishes only for later washing. A "pots and pans" setting omits the drying phase so that sticky food particles will stay soft and easy to remove with a scouring pad. This lets the dishwasher give you a head start on washing tough baking dishes, broiler racks, and so on, and you clean up stubborn spots by hand. "Wash only" lets you wash heat-sensitive dishes, such as plastics, without exposing them to the heat of the drying cycle. "Fine-china" cuts the water force to protect good glassware as well as delicate china. (But it's still not advisable to put platinum- and gold-trimmed china or patterns with overglaze decoration through a dishwasher.)

There are built-in dishwashers, portables, and convertible models. The built-in kind is permanently installed in a 24-inch counter space with attached plumbing. The portable usually has less capacity than a built-in, but is less expensive and is rolled to its place of use. It's pipe is attached to the kitchen faucet, its drain pipe hooked over the sink, and its cord plugged in to an electrical outlet. The convertible is the in-between model chiefly for those who want a dishwasher now, but later want to build it into a remodeled or new-house kitchen. It is a full-size unit that will fit a 24-inch cabinet space.

Food-Waste Disposers

A disposer grinds up waste and flushes the small pieces down the drain. It is usually installed directly under the sink. It lets you peel vegetables and fruits in the sink and push the peelings down the drain. It can also take such other waste as fat trimmed from meat, fruit pits, and any bones that will fit. Perhaps its biggest appeal is saving time by letting you scrape and rinse plates directly into the sink.

A disposer will not, however, handle such trash as paper, bottle caps, cans, or other comparable nonfood waste. You still need a trash basket for such waste.

There are two basic kinds of disposers, the batch-feed model and the continuous-feed model. Garbage is loaded into the batch-feed kind, a lid is put over the sink opening and turned to start the unit. A wall switch usually starts the continuous-feed kind and waste is fed in continuously during operation. The continuous-feed kind is somewhat more convenient, but the batch-feed may be desirable in a family with small children (as it cannot operate without its cover in place). Whichever you get, check the quality; it can vary considerably from brand to brand.

Appliance Design and Looks

Stick with a simple design in appliances, and cabinets, too, rather than the elaborate. The simpler the design, the longer they retain appeal. Many elaborate kitchen appliances and cabinet styles tend to be temporary fads that are fashionable for merchandising purposes for a few years then quickly fade out of fashion. They might look exceedingly new and different when you first see them in a showroom but that's why they are there. Like tail fins on cars, they have their moments of great popularity, but a few years later you find that you could well do without curlicues, overdone colonial hardware, and so on. If you truly like such things and know exactly what you want, fine. If in doubt, the best rule is to choose a simple, unadorned style.

Decorating the Kitchen; Paint and Wallpaper

Obviously, the colors used, the cabinet style, and over-all decor you wish depends on personal taste. Light colors, even white, will make a kitchen look and feel bigger than it is. Dark colors make it look smaller, and quite small if you start with a small kitchen. But here you can use off-white and, say, a speckled, light-colored floor, which camouflages the inevitable dirt that lands on it. Of course, light colors also will show dirt quicker, so you may want a compromise.

Light, warm colors, such as yellow, could be used if your kitchen receives limited sunshine. Cool colors, such as blue, should not be used unless there is plenty of warm sunshine to compensate for a cool color.

Paint or wallpaper used on kitchen walls should be grease- and moisture-resistant, and non-absorbent to avoid picking up odors. It should have easy-cleaning properties so that grease and food spatters can be wiped off. Semigloss paint is a good compromise between enamel, which is easiest to wash but glary, and flat paint, which is pleasant but sometimes hard to clean. Any wallpaper can be treated to make it resistant to grease and moisture and easy to clean. But some allegedly "scrubbable" papers are merely treated, not vinyl-coated, and generally won't stand much scrubbing.

Some wallpapers come already treated. Better still, you can choose any paper you wish and have it given an excellent factory treatment for re-

Deceptively handsome "show" kitchen actually has glaring flaws. It pointedly illustrates the importance of differentiating between really good kitchen design and surface glamor. Two of the flaws: refrigerator door opens the wrong way, and inadequate countertop surface, especially between sink and range. It's a nice floor, though.
Kentile, Inc.

sistance to grease and any other kind of dirt encountered (not only for the kitchen but for any other rooms). One such process, is called Resistane. You choose your paper and either you or the seller send it off for a permanent treatment (Resistane Co., 996 Nepperhan Ave., Yonkers, N.Y.).

Cost of a New Kitchen

Don't launch a complete new kitchen unless you're prepared to spend at least $2500 and as much as $5000, sometimes more. Unhappily, it costs this much, despite advertisements to the contrary.

For one thing, the prices you generally see in ads are for equipment only, a disposal, say at $69.50, but it costs another $35 to $50 to install it. The cost of all equipment and cabinets, in other words, accounts for only about 50 to 60 per cent of the total kitchen cost; the balance goes for installation labor, new wiring and piping, plus a variety of other installation necessities most of us do not think of.

For another thing, there are the notorious bait ads seen regularly in newspapers; for example—"Complete New 16-Foot Kitchen for $589!" Fall for this and a slick dealer will unload a pile of kitchen cabinets on your doorstep, then demand another $1000 if you want them installed. With new appliances, too, the price goes even higher.

Many of us feel that we would never be taken in by such larceny. Nevertheless, having seen such ads, we get a deceptively low idea of kitchen costs. We are later shocked when a reputable dealer quotes upwards of $2500, which is actually a low figure for a complete kitchen. From $3000 to $4000 would be about average for a typical house.

Sometimes money can be saved if you buy the appliances yourself. You may be able to obtain them from an appliance dealer who will give you a special deal. But not always. A kitchen remodeler gets his appliances at a low wholesale cost and you may be charged only a small nominal markup. You could ask for a price breakdown of the work to be done with and without appliances, then compare it with the cost of appliances if you furnish them.

After a full complement of appliances, the kitchen cabinets generally account for the next biggest portion of the total price. By and large a low bid for them generally indicates inferior quality. You'll be cursed with infuriating doors and drawers, plus poor finish and paint. This means that cabinet specifications should be carefully checked against the standards in this chapter.

The plumbing and wiring hookup also cost money. The amount depends on how much of each is required for your kitchen. Plumbing costs are lowest when your existing water supply and drain pipes can be utilized with a minimum of alterations. Wiring cost is unpredictable. If much new electrical equipment is installed it may be too much of a load for the capacity of your present house-wiring system; then a whole new and larger electrical service may be required. And then, of course, structural alterations, if required, are not done for nothing.

First get bids on the whole job installed in the ideal way you want it. If the cost is higher than you can pay, as is often the case, then begin shaving here and there. Ask contractors how they can best come down in price. What is expendable? What can be omitted at the greatest savings and then perhaps installed at a later time when you're back on your feet financially. Sometimes a minor change in the plan can affect a major price reduction by eliminating a knotty installation chore. But don't save pennies by compromising on quality products and easy-maintenance materials. What you save initially you lose several times over in increased service and upkeep costs.

A final note: When work starts on a new kitchen your household will be disrupted, to put it mildly. Allow at least a week or two for completion, regardless of what the contractor may say. Your kitchen may be out of business even longer. Hook up a temporary stove in the dining room or at least have a few electric hot plates to fall back on. You could also arrange to leave children with nearby relatives or friends (and you can reciprocate when *they* redo their kitchen).

Chapter 12

Bathrooms:
Avoiding Common Pitfalls
When Remodeling
or Adding a Bathroom

Unhappily, the same mistakes are perpetrated over and over on nearly everybody who installs a new bathroom or remodels an old one. These can and do happen even if you have been burned once and do over a second bathroom, as I found out, red-faced.

You can't count on most plumbers for an inspired job partly because the nature of the business rules out imaginative work and also because a good many plumbers generally install the cheapest fixtures and parts on every job, even for people who are eager and willing to pay a little extra for better-quality products.

Most plumbers also tend to stick with the standard product line of one manufacturer even though new products of other manufacturers excell for a particular job. One of the finest wall-hung (above-the-floor) toilets on the market, noted later, is made by a comparatively unknown manufacturer. Other examples of special products and features to look for, regardless of brand, are sprinkled through this chapter.

The best plumbers usually belong to the local association of plumbing contractors or master plumbers. Call them for a few names to choose from.

In addition, it falls on each of us by default to learn a bit about bathrooms before we remodel. Nearly every component in a bathroom can be had with special features, which you may or may not desire. Even the best plumber, being human, may neglect to mention features you may particularly desire, or on the other hand automatically give you what other people think is special, though it appeals little to you.

Wall dividers with tile skin neatly set off lavatory zone of this bathroom. Wall-hung toilet (right) permits easy floor cleaning. A wall-hung toilet with a low-slung tank, however, is quieter in operation than the conventional-tank model shown here.

Tile Council of America.

This chapter deals in detail with the varying characteristics of bathroom equipment so that you can decide exactly which you want. It also stresses the high importance of getting good-quality products.

His and Hers

But before getting into bathroom planning, here are a few apt words about what a modern bathroom (and preferably two of them) can do for us nowadays, from Ann David, woman's service representative of the American Standard Corporation. Miss David's firm is in the business to sell bathroom fixtures, to be sure, but her comments are of interest. She says:

Sibling rivalry never gets such a clear expression than in the carryings on of the child who is second in line to his sister in the morning use of the bathroom. And what a fiasco when mother and father go out at night. Powdering starts in the bedroom; shaving in the bathroom. Much running, hurrying, and

Broad countertop is an excellent feature for bathrooms. Large sliding mirrors add to feeling of space and are part of the built-in medicine cabinet.

Tile Council of America.

switching of rooms goes on until they can emerge coordinated and groomed . . . and exhausted. Heaven help the child who, in the midst of this crash program, has to use the bathroom . . . it's regarded as little less than sabotage. Add to this picture a guest or two for a short time, or a hot summer, and you have an absurd story—absurd because it is unnecessary.

Aside from the fact that one bathroom just can not bear traffic for four people, let me review a few other reasons for at least two bathrooms. First, the bathroom should offer complete privacy. One bathroom should offer this for the adult; another for the child. With the heightened pressures of life and heightened activity, there must be more room to relax and be alone.

House designs allow for this generally—we have family rooms, dens, workshops, sewing rooms, children's play areas, etc. The same should apply to the bathrooms in the house. Two bathrooms are not a luxury, they are a necessity. If you figure that two adults share the master bathroom, and probably two or more children share a second bathroom . . . that's sharing enough. Some people still may think that a separate bathroom for children is paying too much attention to them. Believe me, it's not. Children have a sense of privacy and possession. You see it with their toys; you see how much they love their own bedroom if it's decorated with their books, their pictures, their heroes. I bet the legend that children have to be kept clean would have much less substantiation if children didn't constantly have to wash in their parents' bathroom.

I've seen lovely bathrooms, smaller and perhaps more modest than the master bathroom, decorated for children. Just as the master bathroom is no place for soap duck decorations, children could do with other than His and Her towels. We all want children to take an interest in their grooming, and many books have been written on the importance of early training to encourage clean habits. The answer may not be in directives or washing schedules. It may be in a separate bathroom for the younger set. And besides the use of the second bathroom for children, it is very useful when you have guests, be they young or old.

Large medicine cabinet with front mirrors plus broad counter are not only a boon for bathroom storage but eliminate lavatory clutter. Open shelf is optional and could be omitted to give a simpler, more attractive appearance. *American-Standard.*

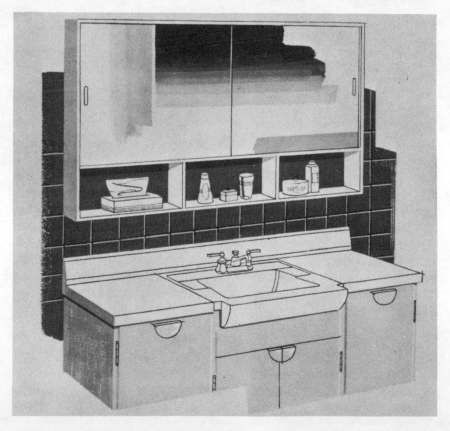

Now to the master bathroom. Many a man will say all he needs is a small bathroom for a quick shave and shower. That's all right if, as I mentioned earlier, his wife isn't trying to powder her nose under his elbow. Besides which, his wife probably likes nothing better than a luxurious bath when her housework is done and the children are still at school. The decor can make the bathroom a place for quiet and relaxed washing and grooming.

I am not exaggerating the importance of this comfortable and attractive atmosphere. I've read articles by doctors and beauticians who say the best therapy for fraught nerves and tired limbs is a long and relaxing bath. The master bathroom is a place where the housewife escapes the perpetual motion of her household management, where she can enjoy the private application of as many beauty creams as she chooses to try. As dedicated as she is to the home, the family, and everyone's welfare and nutrition, there must be a spot where she can feel a dedication to herself, her femininity, and her grooming.

Before: Run-down old bathroom cried out for modernization. Plastic tiles were falling off, floor was rotted, whole room was grim indeed.
After: Combination tub and tiled shower stall replaced old tub; custom lavatory replaced old sink; wall-hung toilet (left out of view) replaced old toilet. Linen closet was put in low-ceiling space, far left. Note overhead globe located so that its light is reflected from mirror to illuminate your face when washing or shaving. Slide-out drawer of lavatory cabinet is a laundry hamper divided for different wash.

© *Curtis Publishing Co., courtesy The American Home. Fred Rola.*

Adding a New Half-Bath

One of the biggest needs today is for a new "half-bath," euphemistically called a powder room. But where can it go? Finding the space for it can be tough.

A perfectly adequate half-bath (no tub) can be installed in a space as small as 24×42 inches. This will give minimum space for a toilet and wash basin. A friend of mine proved it by installing one in a former closet of exactly that size. Even more space can be borrowed from a downstairs clothes closet (which I did in my house), from unused space under a stairway, carved out of a center hall, or a utility room.

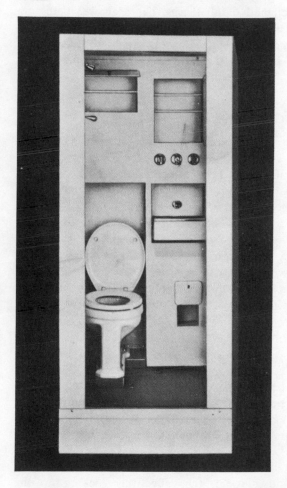

Packaged bathroom, called Bath-O-Lett, may be pullman size but costs less than $500, plus installation. It includes a shower (you cover toilet, close doors over shelves and sink, close outside door, and turn on shower). Outside dimensions: 34 inches wide, 42 inches deep, 84 inches high. Be sure it satisfies your local plumbing code before ordering.

An exterior wall location is not essential for every bathroom. A few obsolete building codes may require a window, but most codes now permit an interior location with ventilation by means of exhaust fan or ceiling skylight.

When looking for a location don't be blinded by existing walls. Determine whether enough of the wall can be moved or altered easily to permit a small half-bath. If not, and appropriate unused space is not apparent to the eye, consider building it into the corner of a large foyer, say, or an expendable corner of a nearby room.

Space for a full, new bathroom should be at least 5×7 feet, inside dimensions—but this is the absolute minimum. If you don't mind a pullman bathroom, at least one is now on the market. It comes as a complete unit only 34 inches wide, 42 inches deep, and 7 feet high, contains a pull-down washbowl, toilet, and of all things, has a shower bath too. Price is under $500 for a complete unit but installation cost is extra. It is called the Bath-O-Lett and made by Morse Boulger, 80 Fifth Ave., New York 11, N.Y. Make sure it will pass your plumbing code before ordering.

Location vs. Installation Cost

Installation cost is directly related to the bathroom location. The closer the location to the existing water and drain pipes, the lower the plumbing cost. Best location is above or below another bathroom, or close to the kitchen pipes. It is particularly important to try to use the existing bathroom-pipe vent, if possible. A new vent is expensive.

The vent is usually a 3- or 4-inch diameter pipe for exhausting waste gases and can be seen coming out of the roof over an existing bathroom. Depending on your plumbing code, you sometimes can use the same vent for a new bathroom and save the cost of a second vent. Managing such economy will depend on the new bathroom location and fixture arrangement. Discuss it with your plumber. Can he save you money by connecting to the existing vent?

Location vs. Convenience

A new bathroom should be located so that it is easily accessible to all the rooms around. Several points about bathroom location, noted earlier in Chapter 12, should be emphasized again here. A bathroom location decidedly should not require passage through a bedroom for access, a major blunder.

Even worse is a location that requires passage through the bathroom, of all things, to reach another room, thus effectively locking up the occupants in the shut-off room. This was done during remodeling of a house I know of, making access to one of three bedrooms possible only by going through the main bathroom. It is a glaring defect that made the house difficult to sell when it was later put up for sale.

The same rule generally applies to the location of your master bathroom. We like to think of the master bathroom as a luxury for privacy so it is often isolated next to the master bedroom where guests cannot use it. Guests end up in the children's bath, which is often a mess. Locating the master bath off the center hall instead and making it off limit for kids avoids conflict. It also obviates the hectic clean-up of the children's bath when guests are expected any minute or, unhappily, arrive unannounced. You may not have children to contend with, but if you decide to sell some day a prospective buyer might well have half a dozen kids. So make the master bathroom accessible.

Interior Planning

A full bathroom should be large enough to accommodate two people at once. Though a 5×7 bath will do if planned well, this is generally the smallest space you can get away with (and is the usual size of the small bathroom in many builder houses—it would be even smaller if they thought it possible).

Remodeling an old bath does not mean that you are restricted to the same fixture location as before. Many bathtubs are thoughtlessly put under windows, causing naked exposure to chilly drafts as well as the need for acrobatics to open or close the window when not in the tub. Keep a tub or shower stall away from the window. It is best, in fact, when no fixture is located directly under a window.

The washbowls should be where they do not interfere with traffic through the room. They need plenty of light, and the more space you can give them, the greater the countertop area possible on each side. Two washbowls in tandem is an excellent way to solve the morning rush-hour problem; sometimes it also can be a low-cost alternative to adding another bathroom. As for the toilet location, many people find it objectionable if it can be seen when the door is open. Put it out of sight if possible.

Getting Good-Quality Fixtures

Poor fixtures are a common cause of trouble. We are given ordinary fixtures that soon rear up and plague us with exasperating shortcomings —chipping, leaks, noise, balkiness. Each of the three principal fixtures therefore should be discussed in detail.

The bathtub. A spanking new tub is installed but you unhappily discover that it's too small, too shallow, or both. Conventional bathtubs are 5 feet long and 30 inches wide. A mere 2 inches in additional width, a 32-inch-wide tub, is gaining popularity because of the surprising extra convenience it affords, especially when bathing children. But you must specify 32-inch tubs.

A square tub can be particularly satisfying, especially if it is large enough and has a seat at one or both ends. Most families need one *at least* 4 feet square but end up with a smaller, tiny thing hardly larger than a washbowl.

To cut costs, many manufacturers have cut the depth of their tubs down to 14 inches and even 12 inches, an outrage; it hardly comes off the floor. Shallow depth is usually what the average plumber will give you unless you specify a standard 16-inch depth, which is practically mandatory if you like tub baths and want to avoid wild splashing over the floor, especially with children.

An enameled cast-iron tub is generally best. It will neither scratch nor chip. But if it is white, it may suffer if you use the wrong detergent, or leave diapers in it overnight. This can be avoided by spending about $5 to $10 more for an "acid-resistant" enamel surface. (All colored tubs, and all-steel tubs have acid-resistant surfaces.) Though steel tubs cost less than cast-iron ones, they can serve well for years. However, steel offers less variety in design and appearance, and some brands show scratches very quickly.

Avoiding Bathtub Crack

A critical and quite widespread problem with bathtubs is the unsightly crack that gradually develops at the joint between the bottom of the tub and the floor. It is not only ugly, but it is also a hazard as water seepage through it can damage and ultimately rot the wood floor below.

The crack develops as a result of tub settling or constant small movement of the tub as people get in and out of it. It can be avoided if the tub is securely mounted and this in turn normally requires special L-bracket supports under the tub (which are then bolted to the wall). They hold a tub firmly in place. They are not usually provided, so you must ask for them, or for comparable support.

Another tip: Have your plumber load the tub full up with water just before he locks it in place and makes his final connections. This will weigh the tub down to its lowest possible position, allowing little or no room for settling.

The washbowl (lavatory). This stirs anger on discovery that it is too small for washing your hair or a new baby. Once it's hooked up you're stuck with it. Yet the price difference between a luxuriously large 20×24-inch bowl and the smaller but commonly sold 17×19-inch model is as little as $5.

In order of decreasing cost and acceptability, washbowls are made of vitreous china, enameled cast iron, and porcelain-enameled steel (the cheapest). Actually, any one of the three will give rugged service. Vitreous china is considered the highest-quality kind because of its gleaming, unscratchable surface. And it does not chip easily (unless of course you smack it with a hammer).

Enameled cast iron also will not chip and is practically indestructable (the reason why it is often specified for schools and hospitals). It is slightly less costly than vitreous china, but a little more expensive than enameled steel.

Enameled steel is highly resistant to abrasion, is also durable, but because of the nature of its material it is not available in as many styles and shapes as the other two kinds. Thus its main drawbacks are lackluster design and appearance.

Summed up, your best bet is a vitreous china bowl, though the others can be just as rugged. First choose the particular shape and size you want. Availability may dictate the kind of bowl you choose. Many of the appealing new round and oval bowls, for example, are available only in vitreous china.

A washbowl can be bought separately and then mounted in your own countertop or lavatory cabinet. Most manufacturers offer lavatory cabinets ("vanities") complete with countertops and drawers. Or you can draw up your own plans and have a complete cabinet or wall-hung lavatory made to order. This need not be expensive. My cost for a custom-made, 32-inch-wide cabinet, shown in the accompanying photo, was $70. It includes a large, center hamper drawer, plus a gleaming sprayed-on paint job (but the cost of the bowl and faucet set were extra).

There are also what are called pedestal lavatories. These are simply the commonly used sink-plus-floor-pedestal support. Some kinds are mounted on the wall and also may have a pair of vertical leg supports. The pedestal lavatory requires the least space and is a good choice when you want to squeeze two lavatories into a limited space.

The toilet (*water closet*). Cheap, low-quality toilets are a widespread curse. Most manufacturers offer three grades. The cheapest and most widely sold is called a "washdown" toilet, which should be outlawed. It has a low water level requiring hand-washing, is terribly noisy, and requires constant floor cleaning around it. It is generally identified by a round seat and a front drain opening; the better kinds have a rear drain.

The next step up for only a few dollars more is what is called the "reverse-trap" toilet. This term refers to the type of flush action. It is easier to clean and much more sanitary than the washdown, but the quality varies from brand to brand. Some brands are almost as noisy as washdowns so you should check this beforehand. (It's difficult to cite the better brands because models are constantly changed from year to year.)

Even better is the "siphon-jet" toilet. It is more efficient than both the washdown and reverse trap. A good one will cost from $20 to about $40 more than a reverse trap, depending on brand.

Obtaining the quietest model at the least cost is difficult because you seldom can hear one work in a showroom—they are not hooked up. You have to take someone's word. But what may seem tolerably quiet to a plumber may be noisy for you, or vice versa. Keep your eyes out for a good one. Make a special note when you see a quiet model in the home of a friend or relative so that you can get the same kind. Also note those that are particularly noisy so you won't get the same kind.

You could also spend more money and get a top-grade "quiet-flush" model, which is the quietest and most efficient of all toilets, the deluxe kind. Many plumbers will not mention them to you because they automatically assume you don't want to spend that much money ($65 to $75 more than the cheapest toilets). The quiet-flush unit is identified by its one-piece construction, a low-slung combination tank and seat.

There is also the handsome wall-mounted toilet which hangs entirely above the floor. It eliminates the big floor-cleaning problem encountered around a conventional toilet. This kind also can be comparatively quiet in operation if you get the right brand; some wall-hung brands, on the other hand, are terribly noisy. The quieter kinds are identified by their low-slung tank and one-piece construction. A conventional high tank, separate from the bowl, is the tipoff to noisy operation, sometimes as loud and noisy as the cheapest washdown toilet. Check this in advance. One of the best is the Case No. 3000, one-piece wall type. Incidentally, a wall-hung job can be installed in new or old houses. The wall may require some beefing-up (with 2×6 framing) but this is seldom a problem.

Like the floor-mounted quiet-flush toilet, the wall-hung toilet is also expensive—about $75 to $100 more than the cheapest toilet—but nearly every delighted owner of one or the other says it is well worth the expense even if you have to work nights to pay for it.

Good-Quality Faucets and Shower Heads

These are called the fittings or bathroom trim by the trade. They are taken for granted by nearly everybody else and we are then usually cursed with trim that quickly tarnishes or rusts, bathroom drip, and the constant need to replace washers.

In fact, getting the best quality, most expensive fixtures is no guarantee of good fittings. Fittings are made and shipped separately by most manufacturers. In brief, there are faucets and there are faucets. Even the shoddiest kind gleams brightly at first. And like toilet quality, as well as most other parts of houses, practically every manufacturer sells good-and poor-quality faucets.

Most manufacturers offer three different grades. You need not get the most expensive kind. There is an in-between grade that is only a few dollars more in price than the cheapest and about half the price of the

Display board shows handsomely designed faucet trim and a high-quality adjustable-spray shower nozzle. Spray is adjusted by the lever on the nozzle. This is one of the few brands with spokelike faucet handles that are not an indication of low quality. It is made by a leading faucet manufacturer.
Speakman Co. Willard Stewart.

deluxe. You can tell the cheapest kind, regardless of brand, by the handles which have two or more spokes radiating out from the center, like a wheel. The better kinds have solid handles, with a ridged circumference for gripping.

Good faucet sets also can be identified by the manufacturer's name stamped on them. No manufacturer puts his name on his cheapest-grade faucets; you may see a fancy but meaningless emblem, but that's all.

Good-quality faucets are made of thick brass, not zinc or aluminum die castings. The thicker the brass the better. Visit a plumbing supply showroom and the dealer can quickly show you the difference between tough, well-made brass faucets and the light-weight, cheapest kind. Though made of brass, they will have a permanent copper-nickel-chrome finish. Tough protective coatings of nickel, copper, and chrome are applied in the factory over the brass body. This gives a durable finish that will not tarnish and will not require too frequent cleaning.

The exterior appearance still may vary. This is a wide choice of colors and degree of luster, something available for virtually every decor. You can have, for example, a brushed satin finish, polished gold or chromium, or highly polished brass. You can also specify single-lever faucets for a bathroom washbowl, shower, and tub for their finger-touch operating advantages, noted in Chapter 11.

You need not accept a particular kind of faucet with a particular bathtub or sink just because you saw both together in a showroom. Nearly any other faucet set on the market can be specified. (This goes for shower heads too.) They should, however, be sized to fit your tub and bowl, but your plumber can handle this. Standard dimensions prevail throughout the industry so this is seldom a problem.

Shower Nozzles

A good-quality shower nozzle will not clog or corrode. It has a flexible ball joint to adjust the spray direction. It should also have a volume spray control enabling you to obtain a fine or coarse spray or anything in between. If you have hard water, a self-cleaning head is another good feature. The cheapest kinds have a rigid head (which cannot be adjusted) and little or no volume control. Locate the nozzle high enough to clear your head.

Safety Features for the Shower

Two other features are highly desirable in a shower for convenience and safety: automatic temperature control and an automatic diverter valve.

Often while taking a shower the water will suddenly turn scorching hot or icy cold, a maddening if not scalding experience. It happens when somebody else in the house begins using hot or cold water, thus drawing it from the shower.

It is avoided by specifying the installation of a temperature-control valve. The shower-nozzle water is automatically kept at a constant temperature; hot or cold water can not suddenly spurt from it. One kind uses a special pressure control valve (which is what you ask for), while another kind, somewhat more expensive, is called a thermostatic mixing valve. This will cost from about $20 to $40, depending on type and brand.

The basic problem, of course, is inadequate water pressure. It may be due to low water-main pressure on your street, an undersized water supply pipe and meter to the house, or undersized or old clogged-up water pipes in the house. And correcting one of these may be impractical or too expensive.

When you first step into a combination bathtub-shower the water may spurt down on you by surprise from the shower nozzle, rather than out of the bathtub spigot. This can be a hazard if it comes down hot, especially with children. It happens when the water was not diverted back to the tub by the last person using the shower. This must be done by hand every time because a manual diverter control was installed. These are dangerous, yet many are sold.

You should specify an *automatic* diverter control (not the manual kind), which automatically switches the water supply back to the tub spigot when the shower is turned off. It is obviously safer but unfortunately not always used.

New Shower-Stall Units

New shower-stall units on the market represent a big step forward in cutting bathroom costs. Long overdue, a unit stall is complete with two or three rugged Fiberglas walls, floor, plus drain (of the same reinforced Fiberglas construction used for boats). It is shipped in a package and can be installed in a few hours. Some brands already have FHA acceptance, a standard you should specify. Cost runs about $150 to $200 for an average size unit, plus installation.

The walls have a low-gloss finish which is claimed to be impervious to alkalis, mold, fungus, and household solvents. Two-wall models are available for corner locations, three-walls for the usual installation. There are also other kinds of unit shower stalls that come in knocked-down packages for quick and easy assembly.

The next step, obviously, is the development of a complete, low-cost,

New prefabricated shower stall is made of tough Fiberglas-reinforced plastic, same as used for boats. Has rich bonelike surface, is durable, easy to clean, is available in two-sided corner models, and meets FHA requirements. Prices run $150 to $200 plus the cost of installation.
Owens-Corning Fiberglas.

full-size bathroom unit, prefabricated for economical installation. This idea is being mulled over now by manufacturers and may be on the market in a few years.

Tile Walls

Ceramic tile is a top choice for bathroom walls and often floors too. It is handsome, available in a variety of colors, easy to keep clean, and so rugged that properly installed it will last as long as the house. It should cover the entire wall and ceiling area around a shower stall or tub, but a tile wainscot from floor, to say 36 inches high, is all you generally need around the rest of the room. This will protect the low, most vulnerable parts of your walls.

Ceramic tile will cost generally from $1.50 to $2 per square foot, installed. This is for the top domestic tiles. Less expensive imported tiles, mainly from Italy and Japan, are also available. But some imported tiles reportedly come with flaws; choose carefully from samples before buying and ask about a guarantee.

The installation of ceramic tile is crucial. If not put up properly, tiles will begin to loosen and fall off. Best kind of installation is what is called a "mud job." The tile is set in a portland-cement backing which is virtually indestructible.

Tile also can be applied to a gypsum-board wall. This can save money but special care is required. The gypsum board should be primed with a top-grade water seal. Lamar Brown, staff architect of the Tile Council of America, told me for this book that a good marine varnish is one of the best sealers. His group has stepped up research on a new special sealer but the results have not been announced as this is written.

In addition, the gypsum board should *not* make actual contact with the bathtub or floor; there should be a ¼- to ½-inch gap between the top of the tub and the wallboard (which is later covered by tile). This is a moisture gap to prevent water from the tub from rising up into the board and ultimately ruining the wallboard. These two requirements— varnish sealer and clearance between gypsum board and tub rim—are essential for a permanent tile job on gypsum board. Specify them and then make sure they are done before your tile is installed.

The biggest problem with tile is finding a good tile man. This can be so exasperating that you ultimately give up. Call a few ceramic-tile wholesalers and ask them for recommended names. Wholesalers' names are in the telephone book yellow pages.

There are also a variety of plastic tiles and plastic-tile board. These lack the handsome appearance of ceramic tile, and even with regular waxing they may not last more than five to ten years. They can suffice, however, in a half-bath where they are exposed to less wear and no bathtub splashing. New kinds of plastic and Fiberglas tiles and even a handsome sheet aluminum wall "tile" are in the development and testing stages as this is written and are due on the market. They may well eclipse ceramic tile in durability and other advantages.

Because water and water vapor are the chief troublemakers in a bathroom—and a major cause of rotted wood and exterior paint blistering— untiled walls should be painted with a special vapor-barrier paint (at least for the prime coat), an alkyd paint which is also a vapor barrier, or plastic-coated wallpaper.

What Kind of Floor?

Look at almost any old bathroom floor and you will see signs of rot and deterioration, notably around bathtub and washbowl. This is the toughest floor in the house to keep clean, attractive, and free from water damage. Many people prefer a ceramic-tile floor for its good looks and rugged wearing qualities, or a floor of marble, terrazzo, or even flagstone. Drawbacks of these materials, including tile, are that they are cold on the feet, and they are death on accidentally dropped glass and medicine bottles.

For this last reason my wife specified a resilient plastic floor; pure sheet vinyl (Armstrong Cork's rugged Tessera), one of the best plastic floors for bathrooms. Though the most expensive, a sheet, pure-vinyl floor is probably the toughest, best-looking, and easiest to maintain of all plastic flooring.

You can save money—though not much in the usual small bathroom space—with other resilient flooring such as vinyl-asbestos tile, or linoleum. But the loss in wearing quality exceeds the small savings in first cost. A sheet material is better in the bathroom than individual tiles of flooring because with the individual tiles the numerous joints are an invitation to water penetration and subsequent damage.

Compartment Plan

A large bathroom for a large family can be compartmentalized, an idea heavily promoted by fixture manufacturers. Toilets, shower, and sometimes the tub are fenced off by partitions which enable from three to five people to use the bathroom simultaneously with privacy. Partial partitions, dividers, or folding doors may be used. Two toilets are often used, each one in a private enclosure. Two washbowls are mandatory, a second tub or shower stall is optional. A compartment bath is tantamount to having two or three bathrooms, but plumbing costs are lower as a result of grouping all the fixtures together. A space of at least $8 \times 10\frac{1}{2}$ feet is required to start with; 10×12 is better.

The merits of the compartment bath, however, are open to question. It has received much publicity, obviously because the big fixture manufacturers landed on it as a good way to sell more fixtures—two instead of one at a crack. Partitioning off a toilet in a large bath coupled with double washbowls often can serve a family equally well at less expense. Or you may do better with a separate second bathroom elsewhere, especially in a large house.

The Garden Plan

This is another luxury idea. It consists of opening up one wall of a bathroom to a private outdoor patio by means of a large glass window or door. If you don't have a naturally secluded spot just outside, a fence at least 6 feet high can be erected about 10 feet away. The idea, obviously the final touch in bathrooms, is to give you the happy benefits of sunshine and light flooding in and also let you borrow space from the outdoors; i.e., have your bathroom feel as large as all outdoors.

It is also practical for a bathroom with direct access to and from an outdoor swimming pool or sunning spot. It is most popular in warm climates such as southern California. It may be your cup of tea if you think you'd like to lounge in the bath amid glorious sunshine and plenty of light and air—and if you can afford it, of course.

What Colors?

Tread slowly here. Colored fixtures, tile, and floor covering should be chosen with care. Our taste in colors frequently changes from year to year and you may be stuck with colors you no longer like. Exotic-colored fixtures and tiles also tend to drop out of fashion as quickly as they arrived. Colored fixtures, incidentally, generally cost about 10 per cent more than the same fixtures in white.

It's best to paint a bathroom with light pastel colors or white, since dark colors make a bathroom seem even smaller than it actually is. Warm colors like yellow and pink are best in a bathroom with little or no exposure to sun; i.e., on the north side of a house. A cool color like blue generally should be limited to a bathroom with plenty of light and sunshine or else the room will feel cold.

If you wish to indulge your own special color tastes by all means do it up brown, regardless of what anyone else may think. It's your pleasure. But if you may sell your house in a few years, remember that esoteric tastes can put a damper on house resale value.

Special Features and Accessories

A bathroom should include a storage cabinet, ample shelves for towels, bathroom-cleaning materials, linen, and so on. Though not essential, an ample laundry hamper can be a boon; it could be built into the bottom of the lavatory unit. Divide it into sections for white, colored, and other soiled clothes, each of which may require separate washing. You could also install a chute leading down to the laundry.

Get the largest possible medicine cabinet and mirror. A cabinet built into the wall with sliding mirror doors is both attractive and exceedingly functional. The medicine cabinet should be at least 20×30 inches. A smaller, separate cabinet, high up out of reach of kids, is a good idea for keeping medicine that could harm them. Better still, perhaps, this could be accomplished by means of a small, locked-door cabinet section at the top of a bathroom linen closet.

Good light is essential for emotional reasons as well as illumination. There should be a light near the medicine cabinet and over the washbowl so you can see your whole face in the mirror without shadows.

Medicine cabinets can be had with concealed, indirect lighting on each side, or with tubular lights on the sides. But make sure you like the looks of the thing before you order; some are unattractive.

Many contain fluorescent lamps which even with the softest fluorescent bulbs shine a harshly cold light on your face. Incandescent light is far better. A separate light is often needed for over the bathtub and shower compartment. You may also need an overhead light, depending on the bathroom. With or without one, the main light should have its switch convenient to the doorway.

Other ideas: space for a make-up bench at the lavatory; a waterproof light over the tub or in the shower-stall ceiling; auxiliary electric wall or ceiling heater for extra comfort if required (*but keep it well away from the bathtub and shower stall for safety*); built-in electric outlet for shaving (which also should be well out of reach of the bathtub); grab bars for extra safety in the tub or shower stall; built-in towel and soap racks; clothes hooks; and shut-off valves at each fixture, which means you will not have to shut off the water supply to the house for a minor repair.

A few special features will please small children: towel racks within their reach; foot bench for climbing into the tub or reaching the washbowl; a tilt-down mirror; a low shelf for holding their bathtub playthings. Such features probably should be easily removable when the children outgrow them.

Manufacturers' catalogues display additional custom features. These include built-in towel and tissue holders; built-in scales; elegant towel bars and other trim; and of all things, heated towel bars. Some manufacturers also promote the sale of *bidets,* widely encountered in Europe for rectal bathing.

Special Installation Features

Two nagging problems in a good many bathrooms are toilet tanks that drip water on the floor and hot-water faucets that spurt forth with cold water for minutes, it seems, before drawing up hot water.

The first is the result of the cold water inside the tank cooling the entire tank. Water vapor in the bathroom air then condenses out on the cold surface. The antidote is the installation of a hot-water mixing valve in the water supply line to the tank. Enough hot water is mixed in with the cold water supplied so that the tank will not get too cold. Another remedy is an insulated tank. A few toilets can be had with insulated tanks, or a special insulation kit on the market can be bought for about $3 to $4 and installed in your tank.

Cold water pours out initially from hot-water faucets after being chilled in the long pipe run from the water heater. Hot water does not arrive until the water in the pipes has been exhausted and you begin drawing hot water directly from the heater. The remedy here is the use of what plumbers call a hot-water circulating line. A second hot-water pipe is installed up to the bathroom and hooked up so that hot water flows continuously back and forth from the heater, and is therefore always present close to the faucets. Then you can count on quick hot water.

Bathroom Booklets

The following booklets are available for 10¢ each from the Plumbing-Heating-Cooling Information Bureau, 35 East Wacker Drive, Chicago 1, Illinois: *What You Should Know about Plumbing,* with information about fixtures and planning tips for the kitchen as well as the bathroom; *Modern Bathroom Plans,* with a variety of bathroom plans showing good and bad arrangements; and *Plumbing Care and Repair,* tips and advice on the care and maintenance of your plumbing system.

Part 5

NEW WINDOWS, INSULATING GLASS, AND SKYLIGHTS

Probably no other single change can improve a house at such low cost as a large new window. It can replace a small existing window to exploit a good view or greatly improve a room where there was nothing but solid wall before.

Indeed, don't think of a window as merely a sheet of glass. Think of it as a medium for letting sunshine, light, and brightness flood into a room, as well as turning a dark room into a bright, cheerful space. The transformation makes a small room feel much bigger than it is. In addition to conventional windows, the same results can be had by means of a handsome new skylight installed in the ceiling.

The trouble with windows is that they also may be a giant source of chills, drafts, and cold in winter, and of excessive sun-heat entry in summer. The trick is knowing how to do the opposite, planning a window so that it will let in plenty of warm sunshine in *winter* but not in summer, and at the same time not cause you to suffer from cold chills in winter.

Knowing such things is important when a house is remodeled, as well as when merely installing a single new window. This section gives fundamental facts about window glass and windows, when insulating glass or storm windows pay off, and how a new skylight installation can sharply improve a house.

Small corner window was replaced by large window for $187, as described in text.
Home Modernizing Guide.

Chapter 13

How New Window Glass
Can Transform a Room
(Triumphantly!)

The dramatic results obtainable with a new window are illustrated by one I had installed for $187 (see photos). The window was put in a small 8×10-foot second-floor study (though it could have been any other kind of room). It replaced a small conventional window that hardly did justice to a sweeping view of the Hudson River.

I simply hired a carpenter to rip out the old window and replace it with new glass, a wide 4×6½-foot window unit. The room was opened up as if by magic, as a result of what architects call borrowing space from outdoors. The large, new glass opening makes the room feel twice as large and cheerful as before, as well as letting us drink in a five mile view up and down the river and across to Westchester County.

How It Was Designed and Installed

To cut costs the window was made of fixed glass; it cannot be opened. A fixed-glass window costs as little as half the cost of a similar window that opens. Ventilation was not important because the room is air-conditioned, and even if the cooling unit breaks down another window in the room can be opened.

Sealed, double glass (Thermopane in this case) was used to prevent condensation and reduce cold air drafts in winter. This raised the cost but was worth it because the window is exposed to bitter cold winds in winter. A double-glass fixed window is also neater and nicer looking than an openable window with storm sash.

A local millwork shop made the window frame from a sketch I drew for $25 (less the glass). The frame was designed to take three sections of 24×48-inch glass. I used three vertical units of glass set next to each other because I think they look better than one broad sheet of glass.

One error I made, however, was not ordering the double glass far enough in advance. It was not one of the manufacturer's stock sizes (normally stocked by local distributors) so I had to wait three months for delivery. This meant extra expense. The carpenter had to install single glass temporarily and then return later to replace it when the double glass arrived.

Cost Breakdown

Here is the cost breakdown for the window installation:

Wood window frame, 4×6 feet	$25.
Carpenter's labor, including moving old window and installing new one	70.
3 sheets of 24″×48″ sealed double glass	75.
3 sheets of single-pane glass, 24″×48″ (temporarily required until double glass was delivered)	12.
Paint (self-applied)	5.
	$187.00

Because the new window faces east, it receives an amazing amount of morning sunshine the year around. On a typical summer morning the sun will strike it before 7 A.M. and not pass overhead until eleven. Despite the air conditioning, the room gets a little warm and as a result a shading device over the window is needed outside. This was first-hand proof that a window facing east will receive as much sun heat in the morning as a west window in the afternoon.

Importance of Window Location

The best location for a large window is usually on the south side of a house, all other things being equal. It will receive more sun in winter than in summer and is comparatively easy to shade. A window on the north will get much daylight, but little sunshine. It is less desirable because of exposure to cold north winds in winter. This, of course, is not so important if you live in a warm climate. A window on the west is the least desirable because of exposure to searing afternoon sun during the periods of hottest outdoor *air* temperatures.

These rules are flexible. A window can be put in nearly any wall and then shaded if necessary to keep out excess summer sunshine. The principles involved, discussed in Chapter 3, deserve review here:

It's best to shade it on the outside rather then on the inside because outside blinds are about twice as effective for keeping out sun heat. Once the sun gets through the glass even the best blinds deflect only *part* of it. Deciduous trees—those that lose their leaves in winter—are best as they let sunshine through when you want it.

A roof-trellis can be good over south windows. Better still are wide roof overhangs, particularly over south windows. They keep out much summer sun, but let in the winter sun, which strikes at a lower angle from the sky. Overhangs are less effective over east and west windows, as the morning and afternoon sun comes down at such a low angle the year around that all but the very widest overhangs cannot keep much of it out. Sometimes a sun fence 8 to 10 feet high can effectively shade a first-floor window on the east or west; the higher the fence and the closer to the window, the better the shading.

Excess cold can be controlled with double-glass or storm windows and by means of heating outlets under the window. Double-glass or storm windows, however, sometimes may be omitted on a south-facing window even in the temperate North. Wide horizontal windows located well above the floor are best for reducing heat and cold, especially in air-conditioned houses. They are effectively shaded by roof overhangs, and create the fewest floor drafts.

Seven Kinds of Windows

In addition to supplying light and air, windows should be chosen to establish the basic character of a house. Choose the right kind. There are seven basic types:

Double-hung windows slide up or down and are popular for traditional houses. Old-fashioned sash cords have been replaced with special metal holders and spring counterbalances. Air entry is easily controlled by adjusting the amount of opening. The best ones can be removed from their frames for easy cleaning.

Casement windows swing out on a vertical axis by means of a crank or lever and permit the entire window to be opened full to the breeze. Precise control of air entry, however, is difficult, and screens must be placed on the inside of the windows. Some kinds open into the room but this causes interference with curtains and shades.

Multipane windows contain three or more individual panes of glass. Small panes are less expensive to replace if broken. Some of the panes swing out for ventilation while the others are of fixed glass, or all the panes can be fixed glass. Sizes and shapes vary from tall and narrow (for floor and ceiling glass) to very broad units.

Awning windows swing out on a horizontal axis. They usually contain

Six common windows. 1. Double-hung. 2. Casement. 3. Multipane. 4. Awning. 5. Sliding. 6. Jalousie.

two or more separate panes with one crank control. One kind swings the top pane out while the bottom pane is swung in to open up the entire area for ventilation. This is called a hopper window. It provides good protection against rain coming in.

Jalousie windows consist of a series of small horizontal glass panes which swing out and upward like an awning window. One crank swings all panes out together. They are best in warm climates with screens on the inside. Except possibly for summer porches, they are ill-advised in the North because they are often leaky. Get a top-quality brand with a good crank mechanism or they will be troublesome in operation. They should crank open and shut smoothly and easily.

Horizontal sliding windows are just what the term says. Instead of opening up or down like double-hung windows, they slide open to the right or left. They are trim and neat-looking and are easily fitted with screens and storm windows. Get the kind that can be easily removed from their frames for cleaning, or left completely out in summer for that matter, leaving only the screens for ventilation.

Glass block windows are decorative and best when you want light but not much of a view. A variety of patterns and textures are made, and they can be used to build an entire wall or a skylight. Special blocks for venting the window are installed if air is desired. Blocks may be clear to see through or translucent just to let light in.

Obtaining Good-Quality Windows

The market is flooded with a huge variety of window brands, many of which are cheap and shoddy. It pays therefore to get brand-name windows (such as Anderson, Curtis, Malta).

The three main kinds of window frames are aluminum, wood, and steel. Aluminum requires less maintenance than wood or steel and little or no painting.

But aluminum gets cold in winter and moisture condensation can be troublesome. The window panes fog up with moisture and even the frames will drip water. This is minimized only if you use the best brand aluminum

Handsome wood windows open up this dining room. Insulated glass cuts down heat loss and condensation. Imagine the difference with a small window.
Anderson Corp. Hedrich-Blessing.

windows, made so the inside movable section containing the glass does not touch the cold outside frame. This is done with non-metallic fittings, such as nylon, for example, and an insulating layer such as vinyl or neoprene between the window section and the frame. The windows do not get as cold. Look for this feature.

Steel windows require periodic painting and are susceptible to rust and corrosion. Many people prefer wood windows for their appearance. Condensation is much less of a problem with them than with the ordinary aluminum and steel kinds because wood doesn't get as cold as metal.

All windows should come with integral weather stripping. Look for a flexible metal or plastic seal between the movable part of the window and the adjacent frame. They should be tight to prevent air leaks, and easy to wash from the inside.

Choosing the Best Window

The windows you choose should harmonize with the rest of the windows and the style of your house. Look at different kinds in houses while you're out walking. Which look good and would go well with your house? Notice large windows especially and how they are located and placed in the wall. Can you look in easily (not good)? Inside you will want privacy.

Also notice windows from the inside when you visit friends. Do they add to the feeling and character of a room? How far are they from the floor? Would you like them higher or lower? Do they add light and cheerfullness to the room or are they always covered by curtains for privacy? Can they be conveniently opened and closed and washed when necessary? You may think you like a large, bow (curved) window with many little sections of glass, but then ask yourself if you mind the chore of cleaning each section of glass individually.

Looking at a lot of windows will give you confidence and give you ideas that you would never learn otherwise. This is an excellent way to determine the kind of windows you will like best for your home.

Chapter 14

Storm Windows
vs. Sealed Double Glass:
Which Is Better?

Both storm windows and sealed double glass (such as Thermopane and Twindow, which are specific brands) consist of two sheets of glass with an air space in-between to reduce heat loss, window drafts, and condensation. In other words, it's insulating glass.

According to tests at the University of Illinois' Small Homes Council, insulating glass (either kind) brings about "fuel savings of 20 per cent or more," depending on your climate zone and the amount of glass to the house. The 20 per cent savings resulted in an experimental house with 20 double-hung windows in Springfield, Illinois. In a house with a well-insulated structure and a small ratio of glass to over-all wall area, fuel savings with insulating glass may amount to only 10 or 15 per cent a year. In a house with a great expanse of glass the fuel savings may approach 40 per cent.

Ordinary single-pane windows get quite cold—put your hand over one on a cold day. In addition to cold downdrafts swirling into rooms, cold glass also causes chills and goose-pimples (by drawing off body heat from your skin). And it fogs up with icy moisture because of condensation. Insulating glass combats these defects because its inside glass pane is warmer.

The advantage of single-pane glass coupled with storm windows is lower first cost. Using sealed window glass instead will generally increase the total window cost by 10 to 20 per cent. This is not excessive when balanced against the special benefits of sealed double glass: 1. Convenience, as double glass does not have to be put up and taken down every year as with storm windows; 2. Less maintenance, with only two glass surfaces to keep clean instead of four; 3. Easier ventilation, quickly attained the year around with double window units; 4. Neater, better appearance.

If you have air conditioning, you can leave storm windows on all the time. Both storm windows and double glass reduce summer-heat entry from hot outside *air* into a house by roughly 50 per cent. Only half as much outside air heat will enter through a square foot of either kind as will enter through the same area of single-pane glass.

Reducing sun heat, however, is another matter. Despite popular belief, nearly as much solar heat will enter through double glass as through single glass, and solar heat is by far the bigger heat problem. In other words, if you live in the South, spending extra money for sealed double glass will generally not pay for itself in reduced cooling costs. (A shading device is the only way to keep out sun heat.) Like storm windows, double glass pays off most in increased comfort and reduced fuel bills in a cold climate. In general, they are worthwhile if your average daily temperature in January is 35 degrees or colder.

Summed up, sealed double glass is generally worth its cost in a cold climate when you remodel. Window openings should conform to stock-size double-glass units. These are the most commonly used glass sizes, available quickly, and lower in cost than other sizes not kept in regular stock.

Buying Storm Windows and Doors

The cheapest combination storm windows on the market today contain about 10 pounds of raw aluminum at around 50¢ a pound, more or less. Put together at a factory, their rock-bottom manufactured cost comes to about $10 to $12 a unit. Figure in freight charges, dealer overhead, warehousing, and other operating costs, plus delivery and installation in your house, and even low-quality combination windows retail at a minimum of $18 to $20 apiece. Really good combinations cost at least $25 to $30 installed, depending on size and type of installation.

Despite these basic costs you will see ads for combination storm windows at unbelievably low prices, sometimes as low as $5.99 or perhaps $9.69 apiece. These are outright bait ads, usually for windows that are not even available. Answer such an ad and a slick salesman will confidentially tell you that the windows in the ad are so shoddy and poorly made that he doesn't have the nerve to sell them to you. They're junk, he says.

Then with a highly persuasive build-up he switches you to much more expensive combination units selling for $40 to $50 apiece. One New Jersey couple actually signed up for the cheapest windows advertised. The salesman said, "Of course, you'll have to rub them down once a week with steel wool. They still may pit and corrode." The couple was alarmed.

The salesman poured it on. "But you'll never need to wipe these really good windows. They never pit, never discolor. The screen and glass is better made. The frames are guaranteed for a lifetime." An hour later the husband and wife tore up the old contract for a set of windows at $89.95 and were talked into signing an outrageously overpriced $369.95 order.

This example of the gyps' tactics may make us smile sadly because *we* feel that it can happen to others but not ourselves. Actually, it happens to many people, though perhaps not so blatantly. The initial offer may be for $17.50 windows which aren't that bad, but before we know it we are up to $35 windows which may sound like the very best but are not worth more than $25.

What about Weather Stripping?

All good-quality windows come with integral weather stripping. This should be specified when ordering windows (and also doors) when you remodel.

Weather stripping means, of course. snug-fitting windows and doors, thus preventing cold air leaks around the frames. You can tell if your present windows and doors need weather stripping by moving a hand around the frame, at the bottoms of doors, and also across the middle joint of double-hung windows. Do it on a cold day, naturally, and on the windward side of the house.

Various kinds are available, depending on the kind of doors and windows you have. You can see a good selection at a lumberyard, hardware store, or in the Sears, Roebuck catalogue.

Tests at the University of Minnesota show that weather stripping can reduce total heat loss from a house as much as 37 per cent. This is close to the extreme saving. By and large, fuel savings may run closer to 10 or 20 per cent, compared with having no weather stripping at all. Equally important is the sharply increased comfort that results when weather stripping is used to plug up those leaks and air jets that otherwise blow into the house. It sharply cuts down on drafts, often eliminating them entirely.

Chapter 15

New Skylights
for Overhead Windows

It used to be that a skylight was a flat, wire-glass affair with an industrial look. It was a chronic dirt-catcher and let little light into a room.

Handsome new skylights are now available designed especially for houses. Most notable are the plastic dome or bubble kind made of the same tough plastic as the blisters on the old B-17 bomber, and new window skylights designed especially to replace expensive window dormers in attic rooms. They can work wonders!

The principal purpose of a skylight is to shed light and air into the interior of a house. A good example is in the ceiling of an inside bathroom that would otherwise lack natural light. Skylights can permit the use of a low-cost square or nearly square addition to a house rather than a more expensive rectangular shape. Living space in the middle of the addition is enhanced by providing overhead air and light through the skylight. This also reduces the amount of exterior window area needed.

A utility room, laundry area, and even part of the kitchen can be relegated to an interior location, without loss of light and air, and allow more valuable space to face outdoors. Better zoning between living and bedroom areas also can result. A center hall, often a dark pocket, can be made a pleasant space in new additions and old houses.

Plastic Dome Skylights

The new, dome skylights are factory-made and delivered ready for installation. They are leakproof and use the same tough, shatterproof plastic (such as Plexiglas) pioneered in airplanes. Round, square, or oblong shapes are available in sizes less than 12 inches square up to about 8×9-foot rectangular units. Because they are bubble-shaped, looking like part of a large egg sticking above the roof line (but more attractive), rain keeps them washed clean. Prices range from about $50 to $400, plus installation.

Ceiling skylights let light and sunshine pour into normally dark interior of a house. Square or round models are available. Bubble design lets rain keep them clean.

Skydome Skylights. Ben Schnall, Jason Halley, Ben Schnall.

They can be installed in any kind of roof, new or old. This means you can, in effect, punch a hole in your present roof and install a skylight to brighten up an interior room space, or it can let you look up at the stars at night without ever moving from your chair or bed. They can be had in clear or opaque plastic or tinted shades. Most kinds can be opened like a window for air or they have air vents.

Besides the plastic-dome skylight and the special ventilating kind for sloped roofs, several other kinds are made. Glass-block skylights can be built with special frames to fit nearly any opening. There are also flat and curved skylight panels made with glass or with a structural plastic.

The Limitations

Like regular windows, protection from sun heat and glare is imperative with skylights. These are the two main hazards to avoid. Improper location of a skylight can let so much sun pour in that the heat and glare will be insufferable.

Heat entry is controlled mainly by proper location and by limiting the skylight size. A skylight on the north slope of a roof obviously will let in less sun heat than elsewhere on the roof. Heat also can be controlled by means of special inside shade accessories available with most brands. To keep heat entry down (as well as costs), use the smallest practical size rather than the largest.

The glare problem is directly related to the total amount of light entering a room from other windows (the same problem encountered with poor electric lighting). The greater the concentration of light from one source and one direction, the greater the glare problem. Thus, much glare may be expected from a skylight if it is the main source of light in a room. It is particularly hard on the eyes. Then you should definitely consider a tinted skylight or one with a shade. Less glare results when there is another good source of light in the room.

Conversely, a skylight can help reduce an existing glare problem. This problem arises, for example, in a deep living room with a large area of window glass in one wall but little or no glass in the other walls. Your eyes hurt because of the concentration of light at one end with no offsetting light balance from the rest of the room. You will notice that curtains are kept drawn over such windows to reduce the glare.

One good remedy is a ceiling skylight as deep inside the room as possible. The resulting daylight shed inside provides a balance to the high concentration of light from the window. This is possible, of course, only in one-story houses or rooms under the roof.

Avoiding Condensation

Heavy moisture condensation will form on skylights in cold weather just as on regular window glass. It is worse with skylights because it drips on your head. Safeguards against condensation are therefore essential, particularly in a cold climate.

In the North this calls for a double-dome skylight which has two sheets of plastic glass, using the same principle as a double-glass window. Or the skylight used should contain a small gutter around the underside of its frame to catch the moisture before it can fall.

Experts say that condensation is not a problem in a moderate or warm climate with single-skin skylights if the unit is installed close to the ceiling line. This exposes the skylight to inside air circulation for carrying off water vapor before it can condense.

Buying Skylights

Shopping for skylights may be difficult because they are comparatively new and not generally stocked by suppliers. Your best bet is to write to manufacturers for literature and the names of their nearest suppliers. A list of names follows. But because of the variety of product design and product changes every year, I cannot say that all of the skylights made by these firms are of the best quality. You will have to check the specifications against the tips given in this article. Also look for waterproof seals at the frame and leakproof construction.

In general, it is best to buy one made by a manufacturer located in your climate zone. The products of a northern manufacturer are more likely to be designed for cold climate exposure than those of a southern manufacturer and vice versa. Also ask if his skylights are accepted by the FHA.

Skylight Manufacturers

Wasco Products Department
American Cyanimid Co.
5 Bay State Road
Cambridge 38, Mass.

Architectural Products Corp.
1355 River Road
Eugene, Oregon

Architectural Plastics Inc.
Rowayton, Conn.

The By-Products Co.
Bladensburg, Md.

Ventarama Skylight Corp.
Port Washington, N.Y.

Dubl-Dome Division
The Pan Co.
1951 N.W. Wilson St.
Portland 9, Oregon

Plasteco, Inc.
P. O. Box 9123
Houston, Texas

Mid-South Industries, Inc.
Columbia, S.C.

Part 6

CHOOSING TOP-QUALITY BUILDING MATERIALS

The market abounds with a confusing variety of different materials for every part of the house. Some are cheap in price and equally cheap in quality. Others cost a little more for increased quality. Still others are highly expensive though often for reasons other than a proportionate increase in quality.

Quality embraces such characteristics as durability, easy maintenance, good appearance, and long life. These features are emphasized in this section. The same characteristics should be sought whether you are merely repairing your house, modernizing it, or adding new living space.

In the mammoth Sears, Roebuck catalogue most products are labeled "good, better, and best," with a small step-up in price for each and a proportionately larger step-up in quality. The same gradations are found in nearly every kind of product and material sold for houses, including kitchen and bathroom fixtures (in earlier chapters) and everything else, regardless of whether you buy it in a lumberyard, hardware store, or from a builder or contractor.

This is important to know because in virtually all cases the so-called "good" or cheapest version is invariably the cheapest in quality, made and sold chiefly to meet competitive sales pressures. You will almost always do well to avoid it and get the next grade up, the middle-grade version.

As a matter of fact the cheapest, lowest quality grade of building materials is often referred to as the "builder" line, or the "builder" model. It is the grade manufacturers cut to the bone, in price and quality, for sales to builder tract houses where price is the chief buying consideration. It's best to avoid "builder" quality materials and products.

In some cases the best and highest-priced version of the same product may or may not be worth the money. It depends on the product and the particular characteristics you want. Sometimes it is a luxury product given special looks and styling and priced extremely high for a top profit at whatever the traffic will bear. Other times—again depending on the product —you do indeed get a worthwhile increase in ruggedness, durability, or elegant appearance which is worth the extra cost.

Throughout this book I have made distinctions in product quality wherever possible and indicated when the top-price item may or may not be worth the money; this is followed through in the following chapters on materials.

Much also depends on how certain products are *installed,* and this, too, is discussed. Providing detailed installation specifications for all products and materials is beyond the scope of this book. In many cases it depends on the brand used and you must rely on the manufacturer's directions.

For additional data, one of the best sources of information on products and how they should be installed is "FHA's Minimum Property Standards for One and Two Living Units," a 315-page manual obtainable for $1.75 (cloth cover) from Superintendent of Documents, Washington 25, D.C. It is a good guide.

Chapter 16

Flooring and Interior Walls

The principal kinds of finished flooring are hardwood, softwood, and resilient materials. Which to use depends largely on the room, personal taste, and budget.

Hardwood is best for living rooms, dining rooms, and bedrooms. Hardwood is handsome, has a warm look, rugged wearing qualities and is an asset for resale purposes.

Oak and maple are the king and queen of the hardwoods. The top grades of each are the handsomest and best-looking, and are available in blocks such as parquet and in strip flooring in modern or traditional styles. The lower grades are equally strong but lower in cost due to appearance flaws like knots; they can be a bargain for a utility room, closet and attic floors, or kitchen sub-floor. Other hardwoods for floors are beach and birch. They offer less variety and choice of grain than oak or maple but are also strong and durable.

The *softwoods* include hemlock, pine, and fir. They give hard and long service but are not as handsome or durable as oak or maple. Use a top grade and a good finish for best appearance.

Pure vinyl flooring, sometimes called solid vinyl, is the best all-round resilient flooring material. The most expensive, it is exceedingly tough, has a rich appearance, high resistance to oil, grease, water, chemicals, and requires the least attention.

Cork and *rubber tile* are ranked next in quality after vinyl. Both are soft to walk on. Cork is noted for its warmth underfoot—it is a top insulator. It is ideal for a study, say, but not for a room or hall where it will get rough treatment; it soon shows scuff marks and scars from furniture feet, dents, and heavy foot traffic. Rubber is resistant to indentation marks and water, but will show wear unless periodically finished, preferably with a self-polishing wax.

Vinyl-asbestos tile can be used in any room. Because of its durability and low cost it is becoming one of the most popular floor coverings. It is resistant to water, grease, and chemicals, but it is not as durable, hand-

Wood flooring can be had in blocks with rich grainy texture shown here, or in parquet.

National Lumber Mfrs. Assn. Robert C. Lautman.

some, or soft underfoot as the higher priced materials noted above. It should be your minimum choice when you have to save money.

Asphalt tile, the cheapest of all, normally should be avoided. It is widely used because it is cheap in price and people don't realize that it is also as delinquent in quality. It is brittle, the least durable of all the resilients, and highly susceptive to stains, scuff marks, and dents; in short,

Handsome tile-block floor in Michigan house can be had in variety of colors. Principal features are rich appearance and low maintenance.

Tile Council of America. Dale Rooks.

it is the bane of many a woman's existence. Because of poor grease resistance it is decidedly not good in a kitchen. Its best use is over a cement basement floor because of its moisture resistance.

Sheet, roll, and tile linoleum are used widely in kitchens. Inlaid linoleum is best because its color and pattern go all the way through to the base. The inlaid kind provides a hard, durable surface, is greaseproof and easy to clean. But it should not be used on a concrete floor or in a basement, because moisture from the concrete below will cause it to rot.

A point to remember about wood and resilient flooring:

"More floors are washed away than worn away." Use good finishes but don't overdo it.

Marble, Masonry, and Tile Floors

There are also ceramic tile (excellent in bathrooms), flagstone, terrazzo, and marble. All are extremely hard and durable (naturally), and require little or no maintenance. They can mean broken limbs, of course,

Prefabricated fireplaces are available in modern or traditional design. Photos also show the use of cork-tile floor (with modern fireplace) and plywood wall paneling with traditional Franklin stove fireplace.

Armstrong Cork. U. S. Plywood Corp.

in case of a hard fall. Wax will enhance the color and appearance of each and reduce cleaning chores. Brick, stone, and concrete floors are also hard and rugged, of course, but are less attractive and require more cleaning. Concrete requires regular waxing. Except for ceramic tile, which is generally applied over wood, the rest of these materials lack resilience and are hard on the feet. Many people therefore shun them for floors except for occasional decorative use in a special part of the house.

Interior Wall Materials

Gypsum-board walls can be as good as plaster at much less cost. Also called plasterboard or dry-wall construction, it has a bad reputation because the thinnest, ⅜-inch sheets are generally used, resulting in weak, wavy walls. This can be avoided if you specify the stronger ½-inch-

or ¾-inch-thick sheets for only a penny or two more per square foot; a double wall of two ⅜-inch sheets is best of all. The joints between sheets require good taping (spackling). If gypsum board is nailed to green studs in the wall, the nails are gradually forced out as the wood dries and unsightly pockmarks result. This can be avoided if your studs are good, dry, No. 1. framing lumber, and special nails are used.

Plaster walls are solid-looking and handsome. The best kind requires three coats of plaster over lath but this is seldom done. Two coats over gypsum-board lath is good. The lath should be reinforced at the joints between walls and ceilings, at corners and around doors and windows. Even the best plaster ultimately may show cracks due to expansion and contraction and there is little you can do about it. By the way, neither plaster nor dry wall by itself is strong enough to support shelving or bookcases. The vertical 2×4 inside the walls must be located and used to anchor nails and screws.

Paneling is available in a bewildering number of different types and grades of wood (from a good many of the 1100 different species of trees in the country). Pine panels are the current favorite but it doesn't have to be knotty, and don't just ask for "pine." There is Ponderosa pine, Idaho white, sugar pine, and so on, each with its individual grain appearance and pattern. And not all pine requires a yellow cast or a finish that will darken it.

Hardwood paneling gives an elegant wall with such wood as pecan, beech, walnut, and cherry. These are the highest in price. Redwood, cypress, and cedar are less expensive. You can also use prefinished oak flooring for walls with no additional finishing required.

Plywood paneling is also available in a variety of patterns and styles often indistinguishable from solid wood paneling. Durability depends on the particular wood used and its thickness. Fir plywood is a big seller because of low cost, but its quality is also considered low. It is not as good as pine and hardwood paneling and is inferior to top-grade plywood panels such as birch.

The best wood paneling should take a clear finish to preserve its natural color and grain. One of the new pigmented oil stains can be excellent. It is brushed on and then wiped with a cloth.

Other Interior Wall Materials

Fiberboard is made in planks and panels and usually called Celotex (though this is merely one of several brands available). Some kinds offer a little insulating value, others none at all. The insulating kind should not be bought for its insulating value alone, except perhaps in a moderate climate where only a little insulation is required; it doesn't insulate that well.

Composition board is comparatively new and varies greatly according to the brand and grade. The soft ones mar easily, and all are vulnerable to moisture and water and therefore should not be used in a basement or other area where dampness may be present. Its rough texture gives it a decorative appearance.

Asbestos-cement boards are hard and rugged. Although used chiefly on exterior walls it is often suitable for interiors. The premium grade is stronger and longer lasting than the lighter-weight standard grade.

Plastic panels and tiles are commonly used for kitchen and bath walls, offer good looks and long wear, and are easy to keep clean if waxed regularly. A good installation is essential. Ceramic tile, also for kitchens and baths, gives excellent long-term service but should be installed by experts. The glazed kind should not be cleaned with steel wool or gritty scouring powder.

Chapter 17

Exterior Wall Materials
and Aluminum Siding

A few general notes first. The choice of wall material for a new addition obviously will be influenced largely by your present walls. The same material may be desired but sometimes you can use a different and better material with a similar appearance, or a planned contrast.

Regardless of what you use, don't mix a variety of materials together and end up with banana-split walls. Stick to one or at most two different materials. Simplicity is the key to good looks. Besides, a splotch of special wall material added helter-skelter here and there makes a house look chopped up and smaller than it actually is.

Exterior wall siding looks best when it is applied over the foundation walls almost to the ground. This makes a house look large and substantial. (No wood, however, should touch the ground. There should be a few inches at least between the damp earth and the bottom of any exterior wood to avoid wood rot and termite penetration.)

Nearly all exterior wall materials can be applied over existing house walls and some over masonry. The condition of your present walls, however, is of crucial importance. A small section of the wall should be opened up in several places to make sure that the new siding does not close in a bad wall condition.

Here are the most popular kinds of exterior wall materials:

Wood, including clapboard and plywood, is attractive on nearly all houses and can be painted any color. Redwood and cedar give a warm, natural wood finish, are resistant to termites and rot, but usually must be stained or they will turn gray as a result of weathering; some people like it while others think it dull and drab.

Plywood panels are growing in popularity, are extremely strong and durable, and offer many design and texture possibilities. The new kinds are bonded with excellent waterproof adhesives and require no more refinishing than other exterior wood walls (with comparable paint). They are generally best, however, in a temperate climate, since freezing moisture in cold climate can open joints that are not well caulked.

Hardboard (such as Masonite) is tough, durable, rot-resistant, and will not split or crack. Various kinds are available including smooth, striated, grooved, or board-and-batten texture. It may require occasional repainting. A vapor barrier within the wall is particularly important to prevent condensation and paint peeling.

Wood shingles and shakes are usually cedar, sometimes redwood or cypress. Like wood roof shingles, they give a rough-hewn, traditional appearance with much texture. Mostly for traditional house styles, such as the Cape Cod, they are durable and weather well, or can be stained or painted. The best shingles are free from knots and pitch pockets. You can tell the difference between the best grade and lower grades by the grain; it should be regular and clear with few or no defects.

Asbestos-cement sheets and shingles give you a hard permanent wall because of their hard, stonelike surface. Both are exceedingly durable, fire resistant, and rotproof, but somewhat brittle. Though painting is generally not necessary for durability alone, it may be required occasionally to renew exterior looks.

Insulating board siding comes in small, asphalt-surfaced panels with a coarse surface and in large, smooth-surfaced panels. Although its insulating value is greater than ordinary wood, it is not enough insulation for comfort; additional inside wall insulation is required, particularly in a cold climate. It weathers well, but it expands and contracts with temperature changes and knocks can damage it.

Prefabricated wall panels with a porcelain-enamel, plywood, aluminum, or a plastic surface are a new development and a significant trend in home building. Such panels are made in factories and shops and merely assembled on the job. Made under shop-controlled conditions they are usually better made than walls put together piece by piece. A porcelain-enamel surface is virtually indestructible and rarely needs maintenance or upkeep. Being relatively new, such panels tend to be high in first cost but prices are coming down as sales rise. Prefabricated panels should be unbeatable as they become more and more available.

Masonry Walls

The biggest features of brick and stone are beauty, strength, and permanence (painting is seldom required). But a few facts on the other side of the ledger should be known. Insulation is absolutely essential with brick or stone walls, though it is often omitted. (It is recommended for all other masonry, too, not only in the North but also in the South with air conditioning, and even in northern Florida, say, where a good many people wish for a little insulation just for winter comfort). Despite popular belief, even the thickest masonry has exceedingly poor insulating properties, which is why masonry houses are particularly cold and hard to heat. Insist on insulation regardless of the type of masonry.

Brick and stone walls also can be quite vulnerable to water seepage through cracks and joints. Periodic painting will still be required for exterior windows and doors; this often accounts for more than half of total house-painting costs. What you save on wall paint is sometimes offset by increased taxes, since tax assessors make a particular target of brick and stone houses.

Nevertheless, some people are unswerving in their wish for masonry. If you are one, accept it with your eyes open. Masonry gives a house a solid, permanent appearance and increased value. But make sure the space between the masonry and the interior wall surface contains insulation and a vapor barrier. Letting your masonry serve as both the interior and exterior wall will not only mean cold walls, but also dampness coming through the masonry can leave ugly stains on interior surfaces.

Stucco is portland-cement veneer applied like plaster to either masonry or frame walls, with no seams or joints. A variety of textures and colors are used, but its appearance gets mixed reviews—you like it or you don't. A good job requires the right mixture and proper application to prevent cracking and water seepage. Three coats of stucco with a total thickness of ¾ inch are generally recommended. Quality varies according to the ability and conscientiousness of the people who do the job; you are at their mercy. Be cautious with stucco.

There are also concrete block, cinder block, and reinforced cement walls. The block walls, now available in colors or with various designs etched into the blocks, can look quite handsome, particularly when painted; or terribly dingy if raw blocks are left unpainted.

Painting is equally important for cement. In fact, exterior paint or a surface sealer is mandatory to prevent cracking, chipping, and water seepage. The block walls are often used because they are cheap and seem like a bargain. But insulating them is just as important as with brick or stone. And when properly finished, waterproofed, and insulated, they may not be so cheap compared with other walls.

How Will New Materials Affect the Looks of Your House?

Because the exterior wall material you choose has a major effect on house appearance, for good or for bad, the esthetics of your choice should be carefully thought out. Too much brick can be dreary. Large stones on a small house or addition can look absurd. Masonry by its nature is a heavy, massive material that can add weight and a look of permanency to a large house but overwhelm a small house or addition. Wood shakes may be traditional for a Cape Cod house but they are generally too grainy for a modern ranch house (as well as making the house look small). Wood is humble and honest and can be handsome in its simplicity, though again it depends on the house.

Unfortunately, hard and fast rules are impossible to lay down on esthetics. Like taste, your choice will hinge on an accumulation of experience. Before choosing the wall you would like, drive around and note how the same wall looks on other houses. How does it look on houses like your own? How does it wear over the years? Above all, don't mix too many different materials on a house front just for variety. A banana-split exterior is a hodgepodge and looks it.

Aluminum Siding for New or Old Walls

Aluminum siding excels for good looks and low upkeep not only for a new face on an old house but also for a new addition even if your existing walls are not aluminum. It goes well alongside many different conventional wall materials, and is usually indistinguishable from wood clapboard.

The Advantages

Low upkeep and infrequent repainting are two of aluminum's biggest advantages. In addition, aluminum will not rot, tarnish, blister, crack, or peel. It reflects sun heat in summer, which means a cooler house. Contrary to some opinions, hail stones (less than footballs in size) will not pockmark it.

It comes in a variety of colors and repainting should not be required for at least 10 to 15 years. Nobody knows for sure, however, how long aluminum will last before new painting is required. It hasn't been around long enough to tell. An FHA investigation of 10-year-old aluminum siding on houses "indicated" that it should last at least 15 years before repainting is needed. A top-grade kind, properly installed, should last 20 to 25 years because of the rugged new paint finishes now being used.

What Does It Cost?

Installed cost over old walls generally ranges from about $75 a square (100 square feet of wall) up to about $100, depending on where you live and the amount of installation labor required for your particular house. A simple rectangular house with unbroken walls is clearly easier to cover than one cut up with jogs and many windows and doors. Cost is also less for aluminum walls on a new addition.

Aluminum will generally cost a few hundred dollars more in total first cost than the cost of other conventional wall materials, but you get this back several times over in the savings on repainting costs alone.

Obtaining the Best Job

First, specify a top-grade siding. Best safeguard here is to buy a brand name such as Alside, Alcoa, Kaiser, or Reynolds aluminum siding. Some prime manufacturers like Reynolds, however, make only the basic aluminum sheets which are later made into siding by a siding manufacturer such as Alside. Some siding makers, on the other hand, buy the thinnest, cheapest aluminum sheets and turn it into the cheapest siding with an inferior paint finish.

Second, the kind of paint finish is crucial. A first-rate brand will have a factory-applied, baked-on paint. The best kind is a baked-on acrylic paint finish which will last an estimated 20 to 25 years. It is new, however, and these figures are based on laboratory tests. Vinyl paint is good for 10 to 15 years service, and the same goes for alkyd paint. Check on the exact kind of paint used. The price goes up slightly for better paint, but is worth it.

Third, proper application over old walls is essential. One mistake sometimes made by contractors is covering the old walls first with sheets of regular aluminum foil before the siding itself is nailed up. They play this up as if it's a special feature. However, a regular foil backing is a vapor barrier which you decidedly do not want here. It will trap water vapor and moisture inside your walls because they can't "breathe." This in turn can lead to condensation and interior wood rot.

The point to remember is that a vapor barrier is absolutely reprehensible on the *outside* of house walls. (As explained in Chapter 21, a vapor barrier should go on the *inside* of the wall, the warm side in winter, next to the interior wall surface.) To permit the walls to breathe, the backing for aluminum siding should be sheets of *perforated* foil, which contain hundreds of small holes per square foot. Even better, according to some experts, is a backing of black building paper that is not a vapor barrier. And the siding itself also should have weep holes to let vapor out.

Fourth, the installation should include the use of special trim and molding (accessories for sealing the spaces around doors and windows, and making neat corner turns). If a salesman says "They don't make them," buy from someone else. Either he's selling the low-grade material of a supplier who does not furnish accessories or he had left them out to keep his price down.

What about Insulating Value?

Even the best conventional aluminum siding does not provide much insulation for protection from winter cold. Almost any new siding will make an old house somewhat warmer simply because it seals the inevitable leaks common in old-house walls. Aluminum also will cut down summer heat entry by bouncing back the sun's rays.

But if you live in a cold climate don't expect new aluminum siding to pinch-hit for thick interior-wall insulation. Nor is it as good as thick wall insulation for keeping out hot outdoor heat in houses with air conditioning. If you desire really good wall insulation, have it done before new siding is applied.

Some brands of aluminum siding are available with a backing of about a half inch of plastic-foam insulation. This costs about $6 per square (100 square feet) more than the noninsulation-backed siding. It is the equivalent of paying 6¢ per square foot for half-inch-thick insulation. If your walls are already insulated, this kind of siding is not needed. If your walls are not insulated, you could have insulation blown into them at a cost of 15¢ to 20¢ per square foot, depending on the walls, for roughly 3 inches of wall insulation. This is a better buy than insulation backing on new siding.

Having insulation blown into the walls is therefore the better choice over the long run if you live in a cold climate or if you have air conditioning. Reduced heating and cooling bills will pay back its additional first cost in a few years. If you need wall insulation and live in a moderate climate with moderately low fuel bills and no air conditioning, then it may pay to choose the insulation-backed siding.

Two Important Buying Tips

1. How much siding are you getting? Ask how many squares (hundred feet) will be installed? (One homeowner got bids for new aluminum which ranged from $1450 up to $2100 and found that the amount of siding he would get ranged from 18 squares up to 30 squares. No wonder the price differential.) Some installers estimate carelessly and charge you for more than they will actually use. Others cut corners and shave the material off areas where you should have it. The quantity of siding should be specified in your sales contract.

2. Is it a top-grade material made by a national manufacturer? Avoid siding turned out from poor aluminum stock by a local fabricator. Go a step further and compare the technical specifications of the siding against the minimum standards for siding in FHA's *Minimum Property Requirements* book (see page 128). Asking if the siding is "FHA-accepted" may or may not bring a truthful response.

Chapter 18

Choosing Exterior Wall Paint

There are three main kinds of exterior paint: the widely publicized new water emulsions (latex), the alkyds, and the traditional linseed-oil (oil-base) paint. Consider the emulsions first as they are generally the best for nearly all new wood, and for new or existing masonry. They are sometimes, but decidedly not always, best for repainting an existing house.

Latex Emulsion Paints

We'll refer to them as emulsion paints. They are thinned with water and include paints with a rubber, vinyl, acrylic, or PVC (polyvinyl-chloride) base. You may hear them called by any of these names.

The emulsions are highly blister-resistant, nonchalking, easy to apply in dry or wet weather (thus no aggravating delays during wet weather). They should last about 25 per cent longer than an aklyd paint, about 50 per cent longer than a conventional oil paint. They stand up well in areas where industrial fumes exist, and where mildew is a threat.

In a severe mildew area, however, you probably will need extra protection in the form of a mildewcide added to the paint. A good many brands contain a mildewcide to prevent mold growth. If you do not see it mentioned on the can, have the equivalent chemical added to the paint being used. (Many mildewcides contain mercury compounds which may discolor in an industrial atmosphere. This is apparently why all manufacturers do not put them in their paint.)

The emulsions give a good uniform appearance. Like the more familiar interior latex paints, they have little or no odor, and do not leave impossible stains on your hands. But they are available only in a flat finish, thus not desirable if you prefer a glossy finish.

For Repainting Old Walls?

Unfortunately, much confusion exists over the virtue of repainting an existing house with an emulsion paint because it is comparatively new. This depends on your old paint. If your old paint is also an emulsion —though this is unlikely—a new emulsion paint can easily go right over it. If it is not an emulsion but in good condition, experts say you also can paint right over it with a new emulsion, but nobody has successfully defined exactly when old paint is in good condition. It is certainly not in good condition if it is dirty and chalky. No emulsion will adhere to an old, dirty, chalking paint.

One test here is to rub a piece of colored cloth on the surface to be painted. If very little chalk rubs off it is a good sign and a new emulsion will probably stick to it. But to play safe, wash down the old paint first with a paint cleaner and then hose it with clear water to remove all traces of chalk, dirt, oil, or grease. Blistered areas should be scraped or sanded down to bare wood and well back from the immediate area of damage. A coat of blister-resistant primer should be applied over the freshly exposed wood. No over-all priming is required if the rest of the old paint is in sound condition.

An effective paint cleaner can be easily made by mixing a quart of household bleach (such as Clorox or Purex), one ounce of a synthetic detergent (such as Tide, All, Oxydol, Fab, or Dash), and three ounces of trisodium phosphate (Soilax or Spic 'n Span, for example) in enough water to make one gallon of cleaning solution.

If, however, enough chalk rubs off to half obscure the cloth, a coat of special primer designed for emulsion house paint should be applied before the acrylic. Specify a blister-resistant primer; not all are. Instead of a primer, at least one maker recommends an additive stirred into the paint to give it a special chalk-adhering quality. Even with a primer applied first, two coats of an emulsion may be required to give a lasting finish. This depends on the paint quality, how well the first coat is applied, and on the color.

Neither an emulsion nor any other paint is recommended if your house is quite old with many layers of paint on the walls. Chip off a small section of old paint down to the wood. If the paint film is cardboard thick, repainting will only hasten the day when it will crack and peel, requiring complete removal of all the accumulated paint down to the bare wood.

These qualifications and potential troubles raise doubts about repainting a house with emulsion paint. Some experts say it is best not to, at least for a few years until the new paints have had more time to prove themselves. They figure, among other things, that the cost of a primer (needed much of the time) plus the likely cost for two coats make it too expensive, compared with only one coat and no primer needed with an alkyd or oil-base paint.

If in doubt, talk it over with a good painter. Has he had good experience repainting other similar houses with emulsion paint? If your old paint has to be burned off down to the bare wood, an emulsion can be applied in the same way as on new wood.

Note: Just before this book went to press and after the above section was written, the Du Pont people told me that they will introduce a new Lucite emulsion paint for exterior walls. It normally will not need a primer before application over old paint. (You should still apply a primer, though, over blistered areas of old paint that have been scraped down to bare wood.) They say the new paint is the result of nearly ten years of research. It also can be used on new or carefully cleaned masonry, brick, cement block and asbestos-shingle siding.

Like other emulsion paints, it can be applied over damp surfaces, shortly after a light rain, for example, and it dries so fast that a second coat can be applied within two hours after the first coat. They recommend two coats for best results. We can probably expect other manufacturers to introduce new emulsion paints that will not require primers on old paint.

Emulsion Paint for New Wood and Masonry

Here is where emulsions shine. But a primer is essential first on all new wood, sometimes on masonry if the masonry has old, very chalky paint. (A primer is generally needed with any other kind of paint too.) The primer must be the exact companion kind recommended by the manufacturer of the particular emulsion you use. If your house is part siding and part masonry, specify a *nonchalking* brand. Some brands are free-chalking, and rain-water wash-down from them will stain the masonry.

Some woods such as redwood, cedar, or mahogany contain water-soluble stains which may bleed through an emulsion paint. Two coats of primer may be needed. Wait a week after the first coat is applied. If a pink stain shows through the primer, another coat of primer should be applied before final painting.

Alkyd and Linseed-Oil Paints

An alkyd is generally the next best choice if acrylic paint is unfeasible. It comes in flat or gloss finishes with little odor. It offers better color retention and is tougher and longer lasting than conventional linseed-oil paints.

A good alkyd paint job should last about six to eight years on the average before repainting is required (versus seven to ten years for an emulsion paint), down to four to five years for linseed-oil paint. These are approximate figures, depending on the use of a primer and two top coats in each case. Some experts say that a top-grade alkyd properly applied may last ten years or more (and a really good emulsion or acrylic properly applied should be good for 15 years or more).

Suggested color schemes for houses.

If your house has shutters, paint the trim the same color as body of house – or white. If not, use these suggested colors for trim.

If the roof of your house is	You can paint the body	Pink	Bright red	Red-orange	Tile red	Cream	Bright yellow	Light green	Dark green	Gray-green	Blue-green	Light blue	Dark blue	Blue-gray	Violet	Brown	White
GRAY	White	X	X	X	X	X	X	X	X	X	X	X	X	X	X		
	Gray	X	X	X	X		X	X	X	X	X	X	X	X	X		X
	Cream-yellow		X		X		X		X	X							X
	Pale green				X		X		X	X							X
	Dark green	X				X	X	X									X
	Putty		X	X					X	X			X	X		X	
	Dull red	X				X		X						X			X
GREEN	White	X	X	X	X	X	X	X	X	X	X	X	X	X	X		
	Gray			X		X	X	X									X
	Cream-yellow		X		X			X	X	X						X	X
	Pale green			X	X		X			X							X
	Dark green	X		X		X	X	X									X
	Beige			X					X	X	X		X	X			
	Brown	X				X	X	X									X
	Dull red					X		X		X							X
RED	White		X		X			X			X			X			X
	Light gray		X		X			X									X
	Cream-yellow		X		X						X	X	X				
	Pale green		X		X												X
	Dull red					X		X		X	X						
BROWN	White			X	X		X	X	X	X			X	X	X		
	Buff			X				X	X	X					X		
	Pink-beige			X				X	X						X	X	
	Cream-yellow			X				X	X	X					X		
	Pale green							X	X						X		
	Brown		X			X	X										X
BLUE	White			X	X		X					X	X				
	Gray			X		X						X	X				X
	Cream-yellow			X	X								X	X			
	Blue			X		X	X						X				X

Avoiding Paint Failures

Four of the most common troubles with house paint are blistering and peeling, cracking, checking, and mildew blotching.

The most widespread and troublesome is blistering and subsequent peeling caused by moisture—cold-weather condensation under the paint. Water vapor from the house or from a roof leak can't get out through open windows and doors so it pushes through the walls until it hits the underside of the exterior paint.

Most exterior paint on houses today doesn't "breathe" (let vapor out) because it is vapor impermeable oil paint. The vapor is stopped in its tracks. Then on a cold day, the trapped vapor will gradually build up pressure until it forces through the paint film, causing blisters and ultimate paint peeling.

	HOUSE PAINT	TRANSPARENT SEALER	CEMENT BASE PAINT	RUBBER BASE PAINT	EXTERIOR CLEAR FINISH	ALUMINUM PAINT	WOOD STAIN	ROOF COATING	ROOF CEMENT	ASPHALT EMULSION	METAL ROOF PAINT	TRIM-AND-TRELLIS PAINT	AWNING PAINT	SPAR VARNISH	PORCH-AND-DECK PAINT	PRIMER OR UNDERCOATER	METAL PRIMER
CLAPBOARD SIDING	✓.					✓										✓	
BRICK	✓.	✓	✓	✓		✓										✓	
CEMENT & CINDER BLOCK	✓.	✓	✓	✓		✓										✓	
ASBESTOS CEMENT	✓.		✓													✓	
STUCCO	✓.	✓	✓	✓		✓										✓	
NATURAL WOOD SIDING & TRIM							✓							✓			
METAL SIDING	✓.					✓.					✓.						✓
WOOD FRAME WINDOWS	✓.					✓						✓.				✓	
STEEL WINDOWS	✓.					✓.					✓.						✓
ALUMINUM WINDOWS	✓.					✓					✓.						✓
SHUTTERS & OTHER TRIM	✓.										✓.			✓			
CANVAS AWNINGS													✓				
WOOD SHINGLE ROOF							✓										
METAL ROOF											✓.						✓
COAL TAR FELT ROOF								✓	✓	✓							
WOOD PORCH FLOOR															✓		
CEMENT PORCH FLOOR				✓											✓		
COPPER SURFACES														✓			
GALVANIZED SURFACES	✓.					✓.					✓.	✓					✓
IRON SURFACES	✓.					✓.					✓.						✓

✓. Black dot indicates that a primer or sealer may be necessary before the finishing coat (unless surface has been previously finished)

What kind of paint for various purposes?

This can happen to the best linseed-oil and alkyd paints. It is particularly evident on house walls near a kitchen or bath, the biggest sources of indoor water vapor. The remedy can be costly. All the old paint must be removed before repainting, and then it is best to repaint with a new, blister-free, emulsion paint.

Blistering outside sometimes can be controlled by using vapor-barrier interior paint on interior walls, especially in bathrooms. If there are no breaks in the finish, it will prevent moisture generated indoors from infiltrating the exterior walls. The same troubles also can be caused by a water leak from a room gutter, for example, or a wet-basement condition. The obvious cure is eliminating the moisture at its source.

Other troubles, such as cracking and checking, are generally caused by the use of inferior paint, the wrong paint for the particular wall surface, poor surface preparation (such as no primer-sealer used), or poor application (such as an oil paint being applied on damp or wet walls—walls must be absolutely dry except when an acrylic paint is used). Sometimes paint flaws can simply be covered up with a new coat, but more often a bad condition will require complete removal of the old paint before new priming and painting.

Mildew is caused by a fungus that discolors and destroys paint. Before repainting over mildewed paint, the old paint should be washed down with washing soda; if badly stained, with a 0.2 per cent solution of disinfectant. Allow the surface to dry thoroughly before repainting. The new primer and paint should contain a mildew inhibitor.

New Stain for a Natural Wood Finish

The best natural finish for outside wood walls, particularly redwood and cedar, is a new stain developed by the Department of Agriculture's Forest Products Laboratory (Madison 5, Wisconsin). It should last about five years, sometimes more, whereas the best stain formerly available was generally good for only a year or two.

The new stain is apparently so cheap and easy to make at home that few manufacturers, so far, market it. You may have to make your own. Here are the ingredients for a 5-gallon batch (all available at drugstore and hardware stores):

Raw linseed oil	3 gal.
Mineral spirits of turpentine	1 gal.
Burnt sienna (oil color)	1 pint
Raw umber (oil color)	1 pint
Paraffin wax	1 lb.
Penta concentrate preservative	½ gal.
Zinc stearate	2 oz.

Mix it this way: Pour the gallon of the mineral spirits into a 5-gallon can. Put the paraffin and zinc stearate into another pan and heat over a flame, stirring until uniform. Pour this mixture into the mineral spirits, stirring vigorously. *Keep the flame away from the mineral spirits.*

When the solution has cooled to room temperature, add penta and linseed oil. Stir in the colors until the mixture is uniform. Then it's ready for use. The surface should be washed and brushed before application. A gallon will cover about 400 square feet of wall, more or less; the smoother the wood, the greater the coverage.

General Tips on Painting

Regardless of which of the three main types of paint you may use:

1. Get the precise kind needed as marked on the can for "masonry," "outside trim," "wood," and so on. There is no all-purpose paint.

2. Get the absolute best-quality, brand-name kind available even if you have to spend $8 a gallon, and a bargain is available on the next shelf for $5.39. In all, the bargain paint may save you a mere $10 to $15 on all the paint needed for a house, but the same $10 extra for the best available grade will mean a better paint job that will last several years longer.

3. Buy only paint that has its ingredients (iron oxide, titanium dioxide, etc.) spelled out on the label. If you don't see them on the label, beware.

4. Follow the directions on the can to the letter. This is crucial, particularly for what it says about using a primer and the *preparation* of the surfaces before painting. You may have to spend as much time preparing the surface as required for the actual painting but this is essential (unless you don't mind repainting six months later).

5. Don't fall for the two-for-one paint gimmick, "a second gallon free with every gallon you buy." Sometimes it's a second gallon for 1¢ more. Nobody gives away something for nothing. You simply get two gallons of cheap paint for the price of a gallon of good paint.

For Special Information

A good source of information on painting is the National Paint, Varnish and Lacquer Association, Inc., 1500 Rhode Island Avenue, N.W., Washington 5, D.C. They publish a wide variety of free pamphlets on choosing and applying paint for nearly every kind of exterior and interior surface. Specify the particular information you need, or write for the whole series.

Chapter 19

Buying a New Roof

A roof leak is the first sign that a roof has seen its best days and it's time to re-roof. Most leaks result from normal weathering over the years. Once the roof is worn through at one spot, starting the first leak, other worn-out spots show up in progressive order. You can patch here and delay the inevitable, but the signals are clear: it's time to re-roof.

There are a few exceptions. Roof leaks sometimes occur in new houses because of sloppy roofing work and occasionally in a roof that is basically in good shape. Such leaks predominate around chimneys and dormers, usually because of defective flashing (the metal seal at roof joints). Occasionally they are caused by a defective shingle. Repairing the flashing or replacing the shingle may be all you need. But in most cases the first leak unfortunately is your first clear sign that you need a new roof and you had better get out your checkbook, painful as it may seem.

What Kind of New Roof?

There are basically two kinds of roof cover—the temporary, which has to be renewed or replaced periodically, and the permanent materials which last at least 40 to 50 years and sometimes for centuries. The copper roof of Philadelphia's famed Christ Church is over 200 years old and still going strong. Here are facts about each, starting with the renewable kind:

Asphalt Shingles

Asphalt shingles, the most common roof cover, are used on three out of four new houses and are equally popular for re-roofing existing houses. Sometimes called composition roofing, it is what most people have on their houses today and the most likely kind to be put on when a new roof is needed.

There are various types of asphalt shingles differing mainly in thickness and weight. The minimum weight accepted by FHA today is a 235-pound asphalt shingle, weighing that much per 100 square feet of roof. This is the minimum grade to buy today. (It is an increase in FHA's minimum standard over 210-pound shingles, the lowest grade formerly accepted. FHA lifted its standard to the heavier 235 pounds in 1962 in order "to insure greater savings to homeowners through longer life and less maintenance of roofs.")

The 235-pound asphalt shingles can be installed over most old roofs as well as on a new addition. They should last about 15 to 20 years, more or less, depending on your climate. The hotter the sun and the farther south you live, the shorter their life. There are also thinner and cheaper grades down to 150-pound-per-square asphalt shingles. These are inferior materials and should be flatly turned down.

The biggest drawback of ordinary 235-pound shingles is that they flap in the wind. A strong windstorm is likely to blow some away, if not a whole section of roof, particularly if you live in a hurricane area. The remedy is to specify asphalt shingles that come with either: 1. self-sealing tabs, which have a factory-applied adhesive on their tabs to keep them stuck down despite wind; or 2. the interlocking kind, which come with tab slots for hooking each shingle together with adjacent ones. Either of these two special features will cost about $1 per 100 square feet of roof more than regular 235-pound shingles, thus about $15 to $20 more on the average house.

One or the other kind should be chosen for most houses and should be mandatory in hurricane areas such as the Atlantic Seaboard and in areas like the Midwest where a windstorm may come up at any time. The self-sealing kind is generally preferred, as the interlocking kind gives a roof an over-all saw-tooth appearance which not everybody likes. If neither is used and you get ordinary non-stick-down shingles, it will then pay to have their tabs cemented down during application. A glob of roofing cement is squirted by hand under each shingle tab, one by one.

There are also better and heavier asphalt shingles which will give you a 20- to 30-year roof, plus better looks, less maintenance, and longer color retention. Though the exact weight varies with the brand, in general these fall into two higher-quality categories: the 250- to 285-pound per square, the next step up, and the 300-pound or better, the premium grade.

These heavier shingles are less susceptible to wind damage than 235-pound shingles because they are heavier and stiffer. But if you live in a severe hurricane area and use one of these heavier shingles it may be good to have their tabs, too, cemented down during application.

Asphalt shingles generally can be installed over old asphalt or wood roofs, but not if the old shingles are waterlogged and generally not if you already have three or more layers of old roofing. Then the old shingles should be removed first.

Cost of a new 235-pound asphalt shingle roof on an existing house ranges from about $20 to $30 per 100 square foot of roof, more on a complicated roof with many breaks and ridges. The cost of the better 250-pound and 300-pound shingles is about $3 to $7 more per square. Most of this extra cost goes for better shingle quality; labor cost to apply them remains about the same regardless of shingle weight.

If your roof is flat or has a very low slope, asphalt shingles are not recommended. Ordinarily they should not be put on a roof with a pitch of less than 3-in-12; some brands can be used on a low 2-in-12 slope, depending on the brand and the manufacturer's recommendations. (A 2-in-12 roof slope means a roof rise of 2 feet for every 12 feet of horizontal travel.)

For Low-Slope and Flat Roofs

If the roof is flat or low in slope you generally get what is called built-up roofing, alternate layers of roofing felt and asphalt covered with a top surface of gravel or white marble chips. It may last five years or 20 to 25 years, depending on the number of layers or plies.

Five plies are best; fewer mean shorter life and expensive upkeep. Cheap quality two- and three-ply roofing are too often used, which is why flat and low-slope roofs frequently deteriorate and leak in a maddeningly short time. Ask how many plies, or if it is a 10-, 15-, or 20-year roof. This is a key question.

There is also what is called roll roofing, a second-grade material. It comes in rolls of asphalt sheet material, cemented down and overlapped on the roof, one layer after the other up to the top of the roof. It is not recommended for houses.

Wood Shingles

Wood shingles and shakes are generally considered the next steps up in quality and price after asphalt. They cost from 25 to 100 per cent more than asphalt shingles, and are lowest in price in the West near the great lumber forests. Shipping costs make them more expensive elsewhere in the country.

The increased quality over asphalt depends on the kind of wood shingles; the thicker the wood, the better. The cheapest are wood shingles approximately ⅜-inch thick which will last 15 to 25 years, more or less. Then comes what are called wood shakes, which vary from ⅜-inch up to 1¼-inch thick. The best shakes are the heaviest and thickest ones, usually ¾-inch to 1¼-inch thick; they are normally good for 50 years or more.

Wood shingles and shakes have a handsome rough texture that is considered the height of fashion in many circles. On the other hand they can be a distinct fire hazard. Sparks and flames from another house fire, from brush fires, and from almost any other kind of building conflagration have been known, depending on wind conditions, to land on wood roofs and ignite them miles away from the originating fire. For this reason wood roofs are outlawed by many municipalities. If not outlawed where you live, you should nevertheless consider this hazard before buying them.

Permanent Roofing

This includes asbestos-cement shingles, tile, slate, copper, terne, and aluminum. Asbestos-cement shingles are of hard-wearing asbestos fiber and portland cement. They are somewhat higher in cost than asphalt

Wood-shake roof gives grainy rustic appearance, as shown in this California house.
National Lumber Mfrs. Assn. Robert C. Lautman.

Asbestos-cement shingles give hard, durable surface, are available in a variety of colors, and should last from 40 to 50 years.

shingles but are the lowest in cost of the permanent roof covers. They come in various colors, giving a pleasing appearance, often indistinguishable from wood or asphalt, and are growing in popularity because of the much longer service they provide, compared with asphalt, for comparatively small extra cost. They are brittle, however, and may crack if walked on. This is their biggest shortcoming. Use sneakers or soft shoes, and insist that the TV repairman do the same, or lay down walk-boards if he goes on the roof.

Ceramic tile, slate and terne (tin-lead alloy) are the Cadillacs of roofing in quality and price. Most people associate tile with the oval-shaped, orange tiles seen on Spanish and California mission houses. Thick, flat tiles are more common today. They give a rich, substantial appearance. Both kinds will last for generations. But insist on a "hard-burned" tile. When tapped with a coin it will ring with a clear tone. The cheaper, soft-burned kind is of uncertain quality. Hit with a coin, it gives off a flat sound.

Like tile, slate also gives a handsome, durable roof. But because of cost and heavy weight it is usually practical only within convenient ship-

Photo shows the difference between conventional asphalt shingles and the better seal-down kind after Hurricane Carla hit the Gulf Coast in September 1961. House in foreground, roofed with seal-down shingles, suffered no damage. Conventional shingles on houses in background were painfully ripped and torn away by the wind.
Johns-Manville.

ping distances of slate quarries in Virginia, Pennsylvania, and Vermont. Like asbestos, both tile and slate are brittle. A misplaced step or stray home-run ball can crack them. Freezing rain and snow in winter also can mean occasional cracked shingles to be replaced. Terne was quite popular at the turn of the nineteenth century, was not used for a long while afterward, and is now said to be making a comeback. It can be a good choice for a house that you expect to live in for a long time.

Aluminum Roofing

New aluminum shingles, recently introduced, offer long life, low upkeep, and good sun-heat reflectivity. But they are chiefly for new additions and new houses. In general, they should not be put on an old roof. This is because chemical action and corrosion will occur if aluminum touches the steel or galvanized nails of the old roofing and old flashing.

Aluminum shingles have a specially designed striated texture, and come in various colors and conventional shingle shapes. In bright sun, however, they appear glary. They are lightweight, easy to install, and will not rot, curl, or split. Cost for a typical house addition will range from about $100 to $250 more than conventional asphalt shingles. Though the metal itself should last indefinitely, the life expectancy of the bonded enamel surface finish has not been determined for sure; it is known to be good for about ten years at least. They can help a new addition, provided they will blend well with the old roof. Look at other houses with aluminum shingles before you decide. If used, the roof and structure should be well grounded to the earth for lightning protection.

There is also aluminum sheet roofing that is equally permanent but much less desirable for houses because of its industrial appearance. It is used primarily for farm buildings, barns, and industrial structures.

Roof Color

Light colors are spreading in popularity since much publicity has been given to their heat reflectivity. This allegedly makes the house cooler in summer, but it is not always true. Good heat reflectivity requires a smooth surface, as well as a light color. That is why smooth aluminum is even better at bouncing back the sun's heat than white (course-surface) asphalt shingles.

A light-colored roof, any kind, also can get dirty fast and reflectivity drops off sharply. By and large, a white or light-colored roof is good, but don't let it be the tail that wags the dog. Choose a medium or even dark color if it is better for over-all house looks; the house can be kept just as cool in summer by good attic insulation and ventilation (as spelled out in the chapter on air conditioning).

The color and texture of a roof should contrast nicely with the rest of the house to avoid a wishy-washy appearance. In general, a white or light-colored roof emphasizes the vertical lines of a house. It makes a house look taller and slimmer. It is therefore good for long, low ranch houses where you want to de-emphasize the width and low height.

On the other hand, a medium or dark roof is generally best for small houses and two-story houses. In each case, it makes the house look broader and bigger. But don't be hog-bound by rules. Consider the design, color, and proportions of your house as a whole, and choose the roof color that you will like as well as one that will enhance over-all style and looks of your house.

Roofing Tips

Regardless of the kind of roofing material used, its installation, the spacing of the shingles, and even the number of nails used per shingle are important for a good job. Determine exactly how much roofing you are getting in total squares of material to be provided. This is an essential fact to determine before you buy.

Ask about shingle "coverage." This has to do with what roofers call shingle exposure and lap. The exposure simply means the amount of each shingle that is exposed to the weather (the rest of it being covered by an adjacent shingle). It varies according to the size, shape, and kind of shingles used. It is usually a 5-inch exposure with conventional asphalt shingles, sometimes 4 inches. Lap or head lap is the distance that a shingle extends (laps) over the next shingle below it. It is usually 7 inches for asphalt shingles. The smaller the exposure and the greater the lap, the greater the number of shingles required and the greater the protection (roof coverage).

Part 7

THE FIVE BIGGEST CAUSES OF HIGH UPKEEP AND REPAIRS IN HOUSES AND HOW TO CHECK THEM

This section groups together five subjects that commonly account for high housing costs: poor heating, lack of insulation, inadequate wiring, termite and wood-rot damage, and low-quality water heaters.

Nearly all of us are recurrently forced to deal with one or more of them continually in the course of living in houses. It's too bad that each one can't be dealt with once and for all so that we are never again bothered with such problems as high heating bills, or the need for new wiring to keep up with new appliances. Or we find that the water heater, bought only a few years before, has sprung a leak and has to be replaced.

The purpose of this section is to tell you how to cope with each, as well as dealing adequately with each when you remodel.

Chapter 20

How to Buy New Heating or Improve Your Present System

Aside from monthly mortgage payments and taxes, heating accounts for the biggest annual housing expense for most families. And ironically, those who spend the most for heating bills generally suffer the most discomfort from winter cold due to inefficient heating.

It is not necessary, however, for every reader to absorb every word of this chapter. You need only refer to those parts that apply to your particular requirements, depending on the kind of heat you have, whether you desire a few guides on buying a new replacement heater, or want tips on heating new living space.

Warm-Air vs. *Hot-Water Heat*

The two most common kinds of central heat are forced warm-air heat and hot-water heat (sometimes called "hydronic" heating, or wet heat). There are also electric heat and the heat pump, which are discussed later.

Forced warm-air heating consists of a furnace, a blower for pushing the air under pressure to rooms, and ducts, usually of sheet metal, for directing the air to the rooms. The presence of ducts and metal air outlets in the rooms, rather than radiators, indicates a warm-air system.

Some people, particularly in the Northeast and parts of the Midwest, distrust forced warm air; they don't think it heats well. They are more happy with radiators or have had unhappy trials with an old, obsolete, gravity warm-air (no blower) system, or with a poorly installed warm-air system. Actually, warm air can be perfectly good in any house provided a good furnace is used and the system is properly installed.

A big advantage today of warm-air is that central air conditioning can be easily added with it, using the same ducts used for heating. Other advantages: It responds quickly to calls for heat from the thermostat,

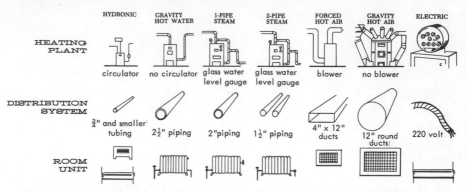

What kind of heating system do you have? The answer will help you determine if your present system can be modernized, or if it can be expanded to heat a new room. Piping in older systems is often covered with insulation, making them appear somewhat larger than indicated above. In gravity or forced-hot-air systems, the registers may be installed in the floors, walls, or ceilings. Electric cables also can be embedded in the plaster.

The Better Heating-Cooling Council.

and a filter with the furnace is supposed to clean the air. Its drawbacks: Openings may have to be cut in rugs or carpets for air outlets in the floor. Furniture placement may be limited to prevent interference with warm-air discharge from the outlets. And air noise may be bothersome (though this is a problem mainly with cheap, poorly installed systems).

Hot-Water Heat

Water is heated in a boiler and flows through pipes to radiators in each room. A pump, called a circulator, is usually located at the boiler to force the water around under pressure. An old system may lack a circulator pump.

Hot water is less susceptible to design and installation errors than warm air (a piece of pipe is a piece of pipe, but air ducts must be sized and hand-fabricated for each house); hot-water boilers are generally smaller and more compact than furnaces, thus require less room; you get more basement headroom because pipes take less space than ducts; a separate water heater for faucet hot water may not be needed—it can be integral with the main heating boiler; some people simply prefer the kind of heat given off by radiators; and a new hot-water system is often easier and cheaper to install in an existing house, particularly a multilevel house (because pipes are easier to run through walls than ducts).

On the other hand, hot water cannot filter the house air; the cost of central air conditioning runs from 10 to 25 per cent more in a house with hot-water than in one with warm-air heat, and a hot-water system must be drained, or given a dose of antifreeze if you leave the house for a winter vacation, or else freezing can burst the pipes.

What Size Heating Plant?

A specific rule of thumb for judging heat capacity is impossible to give. It can vary greatly from house to house and from city to city, depending on your climate. It is figured for a house by what engineers call a heat-loss computation. This takes into account the total wall, roof, and glass area, type of construction, air volume, and so on.

The heating dealer should make a complete heat-loss computation to determine what size heating plant is needed. The output capacity of your old unit, usually marked on the name plate, can give you a good idea of

Many hot-water heating boilers are small and compact, require little space, also contain a built-in heating coil for warming faucet water.

American-Standard.

the new-unit size required, but not always. This assumes that your old unit performed satisfactorily and no changes were made to the house since it was installed.

If your house is in a postwar building development, the old heater is likely to be a borderline case and a larger one may be a good idea. A larger heater than before also will be desirable if you intend to expand your house. Conversely, the house may have been insulated, or have had storm windows and doors installed after the original heater had been put in. A smaller, less expensive new unit may do the job now. A new heat-loss computation by the heating man will confirm this.

A typical house in the North with ordinary amounts of insulation requires 50 to 60 Btu's of heating capacity per square foot of living area. (The Btu stands for British thermal unit, the usual measure of heat capacity. One Btu is roughly equivalent to the amount of heat given off by an ordinary wood match. Technically, it is the amount required to raise the temperature of one pound of water by 1 degree Fahrenheit.) This is the output capacity of the heater, the quantity of heat supplied to the house and marked "output" on the heater. A typical 1000 square-foot house would therefore require a 50,000 to 65,000 Btu heater, twice that output capacity for a 2000 square-foot house. Somewhat more capacity per 1000 square feet may be required in the extreme North such as Wisconsin and Minnesota, less in the South.

A really well-insulated house, however, may require only 30 to 40 Btu's per square foot, or no more than 40,000 Btu's for every 1000 square feet. An electrically heated house, usually the best insulated of all, should require no more than 35,000 Btu's of capacity per 1000 square feet of house area. (Electric heat should not be used unless enough insulation and storm windows have reduced the heat requirement down to this figure. The same thick insulation with oil or gas heat will bring about a proportionate decrease in the amount of heat needed. A smaller, more economical heating plant can be employed and fuel costs will fall to a rock-bottom level.)

When you install a hot-water or steam heating plant its rating may be given in "square feet of heating radiation." This is related to the number of Btu's of heat supplied to your house from every square foot of radiator surface in each room. A boiler should have a Btu rating too. But this is likely to be the "input" rating, particularly with a gas-operated unit; it is the heat capacity of the gas burned. The amount of heat supplied to the house will only be 75 to 80 per cent of the gas input (since no heater is 100 per cent efficient). Thus a boiler with a 100,000-Btu input provides no more than about 80,000 Btu's per hour to your house. If your house heat loss is greater than 80,000 Btu's you need a heater with a larger input. Keep this in mind when dealing with *input* ratings.

There are also times when you may be offered a new heating unit larger than needed, as illustrated by a baffled friend of mine who had to replace a worn-out heating boiler. He had two disparate bids, one for $650 and another for $975. He was afraid of the lower price because the higher bid was from an old-time contractor in his town. Each bid was for a well-known boiler made by a top manufacturer.

It turned out that the low-bid dealer was offering a boiler with a heating capacity of 180,000 Btu's per hour while the old-timer, playing safe, recommended an unnecessarily large 240,000-Btu unit. A glance at the name plate of his old boiler told my friend that its capacity was 180,000 Btu's. Since the old unit, before senility set in, had done well by him, he bought the smaller unit, which saved him a tidy $325 and has worked well ever since.

His experience also illustrates that many a heating contractor, especially old-timers it seems, specify larger heating units than necessary. This is not only expensive but too large a unit will perform almost as bad as too small a unit (as illustrated by the Texas example at the end of this chapter).

Buying a New Warm-Air Furnace

All good warm-air furnaces carry a ten-year guarantee, but they will last for 25 years or more. There are also low-grade furnaces with a one-year guarantee (made chiefly for the tract-house market).

The air blower in the furnace should be belt-driven with a pulley much like an automobile fan belt. Cheap furnaces usually have what is called a direct-drive blower; it is directly connected to the same shaft as its electric motor.

The kind of blower can be determined merely by slipping off the front panel of the furnace. If no fan belt is seen, it is direct drive and the furnace very likely is of poor quality. According to one manufacturer, operating cost alone for a direct-drive blower may cost you $10 to $15 more a winter than for a belt-driven blower; the direct drive requires that much more electricity. A few good furnaces do, however, come with a direct-drive blower and no pulley. But these will have a ten-year guarantee.

These two features—ten-year guarantee and belt-driven blower mechanism—are two of the principal differences between a good furnace and the cheap kind. The good furnace can be guaranteed for ten years because it has a thicker, better-made heating chamber. Brand name means little because most manufacturers make both a cheap unit and a high-quality model. The really good furnace costs only about $25 to $35 more, on the average, than the cheap kind.

Two other facts about furnaces: If it is for gas fuel (a gas-burning unit) it should show the approval emblem of the American Gas Association (AGA), a must for safety. If it is oil-fired, it should carry the UL seal of the Underwriters Laboratories, and also bear a tag saying that it conforms with U. S. Government Standard CS-195-57.

The "Gravity" Furnace

Suppose the furnace being replaced is an old gravity kind, generally a large, bulbous furnace with octopuslike ducts rising up from its body. It has no air blower, its heated air rising to the rooms above by "gravity flow" due to the difference in pressure between warm and cold air.

Should you replace it with a new gravity furnace or with a new, forced warm-air kind containing a blower? If the old gravity unit heated the house satisfactorily, then the same kind should do equally well. But the usual gravity furnace is not the best performer. If in doubt, it's best to order a forced-air furnace, even though this may require additional expenses for modernized ductwork.

Installing a Complete New Warm-Air System

This may be for an old house or new addition. The installation of new ducts, in addition to the furnace, may account for as much as 40 to 50 per cent of the total price of the job. The design of the duct system is crucial for efficient heating operation. A poor duct job more than any other thing is the chief reason why many warm-air heating systems heat poorly.

The best duct system is called perimeter distribution. The warm-air discharge outlets are located around the exterior walls of your house (the house perimeter), preferably under windows. Warm air from the furnace is discharged into rooms at the source of the greatest cold—the key to good heating.

In general, there should be at least one warm-air outlet for every exposed wall, except perhaps in the kitchen and bath where exterior outlet locations may be impossible. Two or three air outlets should be spread out below a long wall, particularly under large windows in a living room. The warm air rising up will counteract cold downdrafts from the windows. This can spell the difference between comfort and chilly discomfort.

You should also request at least two warm-air outlets in bedrooms with two exposures, especially in children's rooms. A perimeter duct system is just about essential for a house in the North without a basement, especially to avoid the curse of cold floors; it is decidedly preferable in all other houses, except perhaps in the South.

The usual and generally second-rate alternate to perimeter ducts is an air distribution system characterized by air outlets located high on interior walls. The warm-air supply has to travel all the way across the room to the critical exterior windows and walls, by which time it has dispersed much of its heat. Spotty heating results. In the cold of winter you cannot sit comfortably near an outer wall. You complain about the heating furnace but in reality your exasperating discomfort stems from inefficient air distribution.

An uninformed heating man may stoutly advocate that the supply-air outlets be located at your interior walls, rather than at the exterior walls. You will also get, he may say, return-air registers under the windows. The cold downdrafts from the window panes, he'll say, are sucked back to the furnace through these intakes before they can spread into the room.

Unfortunately it doesn't work that way in practice. Supply-air outlets on interior walls are recommended only in a house with very well-insulated exterior walls, coupled with storm windows or the double-pane kind; or in houses in the South. Perimeter ducts may cost you a little more but they'll pay off handsomely in warm comfort for years afterward. (You automatically get perimeter heat with radiators located around exterior walls and under windows.)

Special Features to Request with Warm-Air Heat

The air filter should be located so it can be removed easily for cleaning, or you will have trouble. Can you get it in and out easily? Filters require periodic cleaning. Clogged-up filters are a major cause of poor heating. They should not require a $10 service call for a judo expert every time cleaning is necessary.

To avoid noisy operation—the rattling and banging of ducts every time the heat goes on and off—a short piece of canvas "collar" should connect the start of the ductwork with the furnace casing. Metal ducts should not be attached directly to the furnace or furnace vibration will be transmitted to the house. This is another touch that distinguishes a good heating job from a poor one.

Insist that the system be adjusted for what engineers call "continuous air circulation" (CAC), also called "comfort air circulation." The blower is adjusted to operate much of the time in mild weather, most of the time in cold weather. A uniform supply of warm air is supplied in bucketful quantities rather than a truckload blast of warm air once an hour and no heat for the long intervals in between.

The extra fan-operating cost is trivial, especially when balanced off against your increased heating comfort and satisfaction. Continuous air circulation by itself often can turn a sluggish heating system into a top performer. A few changes in the furnace control and blower setting are all it requires.

Obtaining a first-class warm-air system can be assured if it is what is called a "Silver Shield job." This is a rating program initiated by the National Warm Air Heating & Air-Conditioning Association to guarantee good heating for homeowners. Ask if the heating is a Silver Shield job. It is a new program, however, and so far available only in a few dozen cities, including Buffalo, Cleveland, Kalamazoo, Tulsa, Memphis, and Nashville. Even if it is not available where you live, any heating dealer can still conform to the same stiff Silver Shield requirements to give you top-notch warm-air heating. A copy of *Silver Shield Standards Guide* can be had for $1 from the National Warm Air Heating & Air-Conditioning Assn., 640 Engineers' Bldg., Cleveland 14, Ohio.

Planning for Future Air Conditioning

If you plan on central air conditioning in a few years, a few simple provisions made when a heating system is installed can vastly simplify the future installation of cooling and pave the way for a low-cost cooling system later.

The ducts should be designed for cooling as well as heating. Cooling generally requires larger ducts and sometimes a few additional duct runs. Allow for space for the cooling equipment next to or on top of the furnace. A cooling-coil plenum, an empty sheet-metal box, is installed at the same time as the furnace. Later the cooling coil can be easily slipped into place here with a minimum of fuss and expensive alterations. This may cost an additional $15 to $20 when the heating is installed; later the same work will otherwise cost $100 to $150.

Buying a New Hot-Water Heating Boiler

The boiler should have adequate capacity for your house, not too little or too much. Ask if it is a cast-iron or steel boiler. Cast-iron boilers are superior. They are normally guaranteed for 20 to 25 years (but should last about 40 years) and are virtually obligatory if your water supply is hard water. Steel boilers are highly susceptible to rust and corrosion from hard water, and are usually guaranteed, therefore, for only a year. Don't use steel if you have hard water unless you also have a water softener. (Steel, however, is perfectly good for warm-air furnaces as air and not corrosive water is being handled. Nearly all furnaces are steel.

A good cast-iron boiler will carry the IBR seal of the Institute of Boiler and Radiator Manufacturers, which indicates that its heating output has been confirmed by stiff tests. A steel boiler should carry the SBI seal of the Steel Boiler Institute, which is assurance that a steel boiler will deliver its rated capacity. Both cast iron and steel should carry the small *h* insignia of the American Society of Mechanical Engineers (ASME). This indicates that the design and construction conform to strict standards. Look for all of these seals on the name plate. Like warm-air furnaces, cast-iron boilers for gas fuel should carry the American Gas Association (AGA) emblem; an oil-fired unit should carry the Underwriters' Laboratories (UL) approval emblem.

Incidentally, you may not see a name plate on all heating units. Lack of a name plate generally indicates a cheap, low-quality unit. Nearly all good-quality units have a name plate.

Judging New Radiators

The best radiators are baseboard radiators—long, low, spread-out metal units 7 to 9 inches high. They are neater than old-fashioned stand-up radiators and give more uniform heat. There are two main kinds: the cast iron, and the nonferrous (aluminum or copper). The nonferrous are identified by the presence of metal fins along their length.

Like cast-iron boilers, cast-iron baseboard radiators cost more but give better duty over the years and provide more uniform heat. Nonferrous (aluminum and copper) baseboard radiators are often noisy, especially if carelessly installed. Regardless of type, every baseboard radiator should conform to the standards of the IBR. This may not be marked on the radiator; you have to refer to the manufacturer's literature, which will or will not mention it. If unmentioned, the radiators should be rejected. And by all means reject old-fashioned stand-up radiators. Baseboard radiators are far more efficient and far less of an eyesore.

Additional Radiator Tips

You may be stuck with old-fashioned radiators and be unwilling or unable to replace them. Can you improve their looks? Radiator covers will obscure their ugliness, but will also reduce the heat supplied to your rooms. Covers should have as much opening as possible, the greater the total opening, the better. There should be an opening at the front and particularly at the bottom for good air circulation, as well as a large opening at the top for heat discharge into the room.

Paint radiators with an oil-base paint rather than a metallic paint like aluminum or bronze (with or without a radiator cover). A metallic paint reduces heat output by about 10 per cent. If your radiators are now covered with metallic paint, an oil-base can be applied without scraping off the old metallic paint; it is the final paint coat that makes the difference, not what's underneath. The oil-base paint may be any color, since the output variation from color to color is slight. Hence it is feasible to paint radiators any color desired to match your room decor.

The efficiency of any radiator—stand-up or baseboard type—can be increased if a sheet of reflecting metal or aluminum foil is placed behind it, but not in contact with the radiator. It retards the flow of heat from the radiator to the wall, also bounces back this useful heat into the room.

Modernizing an Old, Gravity Hot-Water System

Many old hot-water heating systems are what are called gravity systems. They lack a circulator pump. The hot water from the boiler flows to the radiators by means of gravity flow, in that hot water naturally rises to the radiators upstairs, and the cooler water from the radiators naturally falls back to the boiler (to be reheated).

Nearly every gravity system can be converted to a forced (circulator) system. A pump is merely added. This can raise the efficiency' of the system. It is recommended if a gravity system doesn't heat the house as well as you would like. Another advantage of forced circulation is that you can obtain zoned control by means of two or more circulators, each one regulating the heat supply to separate parts of your house (as discussed later).

Steam Heat

Like hot-water boilers, steam boilers are either cast iron or steel. The cast-iron kind is preferred especially when you have hard water. Regardless of whether it is cast iron or steel, it should show the ASME seal on the name plate.

Steam heat is rarely put in houses today except for replacement of old equipment, which means that both spare parts and expert servicemen for it are rare. If your old system is still performing heroically and all you need, say, is a new boiler, by all means get one and spare yourself additional expense. But if the pipes and radiators as well as the boiler are rundown, then get bids on a complete new hot-water or warm-air system. Hot water may be preferable if the old pipe system and radiators are still good. The same rules for judging hot-water radiators apply for steam radiators.

Can you convert an old steam system to modern hot-water heat? This depends on whether you have a one-pipe or two-pipe steam system. With the one-pipe kind, the pipe that carries the steam to the radiators also returns the condensed steam (water) to the boiler. A two-pipe system has a second, separate pipe for the return leg.

The system can be converted to hot-water heat only if it is a two-pipe job. Unfortunately, the one-pipe system is far more prevalent, and the chances are that you have one and cannot convert unless new piping is installed.

What about Radiant Heat?

The same kind of boiler used for hot-water heat is required when you replace the boiler of a radiant-heating system; thus the same rules for judging hot-water boilers apply. The boiler supplies hot water to pipes embedded in the floor (usually a concrete floor in a house with no basement) which heat the floor and then the house.

If the existing boiler is good but trouble exists within the floor-embedded pipe system, expensive repairs or replacement may be needed. This is a major drawback of radiant heat. If a floor pipe springs a leak or has become gutted with corrosion over the years, the floor may have to be dug up (a messy job at best). At worst, a complete new system of different heat may be required. Sometimes, depending on the house, the existing boiler plant may be salvaged, disconnected from the floor pipes, and hooked up instead to a new system of baseboard radiators installed around the exterior walls of the house. The old pipes are left buried and happily forgotten in the floor.

Other times, however, the high expense of a new system may dictate that you limp along as well as possible with a sick radiant-heat system. Small auxiliary room heaters could be installed to take the chill off excessively cold areas.

Before you do this, investigate the insulation content of your house. It may contain little or no insulation. Adding insulation to the walls, around the concrete floor perimeter, to the ceiling, and the addition of storm windows might bail you out beautifully. New insulation can be the perfect tonic for sharply reducing the amount of heat demanded of the heating system, and for sharply reducing cold drafts and chills that the heating system could not combat by itself. The use of thick perimeter-edge insulation, described in the chapter on insulation, could by itself make an enormous improvement in a radiant-heated house.

Another common trouble with radiant heat is that it tends to overheat the house at certain times, or it cannot provide heat fast enough after a sudden dip in the outside temperature. The entire concrete floor has to be heated up first and this may take an hour or two. If the sun abruptly breaks through again and you no longer need heat, there is little you can do; the floor will continue to radiate heat even though the boiler has gone off.

This sort of thing calls for a special, outdoor temperature control located on an outside wall. It "senses" changes in the outdoor temperature at once and relays the appropriate message to the heating boiler so the heat will go on or off ahead of time, as needed. In other words, it takes into account the time delay necessary for the whole floor to heat up or cool off and starts the process going immediately.

The potential troubles with radiant heat raise questions about the wisdom of using it again when you add new living space to a house. New space can be heated easily by means of baseboard or other radiators hooked up to the existing house boiler. This assumes that the boiler has enough spare capacity for the new addition as well as the main house. Otherwise a larger boiler or a separate heating system is required. (More on how to heat new living space in a moment.)

Radiant heat had a spell of great popularity after World War II, but is far less popular today. It can provide great warmth underfoot, and theoretically it is a splendid idea for removing eyesore radiators from our rooms. But unfortunately its idiosyncrasies can cause anguish. Some banks, in fact, will no longer give a mortgage on a house with radiant heat, and this alone raises a red flag before using it.

Gas vs. *Oil Heat: Which Is Better?*

You can burn either fuel regardless of whether you have warm-air or hot-water heat. You choose one or the other when you install a complete new heating system for a whole house, for a new addition, or if you convert an old coal heating plant to automatic operation.

Gas is generally better, provided low-cost natural gas is available on your street. Gas is lower in first cost, requires less service, and gas burners last longer than oil burners. But beware of gas if local gas rates are steep, for then fuel bills will climb painfully high.

If available, natural gas is generally, but not always, cheaper. Oil costs today average about 15¢ a gallon, more or less. Gas heat is generally competitive with 15¢ oil when gas costs from 12¢ to 13¢ a therm. The therm is a measuring unit for gas, a quantity of gas equal to 100,000 Btu's of heat value. (A gallon of oil gives about 140,000 Btu's, but don't use these figures for a straight comparison of each. For one thing, gas burners generally operate at a somewhat higher efficiency level than oil burners. Other technical factors also intrude.)

If gas costs are more than 12¢ to 13¢ per therm it will generally pay to use oil. Call the gas company to find out the cost per therm. Gas rates are sometimes given in terms of cubic feet of gas. Natural gas has a heat content of roughly 1000 Btu's of heat. If your gas rates are given in terms of cubic feet, have the gas company people tell you its equivalent cost per therm, a better yardstick.

For Lowest Cost Gas Heat

Gas heat is cheapest when you also use a gas range and a gas water heater. Gas is billed on a sliding scale; the more you use, the lower its unit price. A typical family may consume about 800 cubic feet of natural gas, or eight therms a month for cooking, another 2000 to 3000 cubic feet (20 to 30 therms) a month for water heating. After this much consumption the price you pay for additional gas falls to the cheaper heating bracket.

If, however, gas is used for heating only, you are charged for the first two to three thousand cubic feet each month at the higher end of the scale and heating bills will be higher. A typical six- or seven-room house with insulation will use about 20,000 to 30,000 cubic feet of natural gas a month for heating in a climate like that of New York, Pittsburgh, or Indianapolis with approximately 5000 degree-days per winter.

There is also LP or bottled gas, which is by and large too expensive for central heat. It comes closest to being competitive with 15¢ oil in the Midwest where it costs from 14¢ to 16¢ per gallon. This is for propane with roughly 95,000 Btu's of heat value per gallon. LP prices are higher in the East and New England, where it is generally much too expensive for central heating.

If you're uncertain about the relative cost of oil and gas, talk to the gas company people and to oil dealers. If either beats around the bush, or tries to sell you on all of the real and imagined advantages of his particular fuel but will not flatly give you actual cost figures, then beware.

New High-Efficiency Oil Heat

If you get oil heat, insist on one of the new high-efficiency, oil heating units. They are far cleaner and more efficient than conventional oil equipment. They cut fuel bills by about 25 to 33 per cent compared with conventional oil units, and for the first time they make oil heat as clean and efficient as gas. They are called *forced-draft* oil burners; that is what to ask for. Some of the first brands introduced are made by Jet-Heet, Inc., 152 So. Van Brunt St., Englewood, N.J.; and Iron Fireman, Cleveland 11, Ohio. Other new forced-draft oil burners, still in the laboratory as this is written, are expected from such oil-heat people as Shell, Gulf, and Esso.

Electric Heat

Electric heat is an excellent way to heat a new room or two added to a house, and sometimes a new addition. The cost of installation is low, the installation is simply done, you get clean heat that is easier on curtains, drapes, and wall finishes than any other kind of heat, and equipment maintenance is negligible. It may not be practical, however, for some old houses.

There are five different kinds of electric heat: 1. Glass panel units recessed in a wall, which radiate heat into the room; 2. Built-in wall units which contain an integral fan for circulating warmed air around the room; 3. Electric baseboards which work much like hot-water baseboard radiators except that the heat source is electricity rather than hot water; 4. Radiant panels, usually located in the ceiling, for providing radiant heat down over the whole room with surprising efficiency and comfort; 5. Electric furnaces which, like conventional furnaces, supply warm air to rooms through ducts, but are different in that the air passing through the furnace is heated by electricity instead of gas, oil, or coal; and 6. The heat pump, discussed later.

Glass panels are low in cost and easy to install, but their heat is concentrated within a limited area; far corners of the room may not get enough heat. Built-in fan units provide excellent warm-air distribution because of the fans, but some people are bothered by the on-and-off swish noise of the fans.

Baseboard units give pleasant uniform heat but certain types must be cleaned regularly to keep them free of dust and lint. Radiant panels in the ceiling are likely to give the most satisfactory heat of all but they cost more because of the installation required and are generally limited to new houses or additions where they can be installed when the ceiling is being built.

An electric furnace is also limited, as a rule, to new houses and new additions because of the ductwork it requires. It can be a good way to combine electric heating with central air conditioning, with the same ducts handling warm and cool air supply to rooms. On the other hand, it tends to be more expensive than conventional electric heat, because of the ducts and also because a fan must be operated in addition to the electric heating elements. And it does not lend itself easily to individual room-control of heat, which is a big feature of conventional electric heat.

Operating Cost of Electric Heat—Your Biggest Consideration

Monthly heating bills with electric heat will be steep if not crushing, unless your local electric rates are downright low, or unless you live in the South where severe cold does not push up the daily bill. This is the prime consideration with electric heat. It is less important when electric heaters are used only for an individual room, but nevertheless even this small venture rates investigation before you take the plunge.

The cutoff point for economical electric heat in the North is electricity at a cost of about 1¢ to 1.5¢ per kilowatt hour (kwh). The kwh is the standard measure of electrical consumption. If your rate is more than 1.5¢ per kwh, your electric-heat bills will be higher than they would be with gas at roughly 12¢ a therm and oil at 15¢ a gallon. If you install electric heat for only a room or two, you can loosen the rule and not be overly burdened with an electric rate as high as 2¢ per kwh.

Nevertheless, electric heat is being heavily promoted by electric companies whose rates are 1.5 to 2¢. If you pin them down they will frankly concede that the homeowner pays more for electric heat than he would with gas or oil fuel. But they say other benefits offset the "somewhat" higher electric cost, and for that matter they may well be right.

They cite the advantages of clean quiet heat, negligible maintenance (with no furnace or boiler to give trouble) and these are indeed glowing advantages; lower first cost of installation than a comparable gas or oil heat system in a new house (for example, you save the construction cost of a chimney, or about $100 to $150 on the usual prefabricated chimney used nowadays); and the individual room control possible with a thermostat in every room, which is a boon for keeping some rooms warmer or cooler than others, as desired.

But don't accept electric heat until you have talked with other families nearby who have it. Get a line on their operating costs. Are they satisfied with its comfort and other characteristics? Talk to the electric company people and get an operating cost estimate from them.

Electric heat is fine and inexpensive if not downright cheap in low-cost power areas like the TVA region and the Pacific Northwest. Heating contractors in these areas are also familiar with it and make few mistakes. But it is still relatively new and untried in other areas where it has been introduced recently. Here is where a thorough investigation is advised. You don't want to be a guinea pig.

Mandatory Insulation and Storm Windows

Even if electric rates are very low, electric heat demands that a house be insulated to the hilt, and also have storm doors, storm windows, and weather stripping. Otherwise your operating costs can skyrocket.

Such tight construction, however, causes complaints about stuffiness, lack of ventilation, and excess moisture inside of electrically heated houses.

A good kitchen exhaust fan is usually essential for ventilation and moisture exhaust. Bathroom exhaust fans are recommended, particularly if you have two or more baths, but are not essential.

It is also true that if you live where lengthy storm-induced electric failures are common in winter, you will be without heat at such times. However, an electric failure will also put automatic gas and oil heating systems out of business, as their electric controls can't work.

It is generally unwise to install a new, central electric heating system in an old house. For one thing the installation cost can run high because of the heavy-duty new wiring required, plus a special circuit to every room. For another, old houses are not only drafty and hard to heat to start with, thus requiring wholesale quantities of heat, but they also are difficult and expensive to thoroughly insulate in the copious manner required for electric heat.

Heating New Rooms

Remodeling contractors say that many of us omit heating when we add new rooms or a new addition to our houses. Later we find that the space is uninhabitable in winter without heat (naturally) and then it costs twice as much to install. Another mistake is neglecting the heat until a new space is almost completed.

In one case like this the family delayed calling a heating contractor, and then a good part of a brand-new wall had to be torn out to permit installation of the stovepipe vent required for the heater; no other alternative was possible. Heat may seem the least of your worries when you remodel, but it nevertheless should be planned in the beginning.

The existing heating ducts or pipes often can be extended to provide heat to new space. Your heating plant obviously should have the extra capacity for its additional work. A heating contractor can figure if it does or not. If it is a borderline case, sometimes insulation and storm windows added to the entire house may turn the trick, rather than pay for a second heating plant. By reducing the amount of heat output required for existing living space, the added insulation frees existing heat capacity for the new addition. At the same time, the new addition should be well insulated so that it needs a minimum amount of heat.

If you have hot-water heat, sometimes the capacity of the heater can be raised. One way is by supplying hotter water to your radiators. The boilers in a good many houses often can be adjusted to supply water as hot as 220 degrees, sometimes more. As much as 25 per cent more heat output results (by taking full advantage of the maximum capacity available). The increased boiler capacity may be more than enough to handle a new room or two.

The use of interior boiler baffles may increase heat output by 5 or 10 per cent, an extra boost that can be helpful if your boiler is already adjusted for peak supply. Baffles are simply metal forms inserted in the boiler to produce more efficient heat transfer from the fire to the water being heated. Their cost is low.

Regardless of the type of heater, if its capacity is marginal, have the entire system checked, cleaned, and adjusted. This may make a difference. On the other hand, if there is little hope of squeezing enough extra heat out of the unit, don't kid yourself. Figure on a separate heater before the new addition is begun.

Independent Heaters for a New Room

The most common kinds are electric resistance heaters, a built-in wall furnace, a free-standing heater, and a room-size, year-round heat pump. Installation of an electric unit is comparatively simple because no ducts or pipes are required. The various kinds made are noted earlier, along with other facts about electric heat.

Most wall furnaces burn either gas or oil, so having a stovepipe vent to the outside is highly important. Provision for the vent should be made when a new addition is being built. Ordinarily this is a simple job if done during construction. A vent to outdoors is also recommended for free-standing gas or kerosene heaters. All you generally need is a short stovepipe connection from the back of the unit out through the wall.

A year-round, one-room heat pump is simply a room air conditioner that heats in winter and cools in summer. Like a regular room cooler, it can be built into the wall instead of in a window, where it will cut down light entry. It is best in a temperate southern climate because most units have limited heating capacity, which would mean inadequate heating in a cold northern climate.

Another new heating unit designed expressly for single rooms, and just being introduced as this is written, is the one-room gas-operated baseboard heater. Like hot-water and electric baseboards, it is located at an exterior wall at floor level. Gas is supplied directly to the unit for heating; a central gas boiler or furnace is not required. An exhaust vent to outdoors is also provided to get rid of the products of combustion. The result of long research by the American Gas Association, it is a highly promising kind of heating for individual rooms, especially with cheap natural gas available. Approximate cost runs from $125 to $175 per room, depending on your heat requirements.

"Zone Control"

This means a second and even third thermostat for a new addition to a house or for a part of the existing house that has special heating needs different from the rest of the house. A national survey by a large manufacturer showed that nine out of ten houses costing more than $30,000 need two or more thermostats or else a heating system with one furnace for the living areas, another for the sleeping areas.

The survey, made by the Minneapolis-Honeywell people, found that zone control was needed in about 50 per cent of all houses in the $20,000 to $30,000 price class, and in only one of every five houses costing less than $20,000.

The principal condition requiring zoned control is "a spread-out floor plan," the Honeywell people say. This causes widely differing exposure problems under one roof. It explains why the lower the price of a house, the less likely its needs for special controls; i.e., the smaller the house, the less spread-out the floor plan.

Other conditions requiring zoned controls, according to Honeywell experts, are 1. rooms with large glass areas, 2. finished basements, and 3. rooms over a garage. The last two were found to be a chief cause of chronic heating problems in split-level houses. Such problems occur in houses regardless of the kind of heat used.

Zone control also can solve a chronic heating problem in many ordinary two-story houses—too much heat upstairs and not enough below. One imaginative man, long plagued with this problem, was unable to get his heating man to correct it. Taking matters into his own hands, he "ordered" his heating man to "split" the heating system.

He had hot-water heat. The hot-water supply pipes leading to the second-floor radiators were separated from those to the first floor. A second circulator pump was installed so there would be one for each floor level. (A circulator pump starts running when the thermostat calls for

Uneven heating conditions can be corrected by the use of zoned controls, a separate thermostat for each section of your house that may require more or less heat than the heat required by the rest of the house.

heat and pumps hot water to the radiators.) Then a second thermostat was installed upstairs to control the heat supply to this half of the house.

Cost of the change was about $75 and worth it. Uniform heating resulted throughout the house for the first time. Heat was provided upstairs only when needed there and vice versa.

The man, though no engineer, had simply hit on the principle of zoned control. His heating contractor should have known about it but did not. His ignorance illustrates why you can't always rely on heating men.

Zone control of warm-air heat is accomplished in a similar manner. The main trunk ducts that supply heat to each part of a house are each fitted with automatically operated dampers. Each damper opens to let air through, or closes to shut off the air supply, according to thermostat demand in each zone. If one part of the house begins to get cold and the thermostat there calls for heat, the appropriate damper opens and the furnace goes on to supply the heat. If the other zone is warm enough, heat is kept from it by its damper remaining shut. If all parts of the house call for heat, all dampers open.

Thermostat Location

Good thermostat location is necessary for efficient heating. This applies to your present thermostat as well as one installed in a new addition. The thermostat should be on an interior wall, well out of reach of drafts from outside door openings. Drafts from an open door can cause a false alarm, prompting heat when it is not needed.

Other bad locations are near a window with the thermostat exposed to sunshine, in range of radiant heat from a fireplace, exposed to cooking heat from the kitchen, over a radiator or heating outlet, on a wall that contains warm-air ducts just inside, and near light lamps (whose heat can satisfy the thermostat while the rest of the house gets cold). Each of these locations will cause erratic control.

The best thermostat location is usually on an interior wall of the living room or dining room that is free of the above hazards, and a spot that is also representative of the heat needs of the rest of the house.

Solar Heat

Can you harness heat from the sun to heat your house? It is being done experimentally, but unfortunately commercial equipment for it is not yet on the market. You could install a custom-made system designed for your particular house but the initial installation cost would run at least two to three thousand dollars for even a small house. Moreover, such systems are still not foolproof, as many bugs and inevitable problems, as with any new product, are still to be ironed out.

Summed up, solar heat remains in the research and development stage as this is written. A major problem is how to store up sufficient heat to keep you warm in winter when the sun doesn't shine for days on end. Despite the glowing praise of solar heat and the glowing news stories printed about it, it is not yet ready for general use.

Avoiding the Ten Most Common House-Heating Troubles

Since 1949 the National Warm Air Heating & Air-Conditioning Association has been investigating heating complaints in actual houses throughout the country. It uses a mobile laboratory-research truck equipped with $10,000 worth of test gear. Technicians manning the truck visit each house and spend as long as two weeks tracking down the cause of each complaint.

After more than a decade of research, the association's experts found that nearly every heating problem boils down to the following most common troubles. Understanding them can help you improve the efficiency of your heating plant, and also avoid similar troubles when you install new heating. Some have already been noted but deserve repeat mention.

1. *Little or no house insulation.* This causes cold walls, chilly drafts, and discomfort that even the most expensive heating system cannot combat (as explained in the next chapter).

2. *Dirt-clogged air filters,* one of the biggest reasons for poor warm-air heating. The house gets colder and colder as not enough heat gets to rooms. This happens often in new houses as well as in old ones and also after a new addition has been built. Reason: The air filter is clogged with building dust and shavings. Little or no air can pass through the filter and your heat supply is sharply reduced. The same thing will happen in any house with warm-air heat as the filter soaks up dirt and dust removed

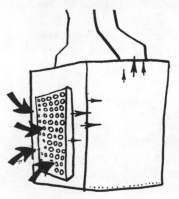  

Dirt-clogged filters.

Heating plant is too big or too small.
Diagrams courtesy House & Home.

from the house air, unless it is periodically cleaned. The filter is simply removed and cleaned or washed. Do this periodically.

3. *The heating plant is too big or too small.* As many as 80 per cent of all houses get an improperly sized furnace, the Warm Air Association experts found. One reason is that many heating contractors persist in figuring the size needed by a fast rule of thumb, scribbling a few figures on the back of an envelope. Another reason is that a skimpy furnace is used to save a few dollars. Still another, at the other extreme, is that many people believe in an oversized unit just to have reserve capacity.

An example, discovered in a Texas house, involved a heating installation that was practically perfect. But although the house heat loss was 97,000 Btu's, an oversized 157,000 Btu furnace had been put in. The supply air to the house got too hot, room temperatures fluctuated greatly, and uniform thermostatic control was impossible. The main lesson here is to insist that the heating contractor make an accurate heat loss and match the equipment size to it.

4. *Erratic heating due to an unbalanced heating system.* This is because many heating men omit the final adjustments necessary for apportioning the proper amount of heat to each room. As a result, some rooms get too much heat, others too little. The furnace blower, duct dampers, and room registers must be adjusted for good heat distribution.

5. *Improper air-control settings.* This is when furnaces are not set according to the CAC principle (continuous air circulation). (Information on CAC operation is available for $1.25 from the National Warm Air Heating & Air-Conditioning Ass., 640 Engineers' Bldg., Cleveland 14, Ohio. If necessary, donate one to your heating man.)

6. *Not enough warm-air outlets in the right places.* To help combat chilly downdrafts from cold window glass, the association stresses the

Not enough warm-air outlets in the right places.

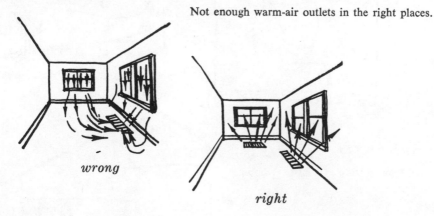

wrong

right

great importance of proper heat discharge into a house; e.g., at least one warm-air outlet (or radiator) should be located under the windows at every outside wall.

7. *Cold floors, particularly in houses with a concrete slab floor and no basement.* The two preventatives: 1. Thick edge insulation around the concrete floor perimeter; and 2. Perimeter warm-air ducts or radiators which supply heat directly to the critical house perimeter.

Cold floors are also a problem in houses with a "crawl-space" (built 18 to 30 inches above the ground with no basement). Adequate insulation is required, as spelled out in the insulation chapter. In addition, heat could be supplied to the crawl-space, providing a cushion of warm air under the floor. Heat bills should rise very little, if at all. Sometimes over-all bills will even decrease, as a heated "crawl-space" does away with the human tendency toward overheating a house just to overcome a cold-floor problem.

The same principle can help solve a cold-floor problem in a house with a basement. You provide a little heat to the basement by means of a single heat outlet there. A cushion of warm air forms under the floor and cold spots cannot develop.

8. *Heating plant starved for oxygen.* This occurs chiefly in new houses built so tightly that you cannot count on outside air leaking in around doors and windows. As a result, the heater does not get enough oxygen to support combustion. The trouble is compounded when you have other air-consuming devices like clothes driers and exhaust fans, which put a pre-

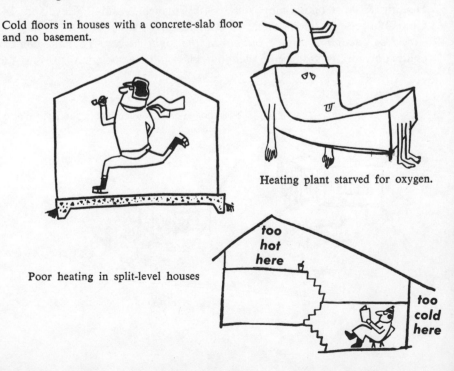

Cold floors in houses with a concrete-slab floor and no basement.

Heating plant starved for oxygen.

Poor heating in split-level houses

too hot here

too cold here

mium on the little air available. Incomplete heating-plant combustion may result, causing the release of lethal fumes into the house. Air must be made available to the heater. A small window opening or vent may be necessary. If the heater is in a closed utility room, a small outside air duct to the equipment room is essential.

9. *Poor heating in split-level houses:* The biggest problem here is the lowest-level room, usually a playroom. It gets so cold that it is out-of-bounds in winter. It's a difficult problem because its floor and walls are

Good comfort with forced warm-air heat calls for a wall of heat supplied around the exterior walls of new rooms or a new addition, particularly in a cold climate. In the South, overhead ducts can be used, bottom diagram. Either system can be used when combining central air conditioning with heating. For summer air conditioning only, overhead ducts are generally better.

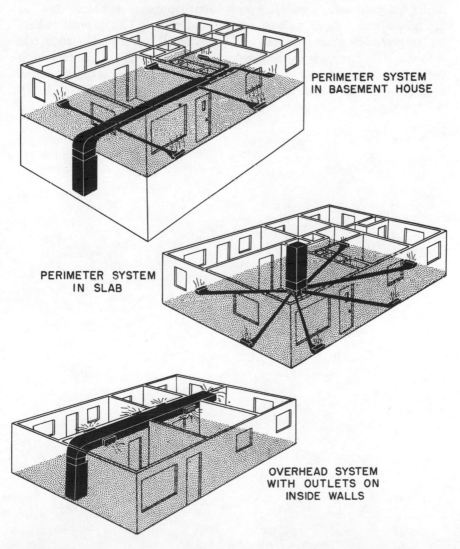

PERIMETER SYSTEM
IN BASEMENT HOUSE

PERIMETER SYSTEM
IN SLAB

OVERHEAD SYSTEM
WITH OUTLETS ON
INSIDE WALLS

generally below ground level, and the only heat supply is often a small duct discharging warm air into it from ceiling level. The floor and lower wall surfaces are not properly heated.

This kind of room, the association says, should be treated like a house with a concrete slab floor; i.e., heat should be provided at floor level and around the outer edges of the room (by means of perimeter floor ducts or baseboard radiators). Insulating the walls and floor also can help greatly.

At the same time, the highest level rooms in a split-level house get too hot because of the natural rise of warm air from below. One solution is cutting down on the direct heat input to the high rooms; another is the installation of a separate thermostat and zone controls to provide heat upstairs only when needed.

10. *Cold ducts.* Supply ducts from the furnace to the house may pass through a cold attic, garage, or crawl-space area, and thereby lose so much heat that little or no heat reaches the rooms. This happens unless the supply ducts in such spaces are insulated. A supply-air duct is one with warm air flowing from the furnace to the house. There are also ducts that return cool air from the house back to the furnace for reheating; these need no insulation when they pass through a cold space.

Chapter 21

Insulation for Your Present House, New Rooms, and New Additions

Most houses do not have enough insulation, if any at all. If your house tends to be chronically cold and chilly in winter, like most people you probably lay the blame on the heating system. Actually it is just as likely to be caused by inadequate insulation.

Most of us view insulation chiefly as a means of reducing fuel bills in winter, but its key role in making a house comfortable is overlooked and unappreciated by a good many people. In short, the *comfort* benefits of insulation should be kept in mind when you consider insulation for new rooms being added to your house, as well as for your present house.

This chapter deals with how to tell if your house needs insulation (even though you may think it is "insulated"), how and where to insulate an existing house or new addition, the fuel savings to expect, how insulation helps keep a house cool in summer, and such things as the common misconceptions about insulation that actually are widespread causes of high fuel bills and hard-to-heat houses.

How Insulation Keeps You Warm in Winter . . .

Thermal insulation is any commonly used material with special characteristics for reducing heat flow in and out of a house. In its broad sense it embraces storm windows and weather stripping.

If a house has little or no insulation, the floors, walls, and ceilings get quite cold. Cold drafts are created. In addition, cold walls and ceilings draw off excessive body heat causing chills and goose-pimples for the same reason you feel chilled standing in front of an open refrigerator.

A cold structure is a common condition even in houses with excellent heating systems. We tend to compensate for it by raising the thermostat setting up to 75 or 80 degrees, but we not only remain uncomfortable but the air gets hot and stuffy.

Various kinds of insulation include rigid board (lower left), pre-cut batts (left), blanket insulation (center), and aluminum-foil-covered blanket insulation.
Owens-Corning Fiberglas.

The basic cause of your discomfort is the cold walls, floors, and ceilings. To keep them from getting cold, an overcoat of thick insulation is required in addition to good heating. Then the house will be supremely comfortable at a lower 70- to 72-degree indoor air temperature (another little-known reason why plenty of insulation reduces fuel bills). In short, insulation is essential for true warmth and comfort with even the best heating system.

. . . and Cool in Summer

The same phenomenon works in reverse in summer, a major reason why summer heat prevents you from sleeping even though the night air outside may be reasonably cool. The chief culprit is a hot ceiling. Heat from the sun-baked roof seeps down to heat up your ceiling, which will get as hot as a cement floor with radiant heat in winter (80 to 85 degrees). It sheds a rain of invisible radiant heat down on you. Hot walls also contribute their share of heat radiated inward (though not as much as ceilings). You are caught in a radiant hot box.

Rigid insulation is excellent for the inside surface of masonry walls.

Concrete floors should be insulated when built. If not, you suffer with cold floors. Rigid insulation can be applied later, if needed, at the floor curb, as shown here.

The hot-box effect can be curbed by plenty of insulation and vastly improve your comfort in summer. Even more insulation is needed than for conserving heat in winter. The amount to use is given on the following pages (including a new way for stopping radiant summer heat).

What about Fuel Savings?

Insulation will reduce fuel bills from 10 to 50 per cent, sometimes more, depending on the house, the type of construction, and the insulation used. Take a typical old house with leaky walls and no insulation whatever. A thorough insulation job coupled with new storm windows should reduce annual fuel bills by a good 40 to 50 per cent. Take a more tightly built, newer house with some attic insulation and storm windows but no wall insulation: merely insulating the walls should reduce over-all fuel bills by 10 to 20 per cent.

One of the most convincing cases for insulation is the results of a study of some 70 actual houses located in every climate zone of the country, which were built by conventional builders and carefully insulated. The results showed that a typical 1200-square-foot house (usually priced from $15,000 to $20,000) can be heated *and* air conditioned nearly anywhere in the nation for no more than $150 a year total cost for winter fuel and summer electricity for cooling.

This averages out to less than $13 a month the year around, based on average national fuel costs of 8¢ per therm and 2¢ per kilowatt hour for electricity. (The houses also embodied certain additional design features, such as window shading and large attic vents, chiefly for reducing summer cooling bills.) The lesson is clear—don't skimp on insulation.

Does Your House Need Insulation?

How can you tell? Hold the palm of your hand flat against each wall of your house. In winter it should not feel much cooler than an interior partition. Otherwise, the wall is losing excessive heat to outdoors and insulation is needed. Do the same for the ceiling and the floor, particularly around the perimeter of rooms near outside walls. Though not infallible, the palm test is a handy way of spotting unsuspected cold sources.

How warm do you have to keep your house in winter? If you are comfortable with the thermostat at 70 to 72 degrees you probably don't need insulation. If you have to set the thermostat from 75 to over 80 degrees, you probably need insulation, since a high thermostat setting is a tip-off to little or no insulation. You have to heat the house air warmer to compensate for the loss of body heat to the cold structure.

Still another indication of insulation or the lack of it is snow retention around the house and on the roof. Does the snow remain piled up around the exterior walls of your house? Or does it melt for about a foot away from the house skirt while it remains on the ground elsewhere? If it melts away, you are paying to heat the snow as well as the house. Excessive heat is leaking out through the floor or the low sidewalls. This is a particularly good indication of whether or not you have adequate floor insulation in a house without a basement. Snow, of course, should remain on your roof as long as it does on other house roofs. Otherwise, excessive heat is leaking up through the ceiling to melt it. Insulation is needed over the ceiling.

Where Is Insulation Required?

It is required in all exterior walls and the ceiling below the attic. Insulation for a ceiling normally is put between the joists at the *attic floor,* not under the sloping roof rafters at the attic ceiling. If, however, the attic is converted to living space with heat, the walls and ceiling of these rooms should be insulated, and insulation is not required between the floor of new rooms and the rooms below.

Insulation is needed for any other wall, floor, or ceiling surface that separates living space from outdoors, or between a room and an unheated space such as an attic, garage, or utility room. One exception is a basement; insulation is generally not needed at the basement ceiling.

Common places where insulation is often overlooked are the walls between the house and cold garage, the garage ceiling under an occupied room (frequent cause of cold bedrooms), around dormers, and under the floor of any part of a house that is raised above ground level and exposed to cold outdoor air. The palm test is an excellent way of discovering trouble spots like these.

It is amazing how much difference insulation can make at such places. I once rented a small bungalow on a lake exposed on one corner to vicious north winds sweeping unabated across the lake and then slamming head-on against a corner bedroom, by far the coldest room in the house. I put up insulation wallboard, not full insulation, on the inside of the two exposed walls of this room which alone made it a warm room.

What Is the Best Kind of Insulation?

In general, the best all-round kind is mineral wool, which means rockwool, slag wool, and glass fiber (such as Fiberglas). It is rotproof, bugproof, fire-resistant, and by and large superior to most other kinds for houses.

It comes in bats (4-foot long material of different widths designed to fit between the studs of walls or ceilings), in long rolls called blankets (cut to the desired length as needed), in rigid, pressed boards (for insulating foundation walls and the exterior edges of concrete floors), and as "loose fill" (that is blown into walls and attics, or simply poured out of bags by hand).

Other kinds of insulation are wood fiber, cotton, cellulose fiber (also called macerated paper), expanded polystyrene, mineral aggregate (perlite and vermiculite), and aluminum-foil (reflective) insulation. Wood fiber, cotton, and macerated paper require chemical treatment to make them resistant to fire and bugs. Their quality can vary greatly from brand to brand. Some are good, some are not so good.

Examples of the wood-fiber variety are pressed insulating board and fiberboard sheathing. Insulating board comes in large sheets about ¾-inch thick and in a pinch can provide an insulated interior wall surface for a room (though it is best to fully insulate the wall rather than depend solely on the board for top protection). Fiberboard is a sheathing (such as Insulite) that is used as an exterior sheathing for houses; it is installed between the wood framing and the exterior wall surface, the siding. By itself it provides some insulating protection but generally not enough in the North for adequate insulation; the walls themselves should be insulated too.

Macerated paper, often called cellulose or cellulose fiber insulation, is a cheap, low-cost insulation made by cutting up old newspaper into shreds. It is widely sold for existing houses (blown into the walls and attic). Experts are wary of it, however, because some brands are so poorly made that they create a pronounced fire hazard, as well as providing tempting food for bugs and mice.

Expanded polystyrene, such as Styrofoam and Scoreboard (made by Dow Chemical) is excellent for concrete floor edges, foundation and basement walls. It is a rigid insulation that comes in boards and sheets, with a high insulating ability. The Styrofoam kind is a neat white material which can be cemented to the inside of masonry walls, in a basement, for example, and then easily plastered.

There is also loose metallic-pellet insulation made of perlite (volcanic glass pellets), and vermiculite (mica pellets). Both come in bags and are poured in place. Perlite is used chiefly for insulating the hollow space inside of a masonry wall, and it is roughly one-third more efficient than vermiculite; i.e., 2 inches of perlite will give you the same insulating protection you would get from about 3 inches of vermiculite (because of perlite's better heat-stopping characteristic).

Vermiculite can be used inside of masonry walls and also between the joist spaces of an attic floor. You will need, however, about 8 to 9 inches of it to give you the same insulating protection you would get from about 6 inches of a good mineral-wool insulation.

Aluminum-Foil Insulation

Aluminum-foil insulation comes in one or more parallel sheets of foil, called multifoil. Many houses get a mere one or two layers, which is not enough. Each layer of foil gives you the equivalent insulating effect in winter of about a half inch of mineral wool. This calls for *at least* three-layer foil for walls and at least four layers for ceilings.

Because of its reflective characteristics, foil is better at keeping summer heat out of a house than at keeping winter heat in. Multifoil insulation is comparatively cheap in cost, but based on personal experience coupled with long discussions about it with engineers, I do not recommend foil for insulating a house or new addition in a cold northern climate.

On the other hand, a single sheet of foil can be superb under the roof to keep an attic cool in summer regardless of where you live. The sheet of foil is stapled to the underside of the overhead sloping rafters in the attic (just under the roof). It bounces back the hot heat from the roof that is normally radiated down to the attic floor. Attic temperatures are sharply reduced, which means much less heat seepage into the rooms below.

However, much heat can accumulate in the small space between the foil and the underside of the roof. This space therefore should be ventilated by the air flow in and out of your attic vents. And because the accumulated heat above the foil will tend to rise to the peak of the attic, do not run the foil all the way up to the attic peak. End it about 6 to 12 inches below the peak, leaving an open space, unsealed by foil sheet, at the top of your attic. This permits the hot air caught above the foil to escape and be carried out of the attic by air washing in and out of your attic vents.

Aluminum-Covered Bulk Insulation

Aluminum foil is also used as a surface cover for regular insulation. This is something else again. The foil serves either one of two purposes. It may be on only one side of the insulation. Then it is a vapor barrier (discussed in a moment) designed to prevent vapor travel from the house into the house structure.

Or the insulation may have foil on both sides. Then the foil adds a little extra insulating value to the regular insulation. This kind of foil-wrapped insulation is best for attic floors. The foil on top of the insulation bounces back heat rays coming down from the hot roof in summer (in which case you would not need a layer of foil under the roof rafters).

The foil on the bottom serves chiefly as a vapor barrier. Foil-wrapped insulation generally does not pay in the walls of most houses; conventional bulk insulation here is just about as good at less cost.

Vapor Barriers

Regardless of the kind of insulation, ask if it comes with a "vapor barrier." This is important to prevent vapor infiltration of the house structure, thus prevent such troubles as exterior paint peeling and wood rot. A vapor barrier is a layer of vapor-impermeable paper or foil on one side of the insulation, or a polyethylene plastic sheet. Vapor barriers should be mandatory for nearly all houses except in a very warm climate. More accurately, they are essential if the average January temperature where you live is less than 35 degrees.

How Much Insulation?

Insulation is cheap, so use plenty of it. But what is the economical maximum amount to use? This depends on your climate, if you have electric heat or air conditioning, and the particular insulation used.

Using a good type of insulation is important because some kinds are much more effective per inch of thickness than others. Putting it another way, you may need 3 to 4 inches of one brand to give you the same protection you would get from only 2 inches of another really good kind.

The foolproof way to choose insulation is by means of a uniform standard that takes into account the effectiveness of all insulation, regardless of the type and brand. This brings up the R value of an insulation, a new consumer yardstick to use.

It stands for resistance to heat flow; the higher the R value, the better the insulation. You can check the R value of an insulation simply by looking for it on the package, since it is now clearly marked on most brands. Not all makers, to be sure, stamp the R value on their products, but then you can specify that the insulation used should conform to recommended R values.

Here is how much insulation to use for maximum comfort and savings, in terms of its R values, if you live in a bone-chilling cold climate, or regardless of where you live if you have electric heat or central air conditioning. Another term, the U factor, is also given here for technical readers. (Unlike R values, the lower the U factor, the better. U is the coefficient of heat transmission, the rate at which heat flows through a building wall, ceiling, or floor, in Btu's per hour, per square foot, per degree Fahrenheit). The R value of your insulation should equal or exceed the minimum values in the following chart:

INSULATION FOR MAXIMUM COMFORT AND SAVINGS

Location of insulation	Minimum R value to look for on the insulation	Approximate thickness you get
Over ceilings (between attic floor joists)	19	Equivalent to 5 to 7 inches thick of mineral-wool insulation (such as rock wool, glass fiber), depending on brand
Exterior walls	11	Equivalent to about 3 inches, depending on brand
Floors over vented crawl space (no basement)	13	Equivalent to 3 to 3½ inches, depending on brand

The above R-value standards, by the way, were used for the test houses that are heated and cooled for less than $150 a year.

Insulation for Reasonable Comfort and Savings

You can save money and get away with less insulation than above if you have conventional gas or oil heat, no air conditioning, and if your climate is not excessively cold (lowest winter temperatures where you live do not fall below about 10 degrees). Then you use the following adjusted R values:

Insulation location	Minimum R values	Approximate thickness you get
Over ceilings (between attic joists)	13	Equivalent to 3 to 4 inches thick of mineral-wool insulation, depending on brand
Exterior walls	8	2 to 2½ inches thick, depending on brand
Floors over vented crawl space (no basement)	9	2 to 2½ inches, depending on brand

This much insulation will save you almost as much money on gas or oil heating as the maximum insulation (first chart above). But you may not benefit from maximum comfort conditions inside your house.

A Word of Caution

When you talk insulation with a salesman you are likely to hear about it in terms of its thickness. You may hear that you are getting so many inches of insulation, and that's plenty. Or you may be told you are getting "full-wall," "double-thick," or "economy" insulation. Such terms can be highly misleading, so be forewarned. Stick with R values to be sure you are getting the best insulation for the money.

When you buy it, first choose the R value you want, then price the various kinds of insulation available that meet or exceed the R value. Then the lowest-cost brand is your best bet, all other things being equal. If the R value is not marked on a particular type you are considering, beware. (That is, unless it is a kind like loose-fill, which does not come stamped with R values, as discussed below.) In addition to most brands of mineral-wool batt and blanket insulation, R values are stamped on new wood-fiber insulation (such as Balsom Wool), and also on at least one widely used aluminum-foil brand (Alfol).

How Much Insulation if You Live in the South?

It depends naturally on how cold it gets where you live; the farther south you live, the less insulation needed. But even a little insulation is decidedly worthwhile as far south as Miami and southern Texas, even though insulation has long been scorned in such areas. It can help keep your house substantially more comfortable when those inevitable cold waves strike that far south. You need only an inch or two of the cheapest kind. It can also mean a cooler house in summer. If you plan on air conditioning, I should again emphasize that the most insulation is the best insulation.*

How to Insulate Your Existing House

Existing walls can be insulated simply by blowing insulation into them even if they have a little insulation but need more. New techniques make it possible to blow insulation into a brick, stone, or other masonry wall (as well as wood walls), provided it is a "hollow cavity" wall (air space between its inside and outside surfaces). A solid masonry wall is

---

* The owners in a development of 22 air-conditioned houses in Austin, Texas, found to their great delight that they saved an average of 30 per cent on winter fuel bills due to the maximum insulation installed for the air conditioning. In the words of one owner, "There are no more drafts and chills in rooms when those cold windstorms from the Great Plains come sweeping down here in winter."

Insulation is easily blown into the existing walls of masonry or conventional frame houses, provided the wall is hollow. *Owens-Corning Fiberglas.*

insulated by lining its interior surface with insulation and closing in the insulation with a new interior-wall surface.

Insulation also can be blown into other hard-to-reach spaces, such as over the ceiling of a flat-roof house, and between the floor joists of an attic. If you have some insulation, but not enough in the attic, more can be put in to beef-up your coverage simply by adding it over the existing insulation.

Blown-in insulation generally will cost from 15 to 25 cents per square foot of wall, depending on the wall construction and competitive rates where you live, more for masonry walls and less for ceilings. Blown-in insulation will be loose fill made of either mineral wool or of cellulose fiber (macerated paper). I favor the mineral-wool kind, even though you may get a lower price on cellulose fiber. This is mainly because of mineral wool's natural resistance to fire, rot, and bugs.

I would buy from a contractor who is an exclusive dealer for a big mineral-wool insulation maker such as American Rockwool, Baldwin-Hill, Johns-Manville, or Owens-Corning Fiberglas. You could phone the nearest office of a firm like these for the names of contractors they would recommend. And, of course, screen your contractor as you would for any other kind of home-improvement work.

If your attic has a covered floor, loose-fill insulation can be easily blown into the space between the floor and the ceiling below. But because loose fill does not carry R values, you have to specify that enough be blown in to conform with the R values you desire (from charts). In general, it should be 4 to 6 inches thick.

A ceiling also can be insulated with thick insulation batts or blankets at 8¢ to about 12¢ a square foot. This is better than loose fill over ceilings. For one thing, you can choose batts or blankets with an integral vapor barrier. For another, the same insulation can be chosen precisely by its R value and you know exactly what you are getting.

Floors of Nonbasement Houses

A concrete-slab floor is insulated with boards or sheets of rigid perimeter insulation, also called edge insulation. It is applied flat against the vertical outside curb of the concrete slab all around the house. It goes down at least 8 to 12 inches below grade. Follow the application instructions with the manufacturer's literature.

The two best kinds of perimeter insulation are mineral wool and the foamed plastics (polystyrene and urethane), both available in rigid sheets or boards. Neither are stamped with R values, however, for highly involved technical reasons. If you use the mineral-wool kind, it should be at least 2 inches thick and preferably 3 inches in a severe, cold climate.

Between 1¼ and 2 inches is required for comparable protection with polystyrene, and only about 1 inch thick is needed with the new urethane, since these materials give progressively more resistance to heat flow per inch of thickness; i.e., an inch of polystyrene is equivalent to about 1.8 inches of mineral-wool rigid insulation in its heat-stopping characteristics. On the other hand, the foamed plastic kinds cost more per inch than mineral wool; so that you may find that 3-inch thick mineral wool costs no more than less-thick amounts of the foamed-plastic kind.

Incidentally, perimeter insulation may have been installed in a concrete floor when the house was built, but you may not see it. This is because in new houses it is placed in from the outside edge of the floor when the cement is poured (the same way it should be installed when a concrete floor is built for a new addition to a house). But if your floor edges are cold and snow doesn't remain piled up against them, you need such insulation even if a little (but obviously not enough) was installed when the house was built.

You will not need insulation under a concrete-slab floor simply because the protected ground below never gets cold enough to warrant it. Much more heat leaks out around the edges (unless they are insulated).

Insulation for the floor of a crawl-space house is easily stapled between the joists under the floor. It should be supported with chicken wire to prevent sagging.

A special point here: Some people erroneously think insulation is not required under the floor of a crawl-space house because they keep the crawl-space vents shut tight during cold weather. This is a mistake. The usual crawl-space should be kept well ventilated in winter, as well as in summer, to prevent moisture damage to the house underpinnings. Insulation is essential under the floor.

Sometimes, however, the crawl-space is heated (usually when the heating unit is located there). Then ventilation is not required. The crawl-space is kept shut, and insulation is applied on the inside surfaces of the crawl-space walls.

In addition, a good vapor-barrier cover should be laid over the crawl-space earth to prevent the rise of insidious ground vapor up into the house. This can be polyethylene plastic sheet (at least 4 mills thick) or 55-pound roll-roofing building paper. A vapor-barrier seal over the earth is less important if the crawl-space is well ventilated at all times. But even then it can be a good idea just for extra safety, and especially if you have wet earth.

Although insulation is generally not needed for the floor over a basement, if your floor is chilly the National Warm Air Heating & Air-Conditioning Association recommends at least one heat outlet for the basement to provide a cushion of warm air directly under the floor.

Insulation for New Rooms or a New Addition

This is easier and less expensive to do than insulating an existing house. Specify the amount of insulation desired according to the R standards given a few pages back. Check your plans and specifications and make sure you are getting enough. In general, it's best to specify batt or blanket insulation even though a contractor can do it a little cheaper with blown-in loose fill. And because a loose-fill job contains no integral vapor barriers, you will need them installed separately at extra cost.

If you are particularly strapped for money when you add new living space, have the walls and floor (if necessary) insulated to the hilt but leave the attic floor till later. Unlike walls, an attic nearly always can be insulated later at no more expense than its cost during construction.

A Final Point about Insulation Thickness

A perennial question raised has to do with the optimum quantity of insulation that will pay for itself in reduced fuel bills. In other words, what is the cutoff point above which the use of more insulation will not pay for itself in reduced fuel bills?

Some people, including some builders, architects, and manufacturers, have long claimed that only an inch or two of insulation is all we need in houses. They say that the first inch or two of insulation produces the greatest fuel savings and that additional thickness is proportionately less effective. So why spend the extra money?

This is a half-truth. It overlooks several things. First, it does not give much weight to the additional *comfort* that results from additional insulation thickness. Second, fuel costs have risen sharply in the last 15 to 20 years while insulation costs have remained comparatively stable; hence the small extra cost for thicker insulation gives proportionately larger savings on fuel. Third, air conditioning requires more insulation than for heating only. And fourth, new research in recent years has shown conclusively that thicker insulation does pay for itself.

Besides, insulation is so cheap that, when in doubt, it is better to use a little more than a little less. It also should be noted that some of the people who advocate using only an inch or two of insulation are generally people who have a vested interest in thin insulation—a builder, say, who is saving pennies, or certain manufacturers who make only thin insulation and don't sell the thicker kinds.

Old Wives' Tales

Insulation is often misunderstood owing to certain wide-spread misconceptions. Here is what they are and why they are misleading:

Thick walls of solid stone or brick are protection against winter cold. "Look at those hefty walls," people say. Their fuel bills are likely to be hefty, too, because heat leaks out through stone, brick, and other masonry much faster than it does through ordinary wood walls. Masonry is an excellent heat conductor—the reason it is used for fireplaces and ovens.

In actual fact, twice as much heat will leak out through a solid stone wall 2 feet thick as through an ordinary uninsulated wood frame wall only 8 inches thick. You would need a stone wall over 10 feet thick to give you the same heat-retaining protection you would get from an ordinary frame wall with 2 inches of insulation. Brick, concrete, and cinderblock walls are almost as leaky. Yet for years it has been common (and penny-wise) practice to omit insulation with masonry walls. Masonry walls require insulation even more than wood walls.

If your house has hollow masonry walls, insulation usually can be blown inside of them with little trouble. If you have solid masonry walls, you have to add insulation to their inside surface, then close in the insulation with a new inside wall surface.

The air space inside of hollow walls helps insulate a house. Wrong again, even with thick block walls with big air cavities in every block. An air space helps you most only if the air is sealed off and inert. Inside of walls, however, cold air currents are constantly circulating, causing heat to leak out almost as fast as if there were no air spaces. Theoretically, the air in a hollow wall should be withdrawn to create a vacuum, as in a thermos bottle, but this is obviously difficult if not impossible. Next-best solution is to fill the air cavities with an insulating material, or better still, insulate the whole wall.

Insulation is more important over ceilings than in walls. After all, heat rises, doesn't it? Most heat therefore tends to leak out of the ceiling, or so you may think. Nevertheless, the walls add up to quite a large hunk of house surface exposed to outside cold. Much heat can leak out through them and much cold air in, particularly when cold winds slam against them in winter. Another important reason for wall insulation, already mentioned, is to prevent excessively cold wall surfaces.

Insulation causes paint peeling. This half-truth keeps many people from insulating their houses because they fear that the exterior paint will blister and peel. Yet it is a scientific fact that insulation, per se, does not and cannot by itself cause paint peeling.

Paint peeling is caused primarily by moisture trapped inside walls. It is made worse by the wrong paint or defective paint. Occasionally, though experts say it is rare, the paint on a house may be on the verge of peeling and suddenly does after walls are insulated.

However, fewer than 3 per cent of the "hundreds of thousands of buildings that have been insulated have developed such problems," according to one top building authority. These 3 per cent would not have suffered, he says, if the chief cause of the problem, moisture, had been properly eliminated. (The moisture may stem from such causes as a wet cellar or crawl-space under the house, a leaky roof, or an unvented clothes drier. It gets into your walls, with or without insulation, and plays havoc with the outside paint.) The overwhelming majority of us need not fear paint peeling with insulation if we do not have it without insulation.

To play safe when you insulate an existing house, track down and eliminate sources of indoor moisture. Make sure gas heaters, stoves, and clothes driers are vented to outdoors. Use vapor-barrier paint when you redecorate interior walls and ceilings. If necessary, have little wall ventilators installed on the outside of the walls. When you remodel, the use of vapor-barrier insulation is one of the best safeguards of all against paint peeling.

Aluminum-foil insulation radiates back 95 per cent of the heat in a house, thus cuts down heat leakage by that much. Foil can be excellent insulation but, unfortunately, it is widely misapplied owing to this misconception. A single sheet of foil will bounce back that much *radiant* heat, the kind of heat that jumps across a space, like the sun's rays.

But inside the house structure, a sheet of foil is much less effective because heat leakage from the house is a sneaky business. Much of it occurs by means other than radiation—for example, by air currents within the walls (called convection). Foil by itself does not prevent these other kinds of heat leakage. Thus, a single sheet of foil does little good in your walls or roof in winter even though it is superb for baking potatoes in an oven. This is why experts recommend foil insulation with at least three to four parallel sheets of foil.

Chapter 22

Rewiring and
New Wiring Ideas

The electrical people say that eight out of ten existing houses have inadequate wiring. This may sound appalling, if not make you angry when you are compelled to spend money to rewire a young house.

You can't avoid it because new appliances will not work unless your wiring is beefed up. The first telltale signals of weak wiring are lights dimming when a toaster or electric coffeemaker is plugged in, TV set flickering, major appliances that run sluggishly, and of course constantly blowing fuses.

The reason is that the usual wiring installed in nearly all houses built up until a few years ago was designed to handle lights (which draw relatively little electricity) and perhaps a handful of small appliances. Today, however, most families have wholesale quantities of electrical devices, usually 30 to 40 per house (count your own, including radios, electric clocks, shavers, and so on).

Some of them, like an electric drier or range, require more electricity than a whole house required before World War II. In all, there are more than 75 different electrical devices for use in houses today and the number is constantly growing. In short, nearly every family is at one time or another confronted with the need for some new wiring if not a complete new wiring job.

The Three Main Parts of a Wiring System

Understanding terms like wiring circuits is less confusing when you know that your house-wiring breaks down into three main parts:

1. *The main electric board.* This is the heart of the electric system; it is sometimes called the electric service entrance. It is to your wiring system what the size and capacity of the water supply main from street to house is to your plumbing needs. If it is not large enough for the house—and it often isn't—you'll never have adequate electrical capacity.

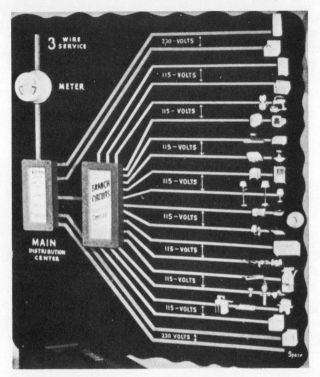

House wiring consists of a central electric board (distribution center), from which a series of branch circuits (separate wires) carry electricity to your lights, outlets, appliances, and other equipment.

The absolute minimum-size service for most houses today is a 3-wire, 240-volt, 100-ampere service. A larger 150- to 200-ampere service, also 240 volts, may be needed if you have an electric range, coupled with electric heat or central air conditioning, or a large house of more than 3000 square feet. Its capacity is noted on the main electric box (where fuses or circuit breakers are located). If the capacity of your present electric box is only 30 or 60 amperes, you probably need a larger box. The ampere rating should be marked on the board or on the inside face of the cover.

The term 3-wire service means you can usually see three separate wires running overhead from the street to the house, not just two. Sometimes the wires are contained in a single cable and you count the number emerging from the cable at the point at which the cable is attached to the house. Don't confuse them, however, with your two telephone lead-in cables.

The connections from these wires to the main electric board should be thick No. 2 wires in size, not smaller No. 3 or 4, which carry less electricity; the lower the number, the heavier the wire. Then you will almost always have enough electrical capacity to meet any contingency.

Many people prefer an electric board with circuit breakers rather than fuses. When an overload or short circuit occurs and lights go out, a circuit breaker automatically snaps open, cutting off the electricity. When the cause of the overload is found and corrected, you merely push the circuit breaker back to "on" and electricity flows again. You do away with the fuss and bother associated with changing fuses. If you prefer circuit breakers, make it clear to your electrician.

2. *The number of branch electric circuits (wires) from the main switch box to the house.* Most houses need at least 8 to 10 separate circuits, but have only 6. If you have much electrical equipment, many appliances, or a large house, you need 12 to 15 circuits, perhaps more. Each individual 120-volt circuit is represented by a separate fuse or circuit breaker. Each 240-volt circuit is protected by two fuses or a double circuit breaker.

A typical house requires three to four individual circuits just for lights and outlets, plus two to three heavier circuits for kitchen appliances, and one circuit each for such things as electric range, furnace, washer, water heater, dishwasher, freezer, and attic fan. In addition, it pays to order two or three spare circuits, available for a future drier, air conditioner, or workshop; i.e., two or three spare fuses or circuit breakers at the main board for future use. An electric board with 12 to 20 circuits costs only about $10 more than one with only 6, *if installed when a house is rewired.* Increasing its size later can cost from $50 to more than $150.

3. *Electric outlets and switches.* A good rule for outlets is one for every 12 feet of wall, because lamps and appliances have 6-foot cords; closer than 12 feet when a door comes between two outlets. Otherwise you end up spreading extension cords all around. The kitchen should have a series of outlets above the countertop to handle appliances safely.

You may also want special appliance outlets in the dining room and for an outside patio to plug in a toaster, waffle iron, or coffeemaker. These should be fed by heavier No. 12 wire, not the usual No. 14 wire for ordinary outlets. Light switches should be located at every entrance to every room, at the top and bottom of stairs for safety, and at garage and basement doors. Adding switches and outlets costs about $4 to $5 apiece when new rooms are being built, twice that afterward.

To get good-quality wiring, ask for "intermediate" grade outlets and wiring quality. There are also "competitive" grades, the cheapest in quality though only pennies less in cost, and "specification" grade, best of all but generally recommended only for heavy-duty commercial use or ships. Also ask for no wiring smaller than No. 12. Lights flicker and appliances work sluggishly because so much wiring today is the smaller No. 14 size.

Making a Wiring Plan

You need not be technically inclined to draw up a useable wiring plan. It can save you misunderstandings and money. (I forced myself to do it for my present house, as much as I abhor such detailing on paper. Surprisingly, it was fun.)

You start with a room-by-room sketch of the house, and then mark exactly where you want new outlets, switches, and lights installed. This forces you to go from one end of the house to another and determine in advance where and what you need. Don't worry about which will go on the same or different circuits. Leave this to the electrician.

I made carbon copies, one for each electrician called in to bid on the job. The electricians were both amazed if not pleased. The sketch enabled them to bid exactly on my work. Later, when the electrician who did the work thought he was finished, I mentioned that a couple of outlets and switches had been omitted. The seeds for an argument were there. We pulled out the wiring plan which showed the missing items. He acknowledged his mistakes and installed them with no more fuss (and obviously at no extra charge).

Doing your own wiring, however, is decidedly not recommended unless you really know what you're doing. Such work is loaded with booby traps, it's easy to violate local codes, and you risk loss of fire insurance coverage in case of fire.

Wiring Guides

The easiest way to draw up a wiring plan is with plan sheets and instructions available to anybody. A free *Wiring Planner* is available from Sears, Roebuck; mention Catalogue No. 39K6238. Sears also publishes the *Sears Wiring Handbook,* another excellent guide even though it is primarily for do-it-yourself wiring buffs: Catalogue No. 34K5248, 35¢ plus 9¢ postage from any Sears mail-order office.

Another helpful guide is *Improving Your Home's Housepower,* 15¢ from the National Wiring Bureau, 155 E. 44 St., New York 17, N.Y. Literature like this tells you how to draw up a wiring plan, and also shows the electric symbols for outlets, switches, etc.

One caution here: Don't depend completely on the plan. Give him the plan, then mark the location desired for every wall switch, outlet, and light with a pencil or chalk in each room and exactly on the wall where desired. I did not do this and as a result the electrician simply installed certain switches where it was convenient for him.

A good example is an entrance light switch in rooms, which should be just inside the door so you need not grope in the dark for it. In my house two such switches are so far inside the room that they require a 10-foot reach. I resent that man and my own carelessness whenever I grope for those switches.

Wiring Costs

Prices will vary because of variations in code requirements from city to city, in labor rates, and the amount of work for your particular house. Here is a range of prices:

Complete new wiring for a typical house generally runs from about $300 to $600, depending on the house. A new 100-ampere, 240-volt electric service and board by itself should run from $75 to $125 in most places; more for a larger service.

New wiring inside the house is generally figured at $7 to $10 for each new outlet, switch, or light receptacle (extra for light fixtures). If special work, an extra-long wire connection, for example, is required, the cost may run up to $20. Add up the number desired for a new bedroom, den, or playroom and you can get an idea of the approximate wiring cost.

New circuits for appliances such as an electric range, drier, or air conditioner: from $25 to perhaps $75, depending on the appliance and the distance from the electric board to the appliance.

Adding up each of these individual items is why the total price generally comes to at least $300 and as much as $600. If you have a larger-than-average house and need all new wiring plus the latest wiring features, it can cost as much as $1000.

Costs for wiring new space added to a house should be lower than the above figures, since it is easier to install wiring during construction than afterward.

New Wiring Features

Here is a listing of special wiring features you may want. Although electricians may not mention them, some are good and inexpensive. Others are decidedly luxury features; not everyone will want them. Decide for yourself.

Silent, no-click light switches. These are a delight, particularly if noise irritates you. There are quiet mechanical switches, better silent mercury-action switches, and flat-plate switches set flush against the wall (light finger pressure on the top pressure plate turns the light on, on the bottom turns it off). Cost is 75¢ to about $1.50 apiece or 50¢ to $1 more than ordinary click switches. They can be obtained to replace existing click switches, as well as when rewiring.

No-shock outlets, a safety feature with small children. They are designed so a child cannot jab a hairpin into the outlet and get a shock. Less than $1 apiece.

Ivory or white outlets and switches, rather than the usual brown, which may clash with your decor. The white kind may cost slightly more and takes extra time for delivery.

Grounded outlets, particularly in the kitchen, basement, workshop, and outdoors. This is added protection against shocks. About $2.50 each, and special 3-prong plugs are also needed for appliance cords.

Multiple switch control, which allows you to turn the same light on or off from every entrance or exit to or from a room, or from the top or bottom of stairs. From $10 to $15 each.

Automatic closet lights, which turn on the closet light when the closet door is opened and turn it off when the door is closed, the way a refrigerator light works. From $8 to $15.

Dimmer control, which is actually a dial for adjusting light brightness up or down according to your needs. Illumination in a room can be dimmed to candlelight glow for a dinner party, or turned up brightly for reading. Special bulbs are not needed. Dimmers are chiefly for living and dining rooms. About $50 each for incandescent bulbs, more for fluorescent.

Remote-control lighting, which permits you to turn indoor and outdoor lights on or off from a central location such as the kitchen or master bedroom. A remote kitchen switch can control front-door or garage lights for example, saving steps. A control panel next to your bed will eliminate that final tour of your house and grounds every night to make sure all lights are out. Cost: $50 and up, depending on the number of lights to be controlled.

Automatic garage-door opener, which enables you to open the garage door from a button in your car. About $75 to $100.

Electric snow-melting panels for the front walk, driveway, or both. They are turned on when snow begins to fall. From $150 to $250 for a 40- to 50-foot drive if installed when new paving is put down; more if the paving has to be torn up.

Continuous strip outlets, which consist of a metal or plastic strip of outlets that is installed along a wall baseboard, or at the back of a kitchen counter or workbench. Outlets are spaced at 6 inches to several feet apart. They do away with the need for breaking into walls for new wiring, and provide an abundance of outlets where several appliances are used at once. From a few dollars for a 6-foot long strip up to $30 for longer ones or others requiring special installation work.

Chapter 23

Cures and Controls for Termites and Wood Rot

Consider termites first. What is the first step to take if you discover termites in your house? How do you make a new addition or a whole house termiteproof?

If termites are discovered, the first rule is: don't panic. They work slowly and may take months if not years to do real damage. Even if they have bored deeply into the structure there is almost always time to assess the damage and discuss it with experts. Don't be hasty and don't be frightened into signing up with the first exterminator that arrives. First learn a little about how termites work and what they can and cannot do.

What Termites Do

They usually nest in the ground, as many as 250,000 in a typical colony. Their basic needs are food and water. They build a network of tunnels from the ground into a house for food (dead wood) and make regular round trips back to the ground for water. This is important to know because cutting off their routes to the house will keep them out and also do away with any inside the house by depriving them of water.

If, however, they can obtain moisture inside the structure—from a water leak or other dampness source—they can remain indoors thriving on the house structure. In one case on record a termite colony was found flourishing on the tenth floor of a hotel, obtaining water from a toilet-tank leak and their food, of course, from the structure. For the same reason, they have infested house attics, subsisting on dampness due to condensation.

Their first target is wood closest to the ground: the wood under porches and outside stairs, exterior wood walls close to the earth, trellises, wood fences, and the wood framing of basement windows. They also enter

Mud termite tunnels from ground up to house permit termites to travel without exposure to hated light and air. *American Wood Preservers Institute.*

through cracks as small as 1/32 inch in foundation walls, piers, and concrete-slab floors of houses without basements. A concrete-slab house, in fact, is quite vulnerable, despite what many owners think and sellers say. Slab-floor houses are damaged by termites as much as other houses.

About 95 per cent of all termite damage in the United States is done by the subterranean species of termites. They shun light and air and work in dark places. They are seldom seen except during swarming time in late winter or early spring, their mating season, when clusters of them take to the air. In a day or two they will have found their mates, shed their wings, and disappeared back into the ground. Seeing them swarm or spotting their discarded wings on the ground is the first sign of their presence. This may occur as early as January in a warm climate to as late as May in a cold climate.

They should not be mistaken for flying ants (a different bug), which have a narrow waist. The swarming, subterranean termite is identified by its black body and glassy, translucent wings. The subterranean worker termite does the damage inside houses. It has a large head, grayish-white color, no wings, and a stubby, oblong body which does not narrow down at the waist like an hourglass.

You will rarely see them unless you dig into infested wood, or break open one of their mud tunnels. These are another telltale sign—flattened mud tubes about ¼ to 1 inch wide leading from the ground up the inside or outside of foundation walls or running up a pipe or metal beam into a house. They may be spread over the masonry walls of a house like veins in your hand, but a good many people see only a dirt-streaked wall and don't give it another thought.

You are not safe from subterranean termites even in the coldest northern states, except perhaps Alaska. They have become quite troublesome nearly everywhere in the North as well as in the South. There are also dry-wood and damp-wood termites with similar appearance and habits. These are found chiefly in a narrow band around the southern part of the United States from the Carolina coast around to the San Francisco Bay region.

Termite Safeguards

The best safeguard is a semiannual inspection of the house, especially in an area with a high termite incidence (see map). You can learn to do it yourself, but it's better to have a service contract with a good pest-control contractor. A service contract is cheap if bought before damage occurs and it usually carries an insurance clause. If damage is discovered, repairs are done at little or no additional expense. The exterminator has incentive to check the house regularly and catch potential trouble before he has to make extensive repairs at his expense.

He inspects the interior and exterior wall surfaces, the basement, crawlspace, or concrete floor slab, and probes the vulnerable underpinnings with a knife or ice pick. In a concrete-floor house he looks for cracks in

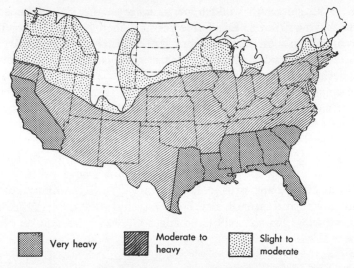

| | Very heavy | | Moderate to heavy | | Slight to moderate |

Map of termite incidence indicates degree of protection needed against termites. Maximum safeguards should be taken in Region I, where termites are rampant; moderate safeguards in Region II; and some safeguards in Region III. Termites are spreading constantly and are beginning to show up in the white areas of the map.

Subterranean worker termite causes the major damage in houses. It is less than ¼ inch long, has large head, no wings, and stubby body.

U. S. Dept. of Agriculture, Forest Service.

the concrete, and especially at floor openings through which plumbing pipes and wires run up into the house. The plumbing supply-pipe box, usually in the bathroom, is a favorite entry route for termites, so opening it and looking in is something that owners should do regularly.

Other precautions include maintaining good drainage away from the house on all sides. All wooden parts of the house should be at least 4 inches above soil level. Dead tree stumps nearby should be pulled and removed because they attract termites and the next jump is into the house. The underside of porches, outdoor stairs, and inside crawl-spaces are especially vulnerable. They should be kept dry and well ventilated. Fireplace wood should not be stacked in or near a house. It behooves us to carry out these precautions—I find it hard to do myself—but by letting them slide we may leave the door open for major damage later.

If You Discover Termite Damage

Unfortunately, there are no hard and fast rules to follow. It depends on where you live and the extent of the damage. Check the phone book and ask friends for the names of reliable termite firms. Call in two or three for an estimate on the repairs needed. Ask each if he is a member of the National Pest Control Association (headquarters at 250 West Jersey Street, Elizabeth, N.J., and a good source for the names of nearby contractors as well as special information on termites and other pests); most good termite specialists are members.

Listening to different termite men can be confusing. They are likely to assess the damage in different ways and their prices will vary. You must determine exactly what each intends to do for your money, the exact kind of repairs, and how much preventative work. Before signing up, ask the nearest Better Business Bureau about the service company.

Wood beams and part of the structure may have to be replaced. He may pump termite-killing chemicals into infected beams, but in some cases even the best treatment cannot be guaranteed. The trouble is that, once termites infect an existing house, a running battle may be required before they are eventually eliminated. You win one skirmish and they regroup under the house and find other weak spots to enter. It pays, therefore, to obtain a service contract along with the repairs being done. The repairs may cost several hundred dollars, but then you agree to pay, say, $25 to $50 a year, for continuing service. If termites rear up again later, the exterminator returns to root them out at no additional expense to you.

Examples of Damage

One friend of mine paid $250 for a termite extermination job on discovering them in his house. He also signed up for a $50-a-year service contract even though the termites were supposedly routed. New termites have shown up nearly every year since and the contractor comes back to get rid of them every time at no additional charge. The house is located near the south shore of Long Island, N.Y., which has become a notoriously bad termite-infected area in the country in recent years. Practically no house there is safe from them.

Another man I know has had termites in his last three houses including his present house. He has learned to accept them, knowing that the land around (Westport, Connecticut) is infested with them. He is taking steps to eliminate them in his present house (by soil poisoning treatment, described below) but he also knows he must maintain constant vigilance to prevent a future breakthrough.

These two examples are in the North. Things are considerably more hazardous for people in the South, Southwest, and in California. Let it go too long and the necessary repairs can cost several thousand dollars. I do emphasize, however, the importance of understanding what can happen and acting ahead of time to prevent it. An exterminator can be called in at any time for an inspection which can be well worth its small cost.

Termite Preventatives

One or more of the following safeguards are recommended when a new addition is added to a house. These are given in the order of importance. The first one, soil poisoning, also can be done for an existing house.

1. Soil "poisoning," the injection of a special chemical into the ground under and around a house. It is anathema to termites for at least five to ten years but harmless to tree roots and plants. After that time the chemical treatment may have to be repeated. Because the chemicals are comparatively new, nobody knows exactly how long they remain effective in the ground. Tests indicate that they may be good for 15 to 20 years.

The most popular brands include Aldrin for new construction and Dieldrin for existing houses (both made by the Shell Chemical Corporation, 50 West 50 St., New York 20, N.Y.); and Chlordane (made by the Velsicol Corporation, 330 E. Grant Ave., Chicago 11, Ill.). Information on other chemicals can be had from E. L. Bruce Co., Memphis 1, Tenn.; Bird & Son, East Walpole, Mass.; as well as from the National Pest Control Association. Cost of chemical treatment can range from $75 for a house addition up to perhaps $200 for a large existing house.

2. Using chemically treated lumber for the main underpinnings of a house, preferably all wood around the base of the walls and under the floor. Pressure-treated lumber should be used, which means a chemical preservative is injected under pressure deep into the lumber.

Pressure-treated lumber can be bought at most local lumberyards. But it should not be confused with paint-on preservatives or wood simply dipped into a chemical bath; both of these cost less, are not accepted by

FHA, and are not worth the money. Special pressure-treated lumber (Wolmanized for example) is also available from factories. Information on the makers of such wood can be had from the American Wood Preservers Institute, 111 West Washington, Chicago 2, Ill.

Pressure-treated wood may cost an additional $100, more or less, for the most vulnerable parts of a new addition, up to $300 or $400 for all the wood used in vulnerable places. It may be expensive, but it is excellent protection not only against termites but also against decay, the scientists' term for wood rot.

Three species of wood are toxic to termites and have natural resistance to rot: foundation-grade California redwood, Tidewater red cypress, and pitchy southern pine "lightwood." The 100 per cent heartwood grade of each must be used, not the sapwood grade. Even then the wood is not absolutely immune, nor as resistant as pressure-treated wood, according to the U. S. Department of Agriculture. For that matter, each of them may be difficult to get in some parts of the country or more expensive than pressure-treated wood. If you do use one of these woods you can figure on fairly good termite protection, but don't count on complete protection over the years.

3. The use of reinforced-concrete foundation walls, rather than walls of concrete block or cinder block. They must be free of cracks and porous areas.

4. A 4-inch-thick capping of concrete laid over the top of concrete-block or cinder-block foundation walls. The hollow spaces inside blocks are an open invitation to termite entry straight up into walls without any exterior signs of them. Capping the top layer of blocks can stop them. Filling the top layer of blocks with concrete is also a good idea, in addition to a 4-inch cap.

5. Metal termite shields placed all around the top of the foundation walls to prevent termite entry into the house. Shields, however, are not the perfect defense. They are, in fact, ". . . in disrepute," according to the man who invented them some 30 years ago, Dr. Thomas E. Snyder of the Smithsonian Institute. They crack, break at the joints, or simply do not extend far enough from the foundation walls. If you have shields on your present house, every inch of them should be periodically inspected for termite breakthrough.

Other Pests

In addition to termites, damage is also caused to houses by other pests such as carpenter ants and the Old House Borer.

Carpenter ants are widespread in the northern half of the country, and extend south to mountainous areas, particularly in the Southeast. They attack houses and dead wood much like termites, especially when the wood is wet. But unlike the white termite worker, carpenter ant workers (the troublemakers) are black and do not shun light and air as termites do. You can often see the black workers going to and from their nests in search of food. Their presence is often indicated by otherwise unexplained sawdust piles beside the timber they are feeding on.

Much the same preventative measures used for termites also apply to carpenter ants: keep your house dry; don't leave wood in direct contact with the ground; provide plenty of ventilation for parts of the house that tend to be damp; and inspect periodically.

The Old House Borer

Despite the name, the Old House Borer most often damages new houses and buildings. (The name has come down to us because it was a major pest in old buildings in Europe.) It causes severe damage chiefly in the eastern part of the country, from Massachusetts down the Atlantic coastline to Florida, as far south and west as Louisiana and Texas, but except for Texas it has not been encountered west of the Mississippi River.

It is a brownish-black beetle about ½ to ¾ of an inch long, slightly flattened in shape, with gray hairs spouting from its head and forward part of the body. Each of its hard-shelled wings has two patches of gray. But it is rarely seen and usually not discovered until it has begun to cause damage.

Signs of its presence include: a rasping or ticking sound made while it is boring or feeding; powdery borings in its tunnels, seen by breaking the wood surface where tunneling exists, wood blistering when its larva are close to the surface; boring dust below infected lumber; or actually seeing beetles in the house.

If they are discovered, the speediest remedy is fumigating the entire house. This takes special care and training. It should be done only by a first-rate pest-control operator. Nobody should re-enter the house until after it has been thoroughly aired. If they are found in a few isolated beams they can be killed by the application of special chemicals. This, too, must be done with care by an expert since the chemicals are highly poisonous to people and animals. It's best not to try it yourself.

Excellent sources of information about house pests are: *Subterranean Termites, Their Prevention and Control in Buildings,* U.S.D.A. Bulletin 64, 15¢; *Preventing Damage to Buildings by Subterranean Termites,* 15¢, and *Control of Non-subterranean Termites* (dry-wood kind) 10¢; *The Old House Borer,* Leaflet No. 501, 5¢; all available from the U. S. Government Printing Office, Washington 25, D.C.

Wood Rot (Decay)

This causes even more destruction than termites throughout the North and South, and particularly in wet and humid climates. The over-riding principle to remember is that a dry house does not rot simply because dry wood does not rot. There is no such thing as "dry rot," a misnomer which came about because rotted wood in the final stage of decay looks dry.

Sometimes rotted wood is mistaken for termite-infected wood and vice versa, even by experts. (I have seen a construction engineer find "termites" in a house's underpinnings when the trouble actually was an advanced case of wood rot.) The difference can be hard to determine at first glance. Wood rot is caused by a minute fungus which eats away at damp wood. The wood becomes mottled as if it had a case of grayish-white measles. The wood can be saved if the fungus is caught in time and the source of the moisture eliminated. Otherwise the infected wood will literally rot away and require expensive replacement.

Here you should differentiate, however, between rotting wood and new "White-pocket" Douglas fir lumber which shows a lot of little white pockets but is nevertheless sound lumber. Such lumber is perfectly good provided it is dry. But if the wood feels damp and soft to the touch, too, it is rotting.

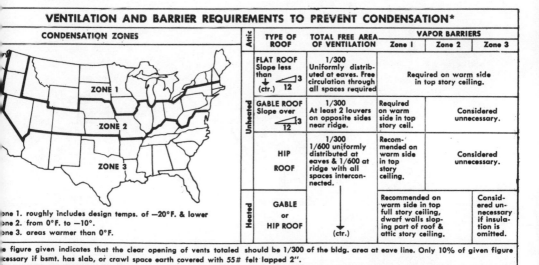

VENTILATION AND BARRIER REQUIREMENTS TO PREVENT CONDENSATION*						
CONDENSATION ZONES	Attic	TYPE OF ROOF	TOTAL FREE AREA OF VENTILATION	VAPOR BARRIERS		
				Zone 1	Zone 2	Zone 3
ZONE 1	Unheated	FLAT ROOF Slope less than (ctr.) ◢3/12	1/300 Uniformly distributed at eaves. Free circulation through all spaces required	Required on warm side in top story ceiling.		
ZONE 2		GABLE ROOF Slope over ◢3/12	1/300 At least 2 louvers on opposite sides near ridge.	Required on warm side in top story ceil.	Considered unnecessary.	
ZONE 3		HIP ROOF	1/300 1/600 uniformly distributed at eaves & 1/600 at ridge with all spaces interconnected.	Recommended on warm side in top story ceiling.	Considered unnecessary.	
ʒne 1. roughly includes design temps. of −20°F. & lower ʒne 2. from 0°F. to −10°. ʒne 3. areas warmer than 0°F.	Heated	GABLE or HIP ROOF (ctr.)		Recommended on warm side in top full story ceiling, dwarf walls sloping part of roof & attic story ceiling.		Considered unnecessary if insulation is omitted.

ᵉ figure given indicates that the clear opening of vents totaled should be 1/300 of the bldg. area at eave line. Only 10% of given figure ᵉcessary if bsmt. has slab, or crawl space earth covered with 55# felt lapped 2".

Wood rot is a widespread problem in zones 1 and 2, where winter cold causes much moisture condensation inside houses. Two best safeguards are ample ventilation and vapor barriers, as recommended in the chart.

Like termites, wood rot spreads first to damp parts of a house near the ground, under unventilated porches and steps, wood walls touching the ground, and in damp basements (spreading to the basement ceiling beams even though the dampness originates at the floor or walls). It also occurs in unventilated attics, and particularly in the floor and walls of a bathroom (due to cracks around the bathtub and shower) and around the kitchen sink.

Rot also can attack wood quite distant from the original source of the moisture because of the insidious ways of water vapor. Water from the basement, for example, is absorbed into the basement air as vapor and then can spread up through the inside of your walls to the attic causing damage there. This occurs more than you may think.

Preventing wood rot boils down to keeping your house dry, which puts additional importance on good drainage away from the house, keeping the exterior wall wood out of touch with damp earth, installing large vents

Here are different vents that can be used to keep a house dry and prevent condensation and wood rot.   *National Mineral Wool Insulation Assn.*

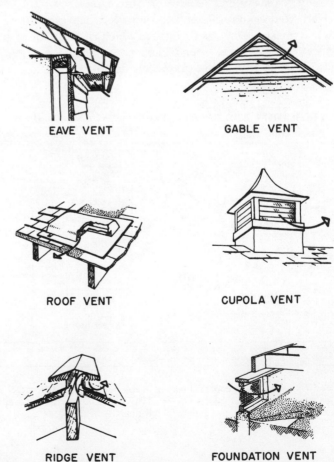

EAVE VENT   GABLE VENT

ROOF VENT   CUPOLA VENT

RIDGE VENT   FOUNDATION VENT

for crawl-spaces, under porches, stairs, and in the attic, and spotting water leaks from roof gutters and drains before they damage the house.

When you build an addition to the house, the appropriate controls should be incorporated in the plan; e.g., built-in vents, vapor barriers, and waterproofing, each of these discussed elsewhere in this book.

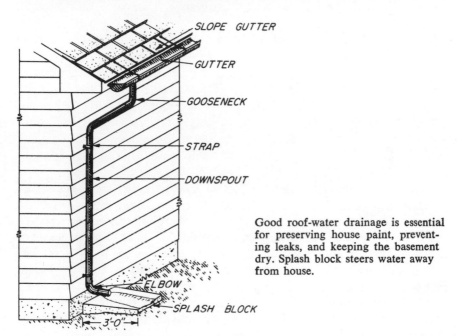

Good roof-water drainage is essential for preserving house paint, preventing leaks, and keeping the basement dry. Splash block steers water away from house.

Chapter 24

Buying a New Water Heater
(for Ample Hot Water
and Long Life)

According to the government's Cost of Living Index, water-heater replacements account for one of the largest single home repair costs for United States homeowners every year. So many heaters are so poorly made that they succumb to rust and corrosion in as little as three years and you must spend at least $100 to $125, often more, for a new one.

For only about $25 more in first cost you can buy a first-rate heater that not only will last 10 to 15 years, but will provide all the hot water you will ever need at one time. But here again you cannot go by brand name alone. Nearly every manufacturer sells both good and shoddy models (though both look equally shiny and new at first glance).

Two Main Kinds of Water Heaters

The usual water heater has its own water storage tank and operates independently of the central heating system. It is found in most houses with warm-air furnace for central heating, but not in all houses with hot-water or steam heat. Another kind of water heater is called an indirect coil heater, used only in conjunction with hot-water or steam heat.

Storage Water Heaters

The two most important things to determine before you buy are the size (capacity) needed for *your family,* and the kind of tank construction that will last the longest with *your kind of water supply.*

In general, the larger the storage tank size, the greater the water-heating capacity. Tanks range in size from a small 20-gallon storage capacity, which stores about enough hot water for a quick bath, up to 100 gallons. The tank capacity needed depends on whether you get a gas or electric heater. The minimum-size model for gas usually recommended for most families is 40 gallons. The exact size needed depends on the number of people in the family and whether or not you have an automatic clothes washer, as shown in the following chart.

If your choice falls between two sizes, from chart below, choose the larger one. This will give you spare capacity for times when everybody in the house needs hot water at once, rather than a borderline unit that has to work overtime. Continually pressing a unit to work at top capacity is a major reason for early failure. Note also that if you have or expect to buy an automatic clothes washer, the next size larger heater should be obtained.

What Size Gas Hot-Water Heater?

Number in family	With no laundering	With nonautomatic washer	Automatic washer
3	20	30	30–40
4	30	30–40	40–50
5	30–40	40–50	40–50
6	40–50	40–50	50–65
7	40–50	50–65	65

Recovery Rate

Regardless of tank size, ask about the *recovery rate*. This indicates how fast a heater can bounce back and provide new hot water when you're drawing a lot at once.

It depends on the size of the burners. The recovery rate normally should be such that the heater is capable of providing at least 30 gallons of hot water an hour, based on heating the water by 100 degrees; i.e., heating 30 gallons of 60-degree water to 160 degrees in an hour.

Sometimes the recovery rate is deceptively based on a 60-degree temperature rise (from 100 to 160 degrees an hour). Look for this on the name plate and don't accept such a unit. A 30-gallon unit with a high recovery rate can be better than a 40-gallon unit with a low recovery rate. The total amount of hot water it can give you per hour is the key fact to know.

Electric vs. Gas Water Heaters

An electric water heater must be larger than a gas one. The smallest electric heater needed for almost any family is one with a 66-gallon capacity tank. With an automatic clothes washer, an 80-gallon tank is usually essential, unless you get a "high-speed" or "high-watt" electric unit. These have greater heating capacity as a result of extra-capacity heating elements. A smaller tank capacity can be used with this kind than is normally required. Not all electric companies, however, permit them.

Gas water heaters generally have the edge over electric ones. Gas units are lower in first cost, provide hot water faster than electricity, and in general are cheaper in operation. Electric units should be used only when you get a low "preferential" power rate for water heating.

There are also oil-fired water heaters. They are high in initial price but can be cheaper per year in the long run if you live where gas is expensive (or unavailable) because operating costs with oil are quite low. They are a good bet in areas where oil has a good edge over gas for house heating, unless electricity is cheap (less than about 1½¢ per kwh) and an electric unit is economical.

Getting Good Quality

Water-heater quality depends largely on the kind of tank and the guarantee you get. The lowest-quality heater—gas or electric—is one with a galvanized steel tank and a one-year guarantee. This kind normally should be shunned—it is likely to rust out in a few years.

Then come glass-lined tanks, the most popular kind. But there are shoddy glass ones as well as good ones. The better ones are guaranteed for 10 to 15 years; one of these is your best bet if you decide on a glass unit. Make sure it has an unconditional guarantee because the guarantee can be tricky.

The usual guarantee for a 10-year model, for instance, promises a new unit free if the unit fails within five years (half the guarantee time). If it fails after that you get diminishing credit toward a new unit on a sliding scale, according to how long afterward the original unit lasted, up to ten years.

Sometimes the guarantee offers only a new tank, not a complete new tank and burner assembly. What's more, you may be charged for shipping costs, freight, and installation labor. Nothing may be said about how you get hot water while the old parts are being inspected at the factory (usually in slow motion). It depends on the particular brand and unit. So read the guarantee fine print carefully.

There are also water heaters with ceramic-lined, aluminum, and copper tanks. These may last even longer than glass but in general are not worth their extra cost unless you have very corrosive water. There are more than 18,000 different kinds of water (in chemical make-up) in the United States, so it is difficult to say when and where one of these special models should be used. Ask local dealers and gas or electric company officials where you live.

Why Soft Water Can Hurt

If you live in an area with soft water, such as New England and much of the South, it is particularly important to get a top-quality, noncorrosive water heater. This is a paradox with water heaters. Women find soft water fine for their hair, but its high oxygen content makes it murder on the ordinary galvanized-steel or cheap glass water heater. A really good glass, aluminum, ceramic, or copper unit is essential.

On the other hand, galvanized-steel heaters can be a bargain in areas with hard water, such as much of the Midwest and California. Lime in the water forms a protective film inside the tanks and inhibits corrosion. A galvanized heater that will fail in three years in parts of Texas may well last over ten years in Chicago. But even in a hard-water city like Chicago, get the best possible galvanized unit, one with the best guarantee; cost is a mere $10 to $20 more than the usual cheap kind.

The Sacrificial-Rod Feature

Galvanized-steel water heaters sometimes come with a special magnesium-rod device inserted down the middle of the tank. The rod inhibits tank corrosion by giving itself up as a sacrificial offering; it draws the corrosive acids away from the tank and lets itself be eaten away first. Much advertising hoopla has been written about the rods. The catch is that they may be used up in a year or two and the tank goes next.

Being human, most of us forget to check and replace them in time. The conclusion here is not to be talked into a galvanized-tank model instead of a better tank, say, just because the galvanized tank comes with a magnesium rod. However, in hard-water areas where a galvanized tank may be used, one with a rod is preferred to one without.

Coil Water Heaters

This kind of water heater, used in houses with hot-water or steam house heat, is also called an indirect or instantaneous water heater. It is integral with the heating boiler, a pipe coil inserted in the regular heating boiler. The same heating mechanism used for heating the house also heats your faucet water. Water-heating costs may be somewhat higher in summer but lower in winter, compared with a separate tank water heater.

One widely mentioned advantage of the coil water heater is that you save the floor space normally required for a separate tank water heater. They are not recommended, however, if you have very hard, mineral-laden water, a hardness rating of about seven grains or higher. Then it is better to have a separate tank-model water heater. Hard water tends to clog up domestic water coils with scale, reducing efficiency, and requiring frequent cleaning. The hardness rating of your water can be determined by having a sample tested by a nearby water-conditioner dealer, usually at a small charge.

Two Crucial Features

Two features of a coil water heater are crucial. First, it should have an IWH seal. This is the seal of an approved Indirect Water Heater, a good-quality unit matched to the boiler. This should be noted on the water-heater coil itself, which can be seen sticking out of the main heating boiler. Insist on an IWH seal.

Second, adequate capacity is plainly essential so you won't be chronically short of hot water. Minimum rating for a one-bathroom house today is 2.75 gpm (gallons per minute) of water-heating capacity; at least 3.25 gpm with two baths. If you have more than two baths, or a big family or use hot water liberally, get a 3.75 gpm coil or larger. Less heating capacity is needed if the indirect water heater comes with a supplementary water tank.

Summed up, the faucet water heater commands special attention. It is often taken for granted and has to be replaced in a short time, or it is so small you never have enough hot water. It is human nature to downgrade your requirements to save a few dollars when you are on the verge of buying. You end up paying twice as much in the long run. And obtain the unit that should be large enough to satisfy future hot water needs if, say, you have a growing family, or don't have an automatic clothes washer but expect to get one.

Part 8

COPING WITH SUMMER HEAT, NOISE, DRY AIR IN WINTER

What is the best way to keep cool in summer (short of fleeing to a cool resort from June to September)? You have a choice between a big fan to ventilate the whole house, and going whole hog for central air conditioning. A fan obviously is cheaper but has drawbacks, as discussed in the following chapter.

We enjoy central air conditioning, indeed demand it, in our offices, in stores, restaurants, and movies (when it is not overused to produce an icy shock). But many of us consider it extravagant or just plain sinful to spend money on a device that merely keeps our homes comfortable in summer. We should bravely put up with torrid heat and humidity the way our ancestors did. (Our ancestors also did not know about central heat, automatic appliances, and electric lighting.)

Air conditioning has much to offer in its way, its price is less than many people think, and it sheds many benefits on a household in addition to merely taming summer heat. It is, in fact, far more of a necessity than you may think at first.

Two other subjects demand attention because they cause much discomfort and anguish in houses: excessively dry air in winter, and noise in a house the year around. Many of us have to cope with one or the other or both so they are also discussed here.

Chapter 25

Ventilating Fans for Attic, Kitchen, and Bathrooms

The Attic Fan

An attic fan draws air through the house and blows it out the attic. Used chiefly in the evening, it cools by drawing in cool evening air after a hot day. It is less effective in a hot climate where the air temperature does not fall much at night. A little cooling effect is realized from the breeze of air over your skin but it is not always satisfactory.

Even the biggest fan doesn't stir up a great deal of air movement through a house. Often the air drawn in is hot, or if not hot, laden with sticky humidity. If evening temperatures fall sharply at night, a properly selected fan can reduce interior temperatures by 10 to 20 degrees.

What Size Fan?

The air-moving capacity of a fan is the chief consideration for successful cooling. In the South, an attic fan should be large enough to replace all the air in a house every minute. A house with a volume of 10,000 cubic feet of air (cfm) therefore requires a fan capacity of 10,000 cfm. In the North, a fan should provide a complete air change every minute and a half to two minutes; the cooler your nights, the less air movement required and the smaller the fan.

To determine the fan size needed, compute the square feet of floor area in your house and multiply by your ceiling height. For example, a 30×50-foot house has 1500 square feet of floor area (30×50). With an 8-foot ceiling this gives 12,000 cubic feet of air volume (1500×8). If you have a second floor, its volume, naturally, should be included too. Deduct the volume of still air in closets, pantries, and any other closed-off space.

Say your house has a total air volume of 12,000 cubic feet. You divide this by the number of air changes required. In the South you would divide 12,000 by 1, as one air change a minute is required. You need a fan with a capacity of 12,000 cfm. In the North, the same house would require a fan capacity of 8000 cfm (12,000 divided by 1½). If you figure that one change every two minutes is sufficient, you will need a 6000 cfm fan (12,000 divided by 2).

You choose the fan with the closest capacity to what you need. You'll generally find that what you need will fall between two available sizes. It's best to choose the larger size rather than the smaller one. You may require a fan with a 13,000 cfm capacity and find that you cannot find one with exactly this capacity. You may choose between one with 12,000 cfm capacity, say, and another with 14,000. Take the 14,000 cfm unit, unless you refigure your needs and the smaller one will do.

A Warning about Fan Capacity Ratings

Choose a fan according to its *ventilation* rating, not its *circulating air* rating. There is a marked difference between the two. The ventilating rating is the amount of air the fan will move through a house when it is

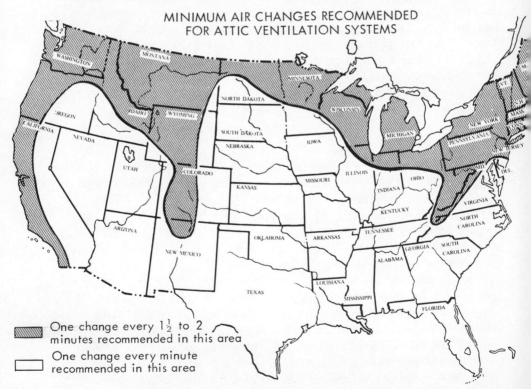

MINIMUM AIR CHANGES RECOMMENDED
FOR ATTIC VENTILATION SYSTEMS

One change every 1½ to 2 minutes recommended in this area

One change every minute recommended in this area

An attic fan should be large enough to pull out all the air in the house every minute in gray area of above map, up to two minutes in dark area.

bucking the inevitable friction encountered by air moving in windows, through the house, and out the attic vents. It is the realistic rating and is given with all good fans.

Circulating air capacity is a tricky figure based on taking the reins off a fan and simply measuring how much air it will move if it were mounted outdoors with no impediments to its air flow. Sometimes it is called free-air capacity. The ventilating capacity may be as much as 25 per cent less than the circulating capacity. It should be discounted by this much. Above all, don't choose a fan according to its blade diameter. Many of us refer to a 36-inch fan, for example, but this is meaningless without knowing its ventilating capacity.

You may see a fan's capacity listed as a "certified rating." This means it is based on stiff industry standards. If you do not see this term, the name plate should say that the capacity is in accordance with one of three standards: the ASHRAE (American Society of Heating, Refrigerating and Air-Conditioning Engineers) code; the National Association of Fan Manufacturers' Bulletin No. 110; or the National Electric Manufacturing Association (NEMA) standards.

Another check on the quality and efficiency of an attic fan is whether it conforms to Commercial Standard CS 178–51, a standard developed by the Department of Commerce and the National Bureau of Standards. There is also a Commercial Standard CS 179–51 which covers how an attic fan should be installed; you could specify that the fan be installed according to this code.

Location and Installation

The preferred location is in the attic floor near the middle of the house and preferably over a central hallway. Provisions should be made for closing off the fan opening in winter so cold attic air will not fall into the house. A trap door, sliding door, or closing shutters can do this. Use a closing shutter which opens only when the fan starts and automatically closes when the fan stops. Hot attic air is kept out of the house when the fan is off.

This location should be your first choice, despite two possible drawbacks: 1. Fan noise may be disturbing, particularly at night. The noise will not bother you, however, if you get a really good fan and it is properly installed. 2. The fan cannot be closed off from the house and used to ventilate only the attic. Cooling the house is far more important, though. If the attic has ample vent openings (and its floor is well insulated), you gain little from fan ventilation of the attic alone.

Second-best installation is locating the fan vertically on the attic floor adjacent to the ceiling intake opening. This requires a special "plenum" box to connect the fan intake with the opening, thus a more expensive installation than having the fan flat on the floor.

The fan should be no closer to the opening than one fan diameter. The box should be lined with sound-deadening material; it should be rigidly built to prevent vibration, and the ceiling opening should have a door or shutters. Main purpose of this setup is so the fan can ventilate the attic only and not the house, if desired, as well as the house at other times.

A third alternative is mounting the fan against the wall at one end of the attic. The fan pulls house air up through a louvered ceiling opening in the attic floor and pumps it outside. An airtight attic is necessary, however, or else leaks from under the eaves, say, will let outside air be pulled in instead of air from the house, which is short-circuited. This installation is used when you wish to cool the attic only (with an intake vent located at the other end of the attic).

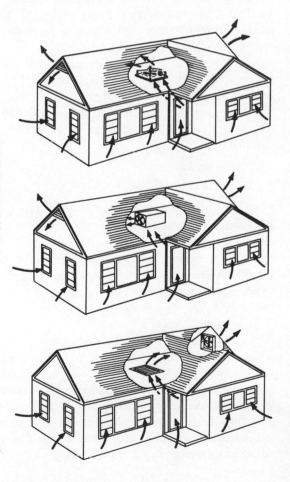

Diagrams show three attic-fan installations. Fan located flat over center of the house is generally best, especially with a low-slope roof. If a flat installation is impractical, fan can be installed vertically in middle of the attic. Locating the fan at the end of the attic requires an airtight attic.

But your living quarters below can be kept just as cool with proper attic insulation (see Chapter 21) coupled with large attic vents for natural ventilation. You save the cost of a fan plus savings on its maintenance, service, and operating bills.

If a fan is installed at the end of the attic it should be located so that it does not discharge against the prevailing winds, as far away as possible from bedrooms, and it should not blast air close to a neighbor's bedrooms.

Other Locations Besides The Attic

Every fan need not be located in the attic. An attic may be too shallow or special problems may rule it out. Then another location may be possible, in the garage or breezeway, for example, or at the basement ceiling, with a floor opening for pulling air out of the house. But choose a central location, the main requirement for unrestricted air flow through all rooms.

Safety Precautions

Regardless of the kind of installation, provision should be made for closing off the fan-intake opening automatically in case of fire. A fusible safety link that melts at a predetermined temperature is used for this purpose. It is wired so that it will also turn off the fan motor at the same time. Your local building code may require one.

Another safety measure is an automatic thermal overload switch on the fan motor to protect against overheating. This is additional fire protection and also safeguards the motor against an overload.

Noise Control and Proper Installation

A noisy fan can drive you out of your mind. Quiet operation depends on the fan itself and how well it is installed. The larger the fan diameter the better for quiet operation, simply because larger fans operate at slower speeds. A 36-inch fan, for example, must run at about 425 rpm (revolutions per minute) to remove the same quantity of air as a larger 42-inch fan running at only 270 rpm. Naturally, the slower the speed, the less noise.

The fan should be belt-driven (like an automobile fan belt and the blower of a good heating furnace), and contain sealed "lifetime lubricated" ball bearings for motor and shaft. An all-welded steel frame will reduce vibration. The electric motor should be cushion-mounted. A rubber gasket should be installed between the fan and the house frame to prevent vibration from air turbulance. These are not luxury features; they are automatically provided with a good fan and are essential for satisfactory operation.

Inlet and Outlet Openings

The size of the intake and outlet openings is crucial. If too small, they choke off air flow, overload the fan, and cause noisy operation. Minimum opening sizes required vary with fan size and are given in manufacturers' literature. A good rule is to make the openings large enough so that the air-flow speed through them does not exceed 750 to 1000 feet per minute (fpm). Divide the fan's capacity in cfm by the maximum velocity desired (fpm), and you will get the minimum net area in square feet required for the intake and outlet openings.

Say your fan, for example, has a capacity of 15,000 cfm, and to be assured of quiet operation you desire no more air velocity than 750 fpm. The net intake-opening area needed is then 20 square feet (15,000 divided by 750). Twenty square feet of net outlet area is also needed but this can be divided between two or more separate outlets in the attic.

The term *net free area* is emphasized because the louvers and screening in a vent cut down the effective area through which air can pass. The over-all size of the opening therefore must be increased in size accordingly. Sometimes, in fact, an attic vent must be at least twice the required net opening size because it may have only 50 per cent free area.

Wood-louver openings with screening usually offer only 40 to 50 per cent of their size in net free area. A wood louver 4×4 feet (16 square feet), will give no more than 8 square feet of free area (50 per cent, or one-half of 16). Putting it another way: to get the over-all size required for a wood opening, multiply the net free area required by two.

Thus, if you need 20 square feet of net free area and install a woodlouver vent, the over-all vent size should be 40 square feet (2 times 20), and 50 square feet if it gives only 40 per cent free area. The typical metal louver gives 50 to 75 per cent net free area, hence a smaller over-all opening may be required with a metal louver than with a wood one.

These free-opening figures are based on vents with ½-inch hardwarecloth screening. The exact size louver and free opening required will depend on the specific fan and kind of vents you use. Specific information on each should be provided with the fan you get and the manufacturer's literature. The usual shutter opening provided with a fan is ordinarily specified by the manufacturer based on 90 per cent free air opening. It is best to use the matched shutter made for a particular fan.

Fan Controls

The simplest and cheapest control is an on-off switch. Additional features are also available. Two-speed fan motors are becoming increasingly popular. In the evening after a hot day you turn the fan on full speed to get rid of heat as quickly as possible. Later it can be slowed down to the quieter low-speed setting for a gentle air flow while you sleep.

The same procedure, of course, can be followed during the day, using high speed to cool down the house fast, low speed to keep it that way (unless it is a sweltering hot day, of course, when only air conditioning or quick retreat to a mountain resort will do much good).

You may want the fan blowing part of the night but not all night long. A special time switch does this. You set it in advance for as long as 12 hours so that the fan will cut off any time later. There are also thermostats that automatically turn a fan on or off according to a preset temperature. The thermostat can be located in the house so that the fan automatically starts up whenever the temperature at night exceeds, say, 80 degrees; or in the attic to exhaust hot air when the attic heat exceeds a predetermined temperature.

Costs

Manufacturers say that fan costs average from $125 to $150 for most houses. This is the nationwide average for the fan alone, excluding its installation—another $35 to $75 at least. A fan for a small house can be had for less than $100, and at the other end of the scale up to $250 to $300 for a large house.

On top of this the installation cost can push total charges as high as $350 to $400. If you have to spend this much, don't compromise and save a few dollars on a too-small unit. You'll be sorry later. (At this point it can pay to consider central air conditioning, or at least individual room units on the order of $200 apiece.) Fan operating cost is usually no more than $3 to $5 a month, based on 10 hours average operation a day.

Operating an Attic Fan

Be sure that at least one door or window in the house is open before starting up the fan (in a two-story house, one on the lower floor). Otherwise soot from a fireplace chimney could be pulled into the house (with no other route open for air entry). Window and door openings must be regulated for good cooling effect. Doors and windows should be shut in rooms where ventilation is not wanted. Conversely, an open window plus an open interior door are necessary in any room that you wish cooled.

No attic fan will choose the rooms it will cool. It simply pulls up all the air from inside the house, and replacement air is pulled in from outdoors through the nearest open windows. To ventilate the whole house speedily, open all windows at least halfway. To cool the downstairs in the evening, close upstairs windows and leave open only the windows and doors in the rooms being occupied. For the best breeze through bedrooms at night, open windows in the bedrooms only and close all others. Of course, severe drafts should be avoided, especially with children. A little experimenting will soon tell you which windows should be open or closed to achieve the best cooling.

Kitchen Exhaust Fans

As with an attic fan, the prime considerations are adequate capacity (based on kitchen size), location, and quiet operation. The fan should provide a complete air change in the kitchen every three to four minutes. A three-minute air change is best in small kitchens, and the absolute minimum-size fan recommended is one with a capacity of 300 cfm. Additional facts on kitchen fans are given in Chapter 11.

Bathroom Exhaust Fans

A bathroom fan, though not essential in all houses, can be a blessing for removing steam and moisture. It can be located nearly anywhere in the bathroom, but try for a ceiling location near the shower. Its capacity should be at least 100 cfm. Models are available with a built-in light and/or an electric heater for extra warmth when you step out of the bath.

Each should operate independently of the other so that in warm weather you can turn on the fan without the heat. A red light should be included to tell you when the fan is on. Sometimes the fan is wired to the main light switch so both the fan and light go on and off simultaneously. A separate switch for each is better. Safety is obviously important, too, to eliminate electrical hazards. Switches should be beyond arm reach of tub and shower. And make sure the electrician installs a "waterproof" job.

Chapter 26

Central Air Conditioning

Air conditioning is not cheap but it can be less expensive than many people think. It can be installed in old houses with excellent results, as well as in new houses. Operating costs are surprisingly low, less per summer than central heat in the North and not much more in the South.

As my family found out to its delight, it is decidedly worthwhile in a northern climate not only for welcome coolness during hot weather, but also for relief from sweltering humidity. There are other compelling advantages, too. If you can afford the cost, it definitely should be considered for all but the coolest climates.

This chapter gives information on costs and how to reduce them to a minimum; on choosing the right system for different kinds of houses; avoiding the most common errors made with air conditioning; and it also deals with certain misconceptions that should be cleared up about home air conditioning.

Benefits of Air Conditioning

Sheer relief from hot summer heat is the principal advantage. But this is only part of the story. By lowering the indoor humidity in summer, air conditioning banishes mildew and sogginess (permitting salt shakers to flow freely, among other things).

Tests show that it filters out much of the pollen in the air, making the house a haven for hay fever, asthma, and other allergy sufferers. It is a boon for people with weak hearts and a variety of other ailments made worse by summer heat and humidity. Doctors prescribe it for such patients (and then its cost is tax deductible). It means no more heat rash, particularly among infants, and contrary to popular belief, fewer head colds in summer.

A common objection to air conditioning is the assumption that it makes the air cold and clammy. This stems from bad experiences in overchilled restaurants and movies, and from walking into an air-conditioned store and being hit with a shock wave of cold air.

Things are different in houses. For one thing, most movies, restaurants, and stores are deliberately overchilled, particularly the very first ones that were air-conditioned. Present day equipment has been greatly improved and overchilling is no longer a problem. For another, air conditioning in a house is set to the exact temperature and humidity a family desires; it need not be set to an extremely low temperature just to be sure that all the numerous occupants will be sufficiently cool.

What about "thermal shock," the strain on the body experienced when you go from 95-degree heat into an air-conditioned house, or out again? This is not damaging to people in good health, according to exhaustive research at the University of Illinois College of Medicine. It is no more damaging than stepping out of a 70-degree house in winter into the cold 30-degree outdoors—a 40-degree drop.

A sudden, sharp change in temperature and humidity may be distressing to people with weak hearts. Such people should avoid abrupt temperature changes. In an air-conditioned house they could have the entrance foyer set at a temperature about halfway between indoors and out as a sort of decompression chamber. Better still, they should avoid excessive heat and humidity, and during heat waves stay indoors with air conditioning. not expose themselves to the harshly debilitating effects of the hot humid outdoors.

"Air-conditioning a Tough Old House"

Here is what my family and I learned about air conditioning from first-hand experience. Like many women, my wife had mixed feelings about it for our house. She is one of its biggest boosters now because of certain unexpected benefits plus the highly salutary effects it has on our small children.

My house is a 67-year-old Victorian structure that is one of the toughest kinds of houses in which to install air conditioning. How the job was done is a good example of the toughest problems nearly anyone could encounter and what to do about them.

We decided on central air conditioning because we needed a new heating plant. Our ancient furnace was in the last stage of old age, and its fuel appetite was astronomical. This was the time to get air conditioning, too, a combination heating-cooling system rather than just a new furnace. The extra cost for installing the air-conditioning part would be considerably less, compared with the cost of installing a central air conditioner later by itself.

Another element that tipped the scale in favor of air conditioning was that we needed new window screens for most of our 28 windows. They would not be needed with air conditioning. This represented a $250 saving which could be applied against air-conditioning cost. A few screens are left on windows so we may enjoy the breeze on nice days.

Biggest Installation Problem

In most houses the installation of ductwork from the basement to the second floor is the hardest part of the job. We could use the old, existing heating ducts but there weren't enough of them. Ductwork generally accounts for the biggest portion of installation and labor expense in home air conditioning, and it is crucial for good heating and cooling.

I made a room-by-room inspection with the air-conditioning contractor, looking for the best places to run new ducts up from the basement inside of existing interior walls. For one room upstairs, an interior duct was impossible. The alternative was a vertical 4×12-inch duct tucked into an open corner of the living room and boxed in. It is hardly noticed today.

Zone Control

We got a two-zone temperature-control system, a thermostat upstairs and another one downstairs. This cost about $150 over the cost of a single thermostat. It enables us to keep each level of the house as warm or cool as we want, independent of the other level. This is a particular blessing. We found, for example, that the second floor requires more cooling in summer than the first floor (because of the attic above).

On mildly warm summer days, in fact, we found that cooling is often needed only for the second floor. Enough cool air floats down the stairwell to keep the first-floor rooms comfortable. In winter, the reverse is true. Thus, the zone controls help reduce operating cost as well as providing balanced air temperature throughout the house.

Equipment Size and Type

The house required a 2.6-ton air conditioner. This means capacity equivalent to the cooling effect given off by 2.6 tons of ice. At first the contractor specified a larger, 3-ton size. We discussed reducing the summer heat load in the house by adding special insulation (noted later) to the attic and leaving most of the storm windows on all summer long (thus reducing outside air-heat flow into the house through the glass).

This permitted the use of the next size smaller air conditioner at less cost; it has proved more than ample for the entire house on the hottest, most humid days. It automatically cools and dehumidifies roughly 1750 square feet of floor area on two levels—eight rooms and one and a half bathrooms. This works out to 1 ton of air conditioning per 673 square feet of floor area, about par for the course for a well-insulated, two-story old house in a northern climate.

An air-cooled unit was chosen since it does not require a steady supply of water to carry away the heat removed from the house. It works like a large window air conditioner. Air is drawn in over the hot refrigeration coils (called the condenser), cools them like the air breeze through a car radiator, and is ejected back outdoors.

Actually, the air conditioner is split into two sections. The part containing the refrigeration mechanism is located outside under a porch where it has free access to outside air. It is connected by copper refrigeration pipes to the cooling coil section located in the basement on top of the furnace. This is where the house air is actually cooled and dried.

This kind of air-cooled split system is the most popular kind of central air conditioning for houses today and the easiest and usually the most economical to install in old houses (if you have warm-air heat and can utilize all or most of your present ducts).

Additional savings result because the cooling coil could be matched to the furnace and installed at the same time as the new furnace. Only one blower and blower motor are needed for circulating air to the house the year around, and only one filter and one set of ducts are needed.

Two Unexpected Troubles

Noisy operation plagued us at first. Like a refrigerator, even the best equipment generates some noise. The noise, however, comes almost entirely from the refrigerating mechanism outside. We do not hear it inside. But our closest neighbors did, since the unit is not far from their bedroom windows. This was a threat to peaceful coexistence. We licked it by putting up a short, 4-foot-high wooden noise "fence," plus a few shrubs, between the unit and their house.

The second trouble confronted me when I entered the basement a week after the system had been started up for the first time. It was during a wave of hot and muggy weather. I saw to my distress a wide pool of water over much of the basement floor. This represented the literally dozens of gallons of moisture (humidity) removed from the house air at the cooling unit. It was not draining away properly.

The drain pipe fed into a drain hole in the basement floor and had been hooked up this way. But I did not know that the floor drain was simply a small hole under the floor capable of absorbing only a small quantity of water at one time. Both the air-conditioning contractor and I had thought it connected to a pipe drain under the house. Because it did not, a new drain system had to be installed. This is mentioned because even when you have an air-cooled system a drain must be installed to carry off the humidity moisture removed from the house air.

Overcoming Common Pitfalls

Two of the most widespread obstacles to air conditioning in old houses are overloaded wiring and no thermal insulation. Without the first, air conditioning is impossible; without the second, it is unwise. Our house previously had been rewired with a 100-ampere, 220-volt main electric board, the minimum size recommended today. This handles the central air conditioner without flinching.

After buying the house I had insulation blown into the exterior walls for heating comfort and lower fuel bills. The attic floor had been previously insulated with 3½-inch mineral wool batts.

I went a step farther in the attic, since roof heat seeping down into a house is one of the biggest single entry routes of summer heat. Following the advice in the insulation chapter, I had sheets of aluminum foil stapled under the roof beams at the attic ceiling. This sharply reduces the amount of roof heat that is normally re-radiated from the underside of the roof down to the attic ceiling and then into the bedrooms. The foil bounces the radiant heat back.

At the same time large aluminum vents were installed at the gable peak at each end of the attic. These are imperative not only to let outside air wash in and blow away the accumulated heat in the attic, but also to prevent condensation in winter.

Because of the foil cover over the attic interior and the new vents, I found that the attic is much cooler in summer than it formerly was. Without these heat controls and without insulation the house would have required a larger and more expensive 5-ton air conditioner and operating costs would be considerably higher.

What About Costs?

It should be firmly emphasized here that air-conditioning cost depends primarily on the house, on how much ductwork and installation labor are required, and, of course, on the contractor's know-how plus competition from other contractors. Cost of my job (in 1959) for central air conditioning plus new heating was $2372. The new furnace and its installation account for about 25 per cent of this. An optional air purifier and winter humidifier were installed for an additional $300. Here is the breakdown:

2.6 ton air conditioner	$824.
New furnace	272.
Installation of equipment, new ducts, labor, cost of zone temperature controls and their installation	1096.
Wiring	105.
Carpentry (for installing new ducts)	75.
Total	$2372.
Optional air purifier and winter humidifier	$300.

A similar air-conditioning system without new heating in a two-story house like mine normally will cost between $1500 and $1850, depending on the installation labor required; less for a one-story house.

The cost of adding central air conditioning to smaller existing houses will range from $1500 to under $1000, depending again on the house. Conversely, the cost is more in larger houses, but the larger the house the less the cost per square foot of house. Costs are 10 to 20 per cent lower in new additions to a house and in new houses, compared with installing air conditioning in existing houses.

Operating Costs

Our operating costs come to only $24 a month, on the average, or a total of $72 for a three-month cooling season. This surprised me, because on the hottest days the unit was running nearly 24 hours a day, and also because we have comparatively high electric rates where we live (2.3¢ per kwh).

We formerly had a ¾-horsepower window air conditioner upstairs, and it alone cost from $20 to $25 a summer to operate. We get our whole house air-conditioned for roughly $50 more each summer than we formerly spent to air-condition just one room.

Our winter fuel bills used to average approximately $285 a winter with the old furnace, over $300 before the house was insulated. The new furnace shaves this by about 30 per cent, cutting cost to around $200 a winter. Thus total operating cost for heating and air-conditioning my 1750-square-foot old house with its high ceilings will average around $270 a year, or under $23 a month—less than I formerly paid for heating alone.

Operating Costs in Other Parts of the Country

Operating costs to air-condition a typical 1200 to 1500-square-foot house in the North will average about $50 a *summer,* up to $100 to $125 a *summer* in the South, based on average national electrical rates of 2¢ per

These two Midwestern houses are completely air conditioned for less than $75 a summer. They are two of 70 test houses which showed that the average house can be heated and cooled nearly anywhere in the country for no more than $150 a year, per 1200 square feet of living area. Insulation and other design features, such as window shading, must conform to standards noted in text.

Owens-Corning Fiberglas.

kwh. It breaks down to an average of $17 per month for three month's use in the North, an average of $23 a month for five and a half months in the South, Southwest, and hot areas of Southern California.

Costs for a particular family will obviously vary up or down from these figures depending on the house size and design, your family's living hab-

	CENTRAL AIR CONDITIONING		OPERATING COST	
	Approx. elec. rate for cooling ¢ per kw-hr	Approx. hours of operation per summer	Cost per ton of cooling capacity, per summer	Average total cost for typical 1200 sq. ft. houses (2 tons)
Akron, Ohio	.0185 cents	600	$18 per ton per summer	$36
Charlotte, N. C.	.02	1000	31.40	62
Chicago, Ill.	.025	500	18	36
Corpus Christi, Texas	.02	3500	53	100
Denver, Colo.	.02	1000	25	50
Detroit, Mich.	.02	500	12	24
Ft. Worth, Tex.	.02	1400	50	100
Kansas City, Mo.	.025	900	33	66
Madison, Wis.	.023	300	21	42
New York, N.Y.	.021	500	21	42
Okla. City, Okla.	.021	1000	32	64
Salt Lake City, Utah	.0155	750	11.50	23
Phila., Pa.	.018	800	20	40
San Francisco, Calif.	.0128	1000	30	60
St. Louis, Mo.	.02	1000	28	56
Tampa, Fla.	.015	1750	30	60
Tucson, Ariz.	.0165	2200	65	125
Long Island, N.Y.	.02	750	25	50

Chart gives average operating costs for central air conditioning for random cities. To estimate costs if your city is unlisted, choose closest city and adjust according to your local electrical rate.

The American Home.

its, and whether electricity rates are higher or lower than average. You can normally count on costs being reasonably close to these just given. In other words, costs in the North for a 2500-square-foot house, two-thirds larger than a 1500-square-foot house, should run about $85 to $90 a summer with 2¢ electricity.

Operating costs are even lower in houses thoroughly insulated and well-shaded from the sun. This is borne out by the 70 guinea-pig houses, noted in Chapter 21, which showed that a typical 1200-square-foot house can be completely heated and air-conditioned the year around nearly anywhere in the country for no more than $150 a year.

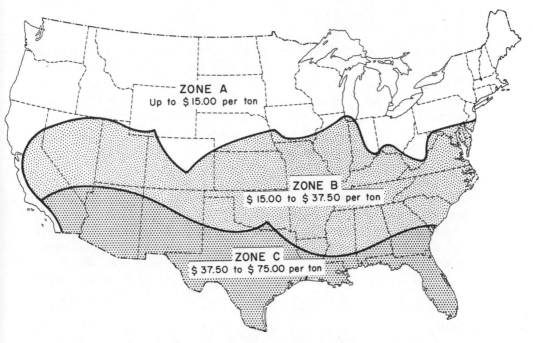

Map gives approximate operating costs for central air conditioning for a complete summer, based on an electrical rate of 1½¢ per kilowatt hour. Your exact cost will vary according to your particular power rate, equipment quality, and house design.
Carrier Corp.

Central Air Conditioning vs. Room Coolers

I might have used four or five individual room coolers for my house. I did not, chiefly because they shut out window light and are less efficient than one large unit, therefore cost more to operate than a central unit for the same amount of house.

If I had installed them in the walls under windows, the cost of the entire job, including new wiring for each, would have brought the total cost almost up to the cost of complete central air conditioning. And regardless of where they are installed they detract from the inside and outside appearance of a house.

On the other hand, one or two room coolers can be perfectly satisfactory for partial air conditioning or for a new addition. A through-the-wall installation is obviously neater than in a window, as well as not obstructing window light. Most models can be installed either flush with the interior wall surface or flush with the outside, but check this according to your requirements. (More on room air conditioners in the next chapter.)

Choosing a Central System

If you have warm-air heat the heating ducts generally can be utilized for cooling too. This facilitates the easiest and least expensive air-conditioning installation. A conventional air conditioner is hooked up with the furnace so that cool air is provided through the same ducts in summer, warm air in winter. Best bet, usually, is an air-cooled split system, as described for my house, with the refrigerating compressor unit located just outside the house. This is sometimes called a remote compressor system. Additional ductwork may be required.

If you have hot-water heat, electric heat, or no central heat a separate central air conditioner is the solution. It operates independently of the heating system. Air ducts will be needed, but they are simpler and less expensive to install than when needed for both heating and cooling. In a one-story house, for example, they can be installed between the basement ceiling beams with discharge outlets in the floor to each room. Without a basement they can be built-in under the ceiling of a central hall with short

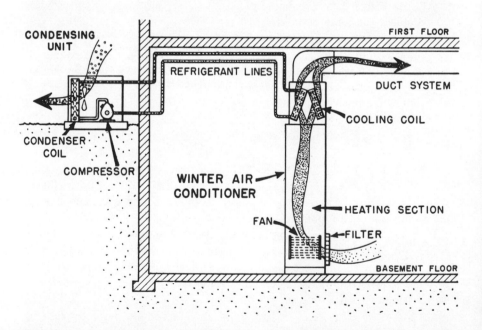

Diagram shows the most common kind of central air conditioning for houses. Cooling-coil section is installed on top of furnace inside the house and connected by refrigerant pipes to the compressor section located outside (for access to outdoor air). It is an air-cooled system, thus no water is required for operation. Same system can be employed in nonbasement houses with the cooling coil located with the furnace. The ducts used for winter heating are also used for summer cooling.

stub duct connections to the rooms around. This last is much better than having cool-air ducts in the attic (which require expensive insulation).

Installing new ducts in a two-story or split-level house can be vastly simplified by the use of a special new "small-duct" system. Made by such firms as the Jet-Heet Co. of Englewood, N.J., this system uses flexible 3-inch ducts that are snaked through walls almost as easily as wiring conduit. It is available for the installation of heating or cooling or both and for new houses as well as old ones.

There is also what is called *chilled-water air conditioning,* long used in big building air conditioning. Cooling is combined with hot-water heating. The same pipes used to distribute hot water in winter are used to distribute chilled water for summer cooling. The water is supplied to special heating-cooling coils encased in small cabinets, instead of radiators, in each room.

Each cabinet contains a filter and small blower. Air from the room is drawn into the cabinet, filtered, cooled, and dehumidified, then discharged back into the room. In summer, the water pumped to the coils is chilled by a refrigerating mechanism (water chiller) located next to the boiler. In winter, hot water from the boiler is pumped through the system to each room cabinet, and the room air drawn into each cabinet is filtered and heated.

A chilled-water system is expensive, however, about 20 to 25 per cent more costly than comparable air conditioning with ducts—its main drawback. In addition, it does not lend itself easily to air-conditioning an existing house simply because all the supply pipes inside walls would have to be insulated first (to avoid sweating in summer).

Chilled water is chiefly for new houses and new additions to existing

Outdoor compressor section of the air-conditioning system should be close to the interior equipment to keep down connection costs, and located where its operating noise will not annoy neighbors.
Carrier Corp.

houses when new heating and cooling are also required. Its biggest advantages are that it eliminates ducts, using pipes instead, and the individual room units permit individual control of the temperature and humidity in each room (but such control must be specified).

Attic Air Conditioners

These are widely sold for existing houses because they require a minimum of installation work and therefore come with temptingly low price tags. By installing the equipment and the ducts in the attic, the dealer avoids the usual troubles of breaking into walls. Air is discharged down into each room through discharge outlets in the ceiling.

But beware here. Though seemingly inexpensive, the troubles that can result are intolerable. Equipment in the attic requires an exceedingly careful installation to prevent constant noise and vibration overhead and not all dealers take the time and trouble to do it properly. Even when they do, the equipment should be located as far away as possible from bedrooms if you value your sleep. Servicing the equipment also may be difficult.

Above all, remember that the attic will be crowded with ducts and therefore hardly useable again for storage or any other purpose. An attic unit is recommended only if the attic is too low for other uses, and if only the blower-cooling section of the equipment is located in the attic, and the noisier compressor section located outdoors. Because of attic heat, the equipment as well as the ducts should be very well insulated. The equipment cover should be lined with insulation in the factory—look for this. If omitted the dealer should provide it.

Water-cooled Equipment—Air-cooled vs. Water-cooled Units

Nearly all air-conditioning units, including the heat pump, require either outdoor air (like a window cooler) or a supply of running water to carry off their heat. The air-cooled kind is better, especially if you live where water is scarce or expensive. It not only eliminates the extra operating cost for water used, but it also requires less service and upkeep.

The water-cooled kind, however, is a little cheaper. It is simply hooked up to a supply of water, which runs through the unit to pick up the heat removed from the house and carry it away. Much water is continually used and this is why operation can get expensive. A water-cooled model is a good bet only if you have plenty of cheap water available, an inexhaustible well, or your own private mountain lake.

Water-cooled operation, by the way, should not be confused with chilled-water air conditioning. A water-cooled unit simply uses water for removing the heat accumulated inside the mechanism. The unit itself may supply its cooling to the house via cool-air ducts or chilled-water pipes.

The Central Heat Pump

Most year-round central air conditioning equipment is electrically powered for cooling. The heating side is designed to burn either gas or oil fuel. There is also the central heat pump. Like a room-unit heat pump, it heats in winter and cools in summer by means of electricity only. Its mechanism is a standard refrigerating compressor unit, much the same as a conventional air conditioner. In summer, heat is wrung out of the house air and discharged outdoors. In winter, the cycle is reversed and heat from outdoor air (or water) is pumped indoors.

A heat pump does away with the need for oil or gas fuel, its biggest feature. But it is equivalent to having electric heat in winter. Thus, it is recommended in a cold climate only if your electric power rate is as low as it should be for conventional electric heat, no higher than 1¢ to 1.5¢ per kilowatt hour. A low electric rate is less important in the South.

With a heat pump, a house also should be insulated and weather stripped to the hilt, as with straight electric heat. Summer operating costs for cooling with a heat pump are roughly the same as they are for conventional electric air conditioning.

The heat pump, though heralded as the air conditioner of the future, is an intricate mechanism and comparatively new. Even the best brands on the market are having their birth pains (with homeowners in many cases serving as guinea pigs). The best experiences with them are in the South where your central heat demands in winter are not severe.

But even there I would not recommend a heat pump unless you thoroughly check among homeowners in your area who have the particular brand you may get, and have used it for a couple of years with no trouble. The dealer should be able to give you the names of users. If he cannot or will not, beware. And don't accept a little-known brand.

Buying Air Conditioning

Regardless of the kind of air conditioning or heat pump you choose, check on the contractor above all. This is all-important, as the best equipment can go haywire if it is not properly installed. The contractor should be experienced in home cooling and be able to show you successful systems he has installed in other houses. As a rule, the most competent contractors tend to be those who are franchised dealers of big-name manufacturers (such as Carrier, York, G.E., Lennox, and Westinghouse) and have held their franchises for several years at least.

Get bids from two to three dealers. Don't fall for the lowest bid price or for a flat installation charge.

Make sure that the dealer you select is providing all the equipment, accessories, and ductwork that the others specified.

You sometimes can save money if you subcontract the wiring and piping required for the air conditioner. The air-conditioning contractor usually provides the equipment, its installation, and the ductwork. He normally subcontracts other work required such as wiring and piping and you are charged (justifiably) an additional markup for his handling of these subcontracts, as with other kinds of home-improvement work. Hiring your own "subs" can save you the markup expense.

The equipment you get should carry the certification seal of the Air Conditioning and Refrigeration Institute (ARI). Equipment without this certification generally should be turned down.

How Much Cooling Capacity

This should be given in Btu's per hour. One ton of cooling is equivalent to 12,000 Btu's per hour. In general, one-story houses require 1 ton of cooling capacity for every 500 to 600 square feet of air-conditioned area. A 1000- to 1200-square-foot house therefore would require a 2-ton system. Two-story houses require less capacity per square foot; about 1 ton for every 600 to 700 square feet of floor area. If your house is very well insulated and designed for low-cost cooling, only 1 ton of capacity may be needed for every 700 to 800 square feet of floor area.

How Cool Inside?

The cooling system should be guaranteed to maintain the house interior at 75 degrees and 50 per cent relative humidity during the hottest summer weather where you live. Thus, the equipment should be capable of lowering the house temperature by 20 degrees in cities like New York and Chicago where the highest summer temperature (called outside design temperature) is 95 degrees; and 30 degrees if you live in Phoenix, Arizona, say, where outside temperatures hit 105 degrees.

An air-conditioning dealer may casually say that 80 degrees inside is all you need and that is all he guarantees. Or that an air-conditioning system should be designed to reduce the indoor temperatures by 10 to 15 degrees below outdoors and that's all. This is nonsense, even though mistakenly believed by some air-conditioning people (and some doctors).

Nearly all humans require 75 degrees and 50 per cent relative humidity indoors for comfort in summer, give or take a degree or two. This is the temperature and humidity people require for maximum comfort in summer in offices, factories, and homes. It is borne out by exhaustive research sponsored by the American Society of Heating and Air-Conditioning Engineers. It is the condition required indoors regardless of what the outdoor temperature may be. The body has no built-in radar telling it what is going on outdoors when you are indoors.

Surveys show that most families set their cooling thermostats at from 73 to 77 degrees in summer. Some people are unusual and like their houses as cool as 70 degrees, others as warm as 80 degrees. They set the thermostat up or down until the temperature and humidity are comfortable and these are the settings that result.

If your system is designed to maintain 75 degrees indoors, rather than 80, it is assurance that there always will be capacity to keep you comfortable in the hottest weather. If you like it really cool, plan for extra capacity; this may call for a larger unit.

Chapter 27

Buying a Room Air Conditioner

First, look for a NEMA (National Electrical Manufacturers Association) certification seal. This seal is attached to certified units by the manufacturer. It certifies that the unit's cooling capacity (in Btu's per hour) is up to par, based on stiff industry standards. If you do not see this seal, don't buy. Actually, close to 90 per cent of all room coolers made are so certified.

But a certification seal assures you only that the unit will deliver its rated cooling capacity. You also want a unit large enough for a particular room, one that is quiet, and assurance of service when necessary.

The size of the unit required can be determined accurately only by computing the "heat gain" of the room it will cool. Forms for easily computing this can be obtained from any good room-unit dealer and you can figure it yourself. Or send 10¢ to the Air-Conditioning and Refrigeration Institute, 1346 Connecticut Ave., N.W., Washington 6, D.C., for their standard room air conditioner heat-gain computation form. The computation will tell you how much cooling capacity is needed for a room in Btu's per hour of cooling capacity. Then you choose a room cooler with a capacity equal to or slightly higher than required.

Some brands are noisier than others, and what's more the noise characteristic of a particular brand may vary from good to bad or back again with annual changes in manufacturers' models. A neighbor's 1961 model of Brand A may be nice and quiet, but a later model of the same brand may have turned noisy. You have to listen to models in a showroom, compare one against the other, and listen hard for the quietest ones. Listen with the unit turned on to "cooling," not to its "fan" setting only.

Check *Consumer Reports* and *Consumers' Bulletin* for their latest ratings. Each publishes test data and recommendations on room air conditioners every year or two.

Complaints about poor service are most common with units bought from discount houses or ordinary appliance dealers who have no facilities for service. You can save money, to be sure, when you buy from a discount house, but find out first what kind of service guarantee you get. It's wiser to buy from an air-conditioning dealer who has his own service department. You may pay a little more but the extra money is good insurance for getting service.

Will You Need New Wiring?

As a rule a unit with a capacity of less than 8500 Btu's can be plugged into an ordinary 115-volt outlet. Exactly how much current does the unit draw? It may draw only 7 amperes, which is low, or as much as 15 amperes, which will probably blow fuses, depending on your wiring strength. If in doubt, choose one of the special 7-ampere models, which are most likely to run off an ordinary electric outlet. This assumes that it is a 115-volt model.

There are also 240-volt models which are more efficient, but almost always require a new 240-volt electric line for the air conditioner. Some dealers have special plug-in devices that tell whether or not your wiring will take a room cooler. Ask about this. If you need a new wiring line, it generally costs about $25 to $50.

Installation

There are models that are set in windows, through-the-wall types, and portable units. The usual window model is objectionable because of unsightliness and because it obstructs light entry. It usually requires a window at least 27 inches wide. Special models are available for casement windows. Measure your window to be sure the unit will fit.

The through-the-wall installation costs a little more because the wall must be opened up. But it is far neater, better-looking, especially in a new room or new addition.

The portable unit is designed to be lifted in and out of windows and switched from one room to another as desired. But once it is in place most people don't bother moving it. Because it has small capacity and can't match the cooling power of a permanent model, it is not recommended, unless you take it with you in summer to your vacation place.

Special Features

Other points to look for:

1. Thermostatic control. Is there a control to automatically turn the cooling on and off, according to your preset temperature requirement? Some units lack this control; you turn the unit on and off by hand (a big nuisance particularly at night). Some have limited control, others have a broad range of settings.

2. Good air distribution. Look for adjustable louvers that can aim the air in various directions over the head of people nearby. Some units have louvers that can be adjusted up or down (for vertical loft) or side-to-side control, some one or the other, and some neither. Try for both, or at least adjustable louvers that aim the air up or down.

3. Convenient controls. They should be clearly marked, easy to work, and easy to reach (not so far back that they are blocked by window shades or so hidden you search for them). Some are so complicated they are a buyer's nightmare. Try them out before buying.

4. Ventilation. A good unit can ventilate a room while it is also cooling and also without cooling (for winter use). This is done by a special control which pulls in fresh outdoor air. Other units have an exhaust feature which pumps out stale or smoky room air (but not always possible at the same time the unit is cooling). Look for one or the other, a feature that will be highly appreciated.

5. Accessible filters. Is the filter easy to remove, clean, and replace? Filters are either replaceable glass wool or permanent metal mesh or plastic. Both are roughly equal in filtering ability, but even the permanent kind has to be removed and cleaned periodically. If the replaceable kind is used, find out the cost of new ones.

6. Rustproof construction. Rust and corrosion are the biggest enemies of a room cooler. Whether a unit lasts only six or seven years or twice that time depends chiefly on its resistance to metal corrosion. Better units contain metal parts of aluminum or galvanized steel, usually protected by a baked-on enamel finish. Sometimes it is called "bonderized" paint. Run a fingernail over the cabinet; you should not be able to scratch the paint.

Consult the manufacturer's specifications, usually tagged to the unit, for mention of rustproof construction. Look inside the cabinet, especially the rear end, which will stick outside exposed to the weather, for the silvery glint of aluminum or galvanized steel.

Chapter 28

Dry Air in Houses and What to Do About It

Dry air in houses can cause great distress in winter. It makes your nose and throat hurt and may cause excessively dry skin. Furniture loosens and cracks at the joints, book bindings suffer, and moisture is drained out of practically everything in the house.

It occurs because the outside air is naturally dry in winter. Its relative humidity is low. The same air in a house is warmed up by the heating system, becoming even drier than outside. The relative humidity indoors is thinned out to as low as 5 or 10 per cent, which is quite low. (The average humidity in the Sahara Desert, one of the driest places on earth—outside of centrally heated houses—averages about 22 per cent the year around.)

Relative humidity is the amount of moisture in the air compared with the amount of moisture the same air could hold if it were 100 per cent saturated with moisture. Air at a relative humidity of 20 per cent contains 20 per cent of the total moisture it could hold if it were 100 per cent saturated with moisture.

As a rule, most people require a relative humidity in winter of 20 to 35 per cent for comfort. Some doctors say as high as 45 per cent, but a humidity level that high is virtually impossible to maintain inside houses in winter without making the structure absolutely leakproof.

Things get too dry for comfort when the relative humidity falls below about 20 per cent, particularly if your nose and throat are sensitive. If you think you suffer from dryness you can be sure by checking on your relative humidity. This is done with an instrument called a hygrometer. Obtain a good one, as there are many cheap ones on the market which are notoriously inaccurate. The best kind is one with a human hair element, which will cost about $15 to $20. Cheaper ones (without a hair element) are available for as little as $2, but they are a waste of money.

Buying a Humidifier

This device introduces moisture into the house to raise your relative humidity. Certain kinds are designed to moisten the air of an entire house while others are smaller and good only for single rooms.

Incidentally, you may already have a humidifier on your furnace and still suffer from dry air. This is because the usual small humidifier that ordinarily comes attached to a furnace is not very good. It is much too small in capacity, hence cannot provide more than a minimal amount of moisture. It is also unreliable because it clogs up quickly with impurities found in nearly all water and ceases functioning. With one of these, make sure it is clean and working, and then clean it regularly to keep it working. The chances are, however, that you will need a new and better humidifier.

What Size Humidifier?

Consider the kind for a whole house. You can install one regardless of whether you have warm-air, hot-water, or any other kind of heat. The first and most important step is to determine the size needed, a humidifier capable of providing adequate moisture. This depends on the size of your house, the house construction, and the lowest outdoor temperatures you experience in winter.

The larger the house and the colder your winter climate, the larger the humidifier needed. An old house of loose construction (leaky windows

CONSTRUCTION CHARACTERISTIC TABLE

HOME VOLUME CU. FEET	OUTSIDE TEMP. F	RELATIVE HUMIDITY	MOISTURE REQUIRED (lb./hr.) FOR		
			LOOSE	AVERAGE	TIGHT
8,000	—10	20	2.14	0.85	0.44
	0	25	2.52	1.00	0.50
	10	30	2.98	1.18	0.60
	20	35	3.25	1.29	0.65
	30	35	2.79	1.11	0.56
10,000	—10	20	2.66	1.08	0.54
	0	25	3.05	1.25	0.63
	10	30	3.70	1.50	0.75
	20	35	4.06	1.63	0.81
	30	35	3.48	1.42	0.70
12,000	—10	20	3.28	1.29	0.65
	0	25	3.74	1.50	0.75
	10	30	4.47	1.79	0.89
	20	35	4.66	1.87	0.93
	30	35	4.58	1.68	0.85
14,000	—10	20	3.74	1.39	0.73
	0	25	4.46	1.66	0.82
	10	30	5.20	2.08	1.04
	20	35	5.68	2.29	1.14
	30	35	4.90	1.82	1.00

What size humidifier for your house? 1. Compute the air volume of the house, excluding garage, basement, attic, other nonliving space. Total volume equals floor area in square feet of all rooms multiplied by ceiling height. Thus, a 1000-square-foot house with an 8-foot ceiling has 8000 cubic feet of volume (1000×8). 2. Determine the lowest outdoor winter temperature generally experienced where you live (call the weather bureau). 3. Is your house of loose, average, or tight construction? This is a matter of judgment, with no hard and fast rules to go by. An old house with loose-fitting doors and windows, little or no insulation, and no storm windows should be "loose" construction. With insulation, storm windows, and weather stripping, the same house would be called "average" construction. A new or recently built house with insulation, storm windows, and weather stripping would be "tight" construction.

Knowing the volume of your house, go to the appropriate horizontal column in the Construction Characteristic Table and read across the line with your outside temperature. For example, say your house volume is 12,000 cubic feet and your outside design temperature is 0 degrees. Reading across this line, you will find the moisture required for loose, average, and tight construction. With "average" construction, you need a humidifier that can provide 1.5 pounds of moisture per hour. With "loose" construction, the humidifier should be capable of discharging 3.74 pounds of moisture per hour into the house. This size unit would keep the house at a 25 per cent relative humidity (RH column).

If your house volume falls between the figures given in the table, you interpolate. If your volume is more than 14,000 cubic feet, take half the volume and determine from the table the humidifier capacity required for half the house; double it to get the humidifier size required for the whole house. Say your house has 20,000 cubic feet of volume. You figure the humidifier capacity required for a 10,000 cubic foot house from the table, then double the figure obtained.

The table gives humidifier capacities in pounds of moisture generated *per hour*. Some humidifiers are rated in gallons of moisture produced per day (24 hours). One gallon of moisture equals 8.3 pounds of moisture. To convert from pounds of moisture per hour to gallons per day, multiply the figure from the chart by 24 and divide by 8.3.

Say you require a humidifier with a capacity of 1.5 pounds of moisture per hour, as determined from the table. This is equivalent to 36 pounds of moisture per day (1.5 times 24). Divide 36 by 8.3 and you get 4.34 gallons per day of moisture required.

This method of computing humidifier size, together with the table, was developed by the National Warm Air Heating & Air-Conditioning Assn. It is so far the only industry-wide method of its kind. To be sure, it may sound complicated, but it is the only accurate method of determining humidifier size.

Many manufacturers use a simple rule of thumb which says that you need 1 gallon per day of humidifier capacity for each room of your house. Thus, a seven-room house would need a 7-gallon-a-day humidifier, a nine-room house, 9 gallons per day. This rule, however, applies to the average house and there is no such animal. With it you risk obtaining a unit that is smaller or larger than what you may need.

It's best to use the above table method. If in doubt, choose a slightly larger humidifier, rather than a borderline size. You can guard against excess moisture simply by setting the humidistat control to a preset relative humidity. When enough moisture has been provided to satisfy your needs, the unit will be turned off automatically.

and doors, little or no insulation, and no storm windows) requires a larger humidifier than a new, tightly-built house of the same size in the same climate. This is because moisture leaks out of a loose house much faster than out of a tight house, thus more moisture has to be fed into the loose old house to keep the humidity up.

Each of these three factors is taken into account in the accompanying chart that is used for selecting a humidifier. Figure your house volume and choose the humidifier according to your outdoor temperature and type of house construction, as explained in the chart copy.

Three Main Kinds of Humidifiers

The three main kinds of humidifiers are: 1. The atomizing kind, generally your best choice; it uses a spray nozzle to inject water into the air. 2. The vaporization kind with an electric heating element to vaporize water into steam, which is ejected into the air. Its chief drawback is that an electric heater is required to vaporize the water, thus extra operating cost for electricity. 3. The surface evaporator kind in which water is evaporated from the surface of a small tank, which is not very efficient.

According to objective sources, good humidifiers are made by Walton Laboratories, Inc., Irvington, N.J.; Research Products Corporation, Madison 10, Wisconsin; The Herrmidifier Co., 1810 Hemstead Rd., Lancaster, Pa.; Lennox Industries, Marshalltown, Iowa; and Advance Engineering Co., 69 Dey St., N.Y. 7, N.Y. I would recommend a unit by either of the first two firms mentioned above.

RELATIVE RATING OF VARIOUS TYPES OF HUMIDIFIERS

UNIT	LIFE	UNIT COST	OPERATING COST	RATE OF OUTPUT	INSTALLA- TION	POWER RE- QUIREMENT	HUMIDITY INLET	CONTROL OUTLET
Pan Type	Excellent	Low	Low	Very Low	Simple	None	Float or Counter Balanced Pan	None
Pan Type With 5 Plates	Plates Must Be Replaced	Low	Low	Low	Simple	None	Float or Counter Balanced Pan	None
Additional Immersion Heat Supply	Life of Heating Element	Average	High	Average	Average to Difficult	Electric High Watts	Float or Counter Balanced Pan	Blower Control or Humidi- stat
Additional External Heat Supply	Good	Average	High	Average	Average to Difficult	Electric High Watts	Float	Same as Above
Centrifugal Atomizing	Good	Average	Average	Average	Average to Difficult	Electric Low Watts	Float	Same As above
Spray Atomizing	Good	Average	Average	Average	Average	None	None	Same as Above
Differential Static Pressure Wetted Surface	Good	Average	Average	Low	Average	None	Float or None	Same as Above
Forced Air Wetted Surface	Evapora- tor Media Replaced	Average to High	Low	High	Average to Difficult	Electric Low Watts	Float or None	Same as Above
Wetted Return Air Filter	Evapora- tor Media Replaced	Very High	Average	High	Difficult	Electric Low Watts	Float	Humidi- stat or Acces- sories

Relative ratings of various types of humidifiers, according to the National Warm Air Heating & Air-Conditioning Assn.

Location and Installation

A whole-house humidifier can be located nearly anywhere in a house but it is best to choose a central location. Its moisture is discharged freely into a main part of the house, preferably a living room, dining room, or central hall. Unlike heating, neither ducts nor pipes are needed to distribute the moisture to your rooms. Unlike heat, the water vapor introduced will automatically spread throughout the house and achieve its own level. Its travel may be impeded to rooms whose doors are tightly shut. Doors normally should be left ajar to rooms where moisture is desired.

The installation is simple. The unit can be located at the basement ceiling, in a utility room, or even a closet, with a short duct from the unit

With warm-air heat, a humidifier can be installed on the ductwork near the furnace, its moisture being added to the air supplied to the house. If this is impractical, or with any other kind of heat, the same humidifier can be installed in a closet, utility space, garage, or at the basement ceiling, and discharge moisture directly into the house, as shown in the small diagram.

Walton Laboratories.

to the nearest room. Moisture is supplied to the room through a discharge register in the wall or floor, then to the rest of the house. Depending on the brand, operating noise may bother you, so check this in advance.

Automatic Operation

An automatic humidistat control is virtually essential. Like a thermostat, it turns the unit on when humidity is needed, turns it off when the humidity reaches a preset level. You set it for the relative humidity you desire. Otherwise you must turn the unit on and off by hand. An automatic humidistat control can also save you grief by turning off the unit before the house is flooded with too much moisture; this can be severely harmful to the structure as well as your furnishings and clothing, as noted later in this chapter.

The installation requires a wiring connection to operate the unit, and a simple pipe connection from your main water line (to supply water as needed). You could omit the water pipe hookup, but then be saddled with the chore of filling the humidifier with water every few days.

If you have warm-air heat, the humidifier could be operated in conjunction with the furnace. Its moisture is fed to the warm air being supplied to the house. The chief advantage is that moisture is distributed through your heating ducts directly to all rooms. This hookup is recommended in large houses with many rooms, and particularly if your bedroom doors are kept shut. It will assure you of uniform moisture distribution to all rooms.

The disadvantage of a furnace location is that moisture is distributed only when heat is being supplied to the house. During periods when the furnace is temporarily off—no heat being required—moisture will not be supplied even though it may be needed. You wait for moisture until the heating thermostat calls for heat again.

This also means that a larger humidifier is needed, compared with the size required when a humidifier operates independently of the furnace. In other words, a furnace-attached humidifier must provide its 24-hour quota of moisture in the restricted 16 to perhaps 18 hours a day that the furnace ordinarily runs. Hence, a humidifier that operates in conjunction with your furnace should be sized from 25 to 33 per cent larger than the size normally necessary.

All things being equal, I would choose an independent humidifier. Moisture distribution to all rooms may not be quite as uniform, compared with moisture being supplied via the warm-air duct system, but independently operated humidifiers work satisfactorily in many houses with hot-water heat and therefore should work equally well in other houses.

What about Cost?

A humidifier large enough for a whole house will cost from about $125 to $200 for a typical house, depending on the house size and the amount of installation work required. You have to pay this much for satisfaction. Anything cheaper generally indicates a compromise in quality of moisture capacity or both and you will probably be sorry later. Operating costs for both electricity and water are low. They should not exceed $2 to $3 a month at most.

Single-Room Humidifiers

One of these may be your cup of tea if you are bothered by a dry nose or throat chiefly at night when you sleep (when the air is coldest and driest). They are portable units, sometimes called vaporizers, and are set on the floor and plugged into an electric outlet. They do not require a water supply connection. Instead you replenish their water tank by hand two to three times a week and sometimes every day.

Prices range from about $35 to $60, depending on size, brand, and mode of operation. Choose an atomizing kind, if possible. It is also best to have an automatic humidistat control (optional feature for about $10 to $20 more), as this will automatically turn the unit on and off, as required, while you sleep.

Do You Really Need a Humidifier?

Not every family does. Broadly speaking, you are most likely to need one if you live in an old house for the reasons already given. Excessively dry air is unlikely if you live in a comparatively new, tightly-built house. The water vapor created by cooking, bathing, and moisture-generating appliances is less likely to leak from the house and is usually sufficient to keep the humidity level high enough for comfort.

If your house is a borderline case you may or may not need a humidifier. The house can be made tighter with storm windows, adding weather stripping around windows and doors, and by insulating. Before buying a humidifier, determine first how low your relative humidity is with a good hygrometer. If it falls to only about 15 per cent, you may get it up to a comfortable 20 or 25 per cent by tightening up on house leaks that now permit moisture to escape. Then the moisture ordinarily generated in the house may be enough to prevent dry air. If, however, your humidity level falls to a low 5 to 10 per cent, you probably need a humidifier.

How warm do you keep your house in winter? The warmer you keep it, the drier the air, and the more difficult it is to maintain a comfortable humidity level. For instance, holding the relative humidity at 35 per cent when the house is kept at 80 degrees inside requires one-third more moisture in the house air than is needed to maintain the same 35 per cent relative humidity with the house at 70 degrees.

This means that merely by insulating a house you sometimes can go a long way toward curbing a dry-air problem. As explained in Chapter 21, people in houses with little or no insulation generally set their thermostats at 75 to over 80 degrees in order to feel warm and comfortable. This much heat tends to dry out the air. With plenty of insulation, however, you will find that you can be equally comfortable at 70 to 72 degrees. The air will be less dry at this lower temperature.

Hazards with Too Much Moisture

You should also know that indiscriminately adding moisture can cause structural damage to the house. It seems as if you can't win and, unhappily, sometimes you can't. As an illustration, a woman pianist in Washington, D.C., was plagued with a dry-air condition which was so bad her piano would not stay tuned in winter. She installed a powerful humidifier to overcome the trouble. It helped the piano, but so much moisture was poured into the house that a serious exterior paint damage resulted (explained in Chapter 18). The paint blistered and peeled so quickly that the house required an expensive new paint job every two years.

This is an extreme example, to be sure. But the possibility of such damage cannot be ignored. Reasonable caution should be exerted when you use a humidifier. Don't overdo it. Don't hesitate to buy a humidistat control so you can set a limit on the moisture generated. A little experimenting will tell you how low the relative humidity can be set and still provide adequate moisture, the lower the better.

Does your house have vapor barriers? Since these prevent vapor from infiltrating the structure, they are particularly important when a humidifier is used. They can be had on your insulation when insulation is installed over ceilings. They can be applied on inside walls and ceilings by the use of vapor-barrier paint when you redecorate. You simply specify a vapor-barrier paint, which is available in a variety of colors and tones.

Chapter 29

Quieting a Noisy House

The usual prescription for a noisy house is acoustical tile for your ceilings, but this is only a halfway measure. For one thing, acoustical tile is not as much of a noise reducer as many people think. For another, its effectiveness is limited to reducing only one of the two kinds of noise in houses.

If you are plagued by noise, it is first necessary to sort out the particular kind of noises that most bother you. The problem and solutions are not the same in every household. If the noise assailing your ears is really bad, you could of course flee to an isolated island, but even there civilization and jet planes would ultimately seek you out.

The biggest noisemakers in houses today are children, radio and TV sets, kitchen and laundry appliances (especially dishwashers, mixers, and clothes washers), mechanical equipment (especially fans and heating units), plus the shouts of kids outside, the blaring of car horns, the rumble of truck traffic, and the roar of overhead planes.

Things are not only noisier than ever before but they are compounded because houses today are smaller and more compact than before— 8-foot ceilings instead of 9, for example. Every noise is, in effect, amplified. The trend toward contemporary design and informal contemporary living makes matters worse. With less heavy upholstery, and fewer rugs and drapes in our houses, the inevitable noise in every house has less chance to be absorbed and toned down. Instead, we have more hard surfaces, and more glass, which bounce noise waves back to your ears.

Indeed, the best noise deadeners in houses are thick rugs, upholstered furniture, and window drapes whose very softness absorbs a portion of the noise waves flying around a house. Put down thick rugs and put up curtains and drapes and you take the first definitive step toward reducing noise. Wall-to-wall carpeting is best, the thicker the better (assuming of course that you desire it for other reasons too). Full carpeting over stairs and in hallways is especially good for reducing the spread of noise from the living to the bedroom areas of a house. Rugs and carpeting by themselves can make a remarkable reduction in your noise level.

Acoustical ceiling tiles are made of soft fibrous materials, available in a wide variety of designs. This room is enhanced by its high ceiling and exposed beams.
Armstrong Cork.

Acoustical Tile

Acoustical tile works on the same principle. It is a soft fibrous material, somewhat spongy in texture, which will absorb from 50 to 75 per cent of the sound waves that strike it. The usual smooth, hard wall and ceiling surfaces in a room bounce back nearly 100 per cent of the sound waves present.

Acoustical tile can help most on the ceilings of kitchens, playrooms, living rooms, and hallways. It is recommended especially for kitchen ceil-

These are a few of the different patterns available in acoustical tile.

Acoustical Materials Assn.

ings where the normal clatter of pots, pans, and whirring appliances is made worse by the presence of hard-surfaced appliances and cabinets, plus an uncarpeted floor, all of which bounce the sound waves around like ping-pong balls. An acoustical ceiling, however, will trap many of the sound waves which are absorbed by the spongy tile, thus reducing the pounding on your ears.

An acoustical ceiling can in the same way—though not always—reduce the chatter of children's voices in a playroom, produce a subdued quiet conducive for conversation in a living room, reduce bathroom noises, and enhance the natural quiet of a bedroom.

Special mention should be made of acoustical tile for hallways, which often serve as noise tunnels, letting noise echo back and forth from one end of the house to the other. It works much like heavy carpeting in halls. It is put at the upper wall levels in a hall, as well as at the ceiling. Because the material is soft and fibrous, it should not be installed lower than shoulder height, as bodily contact will rough it up and reduce its effectiveness. One place acoustical tile should not be used is in a music room or hi-fi corner, since it can mute the tone and quality of music.

What Kind of Acoustical Tile?

A large variety of acoustical materials for houses are now on the market. This is a welcome change from a few years back when practically all tiles were 12-inches square, had the same perforated design, and looked monotonously alike. Today there are such varied types as fissured tile which looks like stained marble, finely textured tile with neither the perforations nor deep fissures, tile with striated ridges and different colors, and a variety of more expensive types with embossed designs. The new products that are available range in size from small squares up to large boards.

Acoustical tile is made of such fibrous material as wood fiber, mineral wool fiber (rock wool), glass fiber (Fiberglas), and polystyrene plastic. The wood-fiber kind was first on the market, is generally the cheapest (by a few pennies per square foot), and comes in the largest variety of designs. Its biggest drawback is susceptibility to high humidity and wetness. Excessive moisture will destroy its cement bond, warp the material, and make the individual tiles look pretty bad, if not cause them to fall off. So don't use wood-fiber acoustical tile where moisture is prevalent, such as in a bathroom or kitchen. The others—mineral wool, glass fiber, and polystyrene—are proportionately better in moisture resistance, with the polystyrene being the best for areas where moisture is present.

Each of the various kinds sold has tongue-and-groove edges and extended flanges for covering the nail and staple heads with which they are held up. They can be cemented directly to an existing ceiling if the ceiling is fairly smooth. They also can be stapled to wood furring strips applied over an old ceiling or for a new ceiling in new rooms. A scale plan of the ceiling is made before the job is started. This enables you to figure how much tile will be needed. The work should start at the exact center of the ceiling so the tile comes out even on all sides.

If the installation is done properly and if nonmoisture-resistant tiles are kept free of water and moisture, they should last as long as the walls. While some dust may accumulate on them from time to time, its removal is easy (by means of a vacuum-cleaner extension or by simply wiping with soap and water). But do not paint an acoustical ceiling too often. Too much paint will gradually reduce the effectiveness of the tiles. One coat of washable paint, roller applied, is enough.

Approximate Costs

Acoustical tiles range in cost from about 15¢ to 30¢ per square foot at a lumberyard, depending on type of material, quality, and texture. Add another 5¢ to 10¢ per square foot for application materials and labor to get the approximate total cost when applied over existing ceilings and walls. The cost will be less in new rooms and new additions, since the tile serves as the finished interior surface; you save the cost of a conventional ceiling or wall surface.

Main Limitation of Acoustical Tile

Acoustical tile is not a cure-all for all noise in a house because it is mainly for reducing noise that originates *within* the room itself. This is important to know. It does not help much against noise that originates *outside* of a room or outside the house. Thus, lining a study with acoustical tile will do little to insulate yourself from the sounds of children in a nearby playroom, or from any other noise originating outside the study. This brings up the nature of noise.

Two Different Kinds of Noise

All noises are either: 1. airborne and get into a house through open windows and doors; or 2. they arrive by impact and travel through the walls and frame of a house like little shock waves.

The only way to stop airborne noise is by shutting off all unobstructed openings between you and the noise source. Doors and windows should be kept closed. Weather stripping around doors is also helpful, particularly around bathroom doors. Leaving a window open can undo all of the effectiveness of the most thoroughly sound-conditioned house. (Closing windows in summer will also, of course, shut out welcome breezes, so for this reason many homeowners turn to air conditioning for quiet as well as for coolness.)

Noise waves that arrive by impact are a major problem because they are the hardest to stop. Impact noise can be reduced, if not stopped, only by sheer mass—a combination of thick and heavy walls between you and the noise source, the thicker and heavier, the better. This is another reason why things are noisier today, since the typically light construction of houses is less resistant to noise penetration than the thicker, heavier houses of yesteryear. It is also why the appallingly thin walls in new apartment houses have led to much complaint about inter-apartment noise.

To be realistic, even the thickest solid brick walls can go only so far in reducing really powerful impact noises, such as the heavy rumble of traffic over a nearby highway. You would need a solid wall at least 10 feet thick between you and a nearby highway to bar the entry of traffic noise into your house. Unfortunately, therefore, if you are particularly bothered by terribly loud noise from nearby traffic, trains, or overhead planes, your only recourse is to move.

Soundproof Construction

Much can be done to put a damper on ordinary everyday noises by soundproofing the existing structure or a new addition you build. As noted above, the heavier and weightier the wall, the more resistant it is to noise travel from room to room, as well as resistant to noise impinging on the house from outdoors. The ideal noise barrier would be walls of thick lead. More down-to-earth is the use of heavy masonry walls, especially for exterior walls. If you are deeply concerned for your quiet when you build a new addition, masonry walls of concrete block, say, are best for interior partitions.

Conventional wood-frame walls also can be beefed up to reduce noise transmission through them. They can be filled with special acoustical insulation, which looks like pads of thermal insulation. Another possibility is to ask for what is called "staggered-stud" wall construction. The wall is made with two sets of 2×2 studs, 2 inches apart, one set for each side of the wall. Overlapping sheets of fiberboard or fibrous acoustical insulation are hung in the air space in-between.

Other good ideas are locating new closets or bookcases between a noisy room and one you want to keep quiet. The weight of many books is an excellent noise stop and a key reason why libraries are so quiet.

What about soundproof floors and ceiling to reduce vertical noise travel from one floor of a house to another? Like walls, they can be beefed up with built-in insulation (as well as heavy rugs). Sometimes the problem is due to squeaky floors as a result of flimsy construction. The remedy is crossbracing the floors (easiest to do to the first-floor since you can brace it at the basement ceiling).

Appliance and Equipment Noise

You must strike at the source of the noise, the equipment. Mount appliances, and equipment (a furnace or air conditioner) on a resilient cork or rubber pad to prevent vibration travel through the house structure. Keep equipment oiled and have it checked occasionally for quiet operation.

Excessive noise from heating pipes and ducts is usually due to poor installation. For example, heating pipes bang against floor beams because the opening in the beam was not made large enough to allow for the inevitable pipe movements when water surges through. This puts emphasis on a good installation when new heating is installed (see Chapter 20).

If you are bothered by television used by another person in the family, have a set of earphones hooked up to the set for the use of the viewer. This can be done for as little as $10, including the earphones. Door slamming can be eliminated with automatic door closers, a big step in the right direction.

Above all, choose quiet appliances and equipment when you buy. It behooves us to take the time to check one brand against another for such things as quiet operation when we buy, but this is essential if you demand quiet. It is particularly important for such chronic noisemakers as kitchen exhaust fans and room air conditioners.

The Psychology of Noise

The rest of this chapter has to do with a few fundamental facts about noise, its effect on people, and perhaps how you can come to terms with it, which is sometimes possible. Scientists define noise as "unwanted sound"—sound that bothers you while the same sound is perfectly tolerable to another person.

A power mower next door may drive you insane but it is accepted by the neighbor using it because he is getting a direct service from the noise. The hum of a refrigerator is taken in stride by most of us because we are used to it and because sub-consciously we are benefiting from the cause of the noise (it keeps our food refrigerated). The roar of an overhead jet may be one of the absolutely loudest noises yet inflicted on humans, but it is music to the pilot's (and passengers') ears, since it means safety; the sudden ceasing of the jet's engines would alarm its pilot and passengers, and justifiably so.

The fact is that sheer loudness, per se, is not the only measure of the noise. What's more, loudness by itself is not harmful to our health, despite popular belief to the contrary. The human body has great capacity for tolerating loud noises up to the limit where noise can cause deafness.

The limit is in the neighborhood of 110 to 120 decibels, the decibel being the usual measure of sound intensity. This level is comparable to the intensity of a jet engine when you are standing about 50 to 100 feet away. The farther away you are, the less the decibel intensity on your ears. In addition, the longer your exposure to intense sounds, the greater the potential harm to your eardrums. The classic example here is workers in boiler factories who become deaf.

The usual noises in houses may cause much mental anguish but are practically never harmful to health. The noises that bother us most fall into five main categories.

Five Main Categories of Noise

First is what is called "interference with voice communication." We can dine in a noisy restaurant and not be bothered by the noise around until it prevents us from hearing our dining partner. At home a housewife will tolerate children playing in another room until the children's screams prevent her from talking on the phone or from chatting with a friend while having coffee with her. The surrounding noise level may approach deafening intensity, as in a plane, but it is remarkable how much we can tolerate it until it interferes with our conversation; i.e., voice communication.

Second is unexpected noise, which takes us by surprise, and again almost regardless of its intensity. Examples are the creak of a door at night, which can practically unhinge us, or the barely audible click of an electric blanket thermostat (which Consumers' Union once likened to the "stomping of a robin on the lawn").

Third are intermittent sounds such as a furnace going on and off. You are taken by surprise because there is no rhythmic pattern to the noise. The more regular the sound (the less intermittent), the more tolerant we become of it. People who live near noisy airports or subway trains learn to take them in stride. More complaints about such noise are made by people living farther away who hear the same sounds more intermittently, are less used to them, and are therefore more annoyed.

Fourth are sounds that threaten an invasion of privacy. If you are having a confidential talk in your living room (or office), nearby voices will upset you because they indicate that you may be overheard. This is psychological but nonetheless disturbing. "If we can hear them, they can hear us."

Fifth are what are termed intelligible sounds. A college professor cannot concentrate in his study because of the barely audible voices of others downstairs, yet college students can concentrate amazingly well in dormitories despite radios blaring all evening long. If we can make out as few as six or seven words out of every hundred spoken nearby, they begin to make sense. We are psychologically disturbed because they distract us, largely out of curiosity. This is what disturbs the college professor. It is particularly disturbing when we are reading a book, or engaged in any other solitary activity.

The usual and often accidental remedy for such disturbing noises is raising the background level of sound so you no longer hear intelligible sounds. Thus more than one college professor in a household full of kids has found that he can concentrate again simply by turning on a radio to a low volume of music that serves to cancel out the intruding voices from downstairs. He is using the masking technique, a widely used noise-control technique in office buildings. There the background level of sound is raised by the introduction of artificial sounds through the air-conditioning system, which in turn masks the sounds of voices in other offices. The voices of people nearby are no longer intelligible.

In other words, you may be bothered by noise in a house chiefly because your house is hush-quiet to begin with. Every little sound that is heard, indoors or out, seems quite loud and annoying in relation to the low sound level of your house. If this is your problem, then consider the introduction of masking sounds via a radio, records, or a neat trick if you can swing it—the installation of a water fountain whose constant trickle is soothing largely because it is masking (for much the same reason that the sound of an idyllic little brook is satisfying).

Noise-Sensitive People

Scientists also say that a certain number of people are noise sensitive or just plain fussy about sound. Little or nothing can be done to relieve them of noise irritation, short of seeing a psychiatrist. One reason such people suffer is that they were brought up amid quiet surroundings and therefore not conditioned to the loud environment confronting them later in life. (Being unconditioned to sound is also a painful experience with people with poor hearing who have their hearing restored by a surgical operation. They suddenly find the world around so noisy with sounds other people take for granted, that it takes long readjustment before they again become conditioned to ordinary everyday sounds.)

Another reason is that certain sounds subconsciously remind us of unhappy memories associated long ago with the same sounds. This gets deep into Freudian reasons which we need not explore here, but is nevertheless a well-substantiated reason for some of us being particularly bothered by particular sounds that leave other people cold; e.g., the ring of a telephone which one time brought shocking news; a popular song long ago associated with an unhappy love affair. Finally there are also people who are neurotic for any of a variety of reasons and certain disturbances such as noise will shake them up violently.

The foregoing discussion is given here simply to broaden your understanding of noise and help you solve household noise problems which may or may not be solved merely by spending a lot of money to sound-proof your house. Before you spend the money, consider whether it will really produce the relief you desire in light of the above facts.

Part 9

THE PROCESS OF BUYING AND PAYING FOR IMPROVEMENTS AND REPAIRS

The woods are full of different breeds of home-improvement contractors and repairmen. It's important not only to get a reputable man but also one who is a specialist in the work you need. One, a jack of all trades, may be perfectly good for odd jobs, but a master of none that you require. Hiring the right man for the job is quite important.

What about getting a fair price and saving money, if possible? The price you pay for the same work differs from one firm to another and also from one time of the year to another, sometimes markedly—the subject of the second chapter in this section.

Of course, many of us just do not have the cash available to pay for home improvements; we need a loan. Knowing how to finance work on a house is an art that can also save you much money on interest and credit charges. The various kinds of loans available are reported here along with the pros and cons.

And how can you avoid home-repair bills or at least sharply curtail them? The answer is by preventive maintenance. We wind up with a maintenance program, or check list, for houses, which lists those parts of houses where a stitch-in-time check can catch trouble before it grows into expensive damage.

Chapter 30

How to Hire and Deal
with Contractors

In general, there are three main kinds of contractors and repairmen:

1. *The "one-stop" remodeler,* who is equipped to handle a complete remodeling project; expand the house, add a new room or garage, do over a complete kitchen or bathroom. You deal with one firm and get one price for the entire job. It handles everything. It is best when you do not want to be encumbered with any details whatever, and especially when you know little about construction and you don't want to be bothered dealing with various subcontractors. The one-stop firm generally has carpenters and a few other specialists on its payroll, but generally subcontracts such things as heating, wiring, plumbing, and painting.

Some one-stop firms specialize in kitchens and bathrooms, others in adding new living space, including finishing off an attic or basement or adding new space to a house. Determine what a firm's specialty is and deal only with one that is well experienced in the kind of work you need.

2. *Specialists,* who are, for example, plumbers, electricians, painters, roofers, and carpenters, each of whom confines his work to his specialty. They seldom do anything else (though some plumbers have expanded into bathroom and kitchen remodelers, some carpenters have become "cabinet makers" or "builders"). They will work directly for you, and often they also work for builders or one-stop remodelers as subcontractors. The key point to determine is whether the man or firm you hire will do the work himself or whether he will do little or none himself and instead subcontract it to others.

3. *Home-builder remodelers* who are a good choice for work that involves new construction or structural alterations. A good builder, in fact, can be unbeatable for large remodeling because of his construction experience and because he usually has skilled men on his payroll. More and more builders are taking on remodeling work, especially during slack seasons for new house building, notably in winter. Names of builders who do remodeling can be had from a local builders' association.

Choosing a Reputable Contractor

The stock advice given is to deal only with reputable firms and repairmen. But no one has a sure-fire rule on how to spot a reputable man. We are told to obtain the names of other people that the man has done business with. But no contractor will give you names of his dissatisfied customers. Of course, if he will not give you any names at all, he should be shunned like the plague. If he is the rare man who can give you a list of all his customers, you can choose at random. Merely having such a list says much for him.

Check with friends and relatives for the names of firms that did well by them. When more than two or three mention the same name, you are probably on to a good man. Top priority should be given to the man's place of business, according to Pete Johnson, president of the Hackensack, N.J., remodeling firm, Comfort Control Corporation, and past president of the NERSICA, (National Established Repair, Service, and Improvement Contractors' Association), a national group of home-improvement contractors. "Does he operate from a well-run showroom or office, or from his glove compartment?"

For example, Johnson cites a New Jersey state investigation of one fast-buck operator accused of shoddy workmanship. This gyp was found to be operating under seven different company names with nothing more than a telephone answering service for each. The woman who made the complaint, and the other victims, could have avoided much heartache if they had checked on his place of business beforehand.

Ask the man for bank references, Johnson says. "Not just his bank for desposits, but more important the banks or finance companies that handle his installment-loan paper. If he cannot give you a few bank names, watch out, since many banks (though not all) will not accept business from unethical contractors."

Call a few building product distributors and wholesale suppliers. Ask them for the names of good repairmen. If your man's firm is not mentioned, bring it up. If you get an immediate and unqualified endorsement, fine. If anything else, punctuted by hemming and hawing, it's probably a condemnation. (We have already mentioned that calling local suppliers is also a good way to find contractors when you don't know any.)

Do not deal with a contractor who does not carry insurance to protect you as well as him. If one of his men falls from a ladder and breaks a leg, *you* could be sued. If a stranger passing by is injured by the contractor's truck backing into your driveway, again you may be liable. This depends on the kind of insurance he has. A really good contractor will have three kinds of insurance: public liability, property damage, and workman's compensation insurance. Ask about this.

By and large a good contractor will be a member of his local trade association, such as NERSICA. Go a step further and determine if he is a member of the local Chamber of Commerce, the Rotary, and so on. In any case, a check call to the Better Business Bureau is obligatory.

Calling the Better Business Bureau

This rates special mention because a BBB office may give you inconclusive information and also because some BBB offices are decidedly better than others. It depends on where you live. There are some 120 different BBB offices in the United States and Canada.

In a noncommittal way, the typical BBB person you get on the phone is likely to say that Firm A, the one you mention, has been in business for so many years and there are few or no justifiable complaints in their file about it. In general, this is a good indication. The tip-off to a questionable firm is when you are told that "several" complaints have been made about it. (Before buying an expensive camera advertised at a low price I once called the BBB to check on the store. I was told that it had recently been fined by the city's license bureau for selling second-hand cameras as new. This was enough for me, and I bought elsewhere.)

Some BBB offices, such as the one in Cleveland, will go a step farther and look into a firm for you if they have nothing on it in their files. In addition to Cleveland, other cities that have really good BBB offices are Boston, Akron, Louisville, Cincinnati, Chicago, St. Louis, Los Angeles, and San Francisco.

Getting Bids

Get bids from two or three different firms. This is your only check on the price you pay. But don't buy solely on the basis of low price. This can lead to grief. For one thing, the lowest bid may omit essential work or include low-quality materials. Thus, make sure that each bid is based on the same specifications and the same grade of materials.

The bids you obtain may vary greatly in price. This can leave you totally confused. A Chicago economist, for example, Allen F. Jung of the University of Chicago, had an architect draw up plans and specifications for adding a second story to a typical one-story house. To determine price variations he asked *forty* different contractors to bid on the job. The bids ranged from $6500 to $10,600.

How in the world can such a great disparity result on the same job? No one can say for sure, but several possible reasons are given. For one thing, and in spite of working from the same plans and specifications, some contractors figure on cutting corners and substitute cheaper materials to get their costs down. Others deliberately figure high as they may be loaded with other jobs and not willing to accept new work unless it is highly profitable. Still others make estimating mistakes.

In most cases, however, bids for a job tend to cluster fairly close together with no more than a 10 per cent spread from the lowest to the highest. Any bid that is sharply higher or lower than the rest should be viewed with suspicion. It will bear hard scrutiny and normally should not even be considered. If in doubt, ask each man why his bid may be different from others. Don't be timid.

Incidentally, when you get bids, let each man know that you are getting other bids. Sometimes a salesman assumes that he is the only bidder and will figure that he can charge you all the traffic will bear. Knowing that he has competition will force him to sharpen his pencil and stay within bounds. Also make it clear that you are not necessarily going to buy the lowest-priced job. You want the best-quality job even if it costs a little more.

Also ask, frankly, how busy his firm is and if he is really interested in taking on your work. When can they start? How long should it take? How many jobs like yours have they done?

Understand the Contractor's Problems

Home-improvement work is a tough business. The typical contractor has to deal with a variety of suppliers on the one hand, and with many a fickle-minded and fickle-fingered hired hand on the other. Merely finding good men and holding on to them is a full-time job.

It is also surprising, a good many remodelers have told me, how many homeowners are out to chisel the contractor. Some never pay their bills. Once a contractor gets stung by a chiseling homeowner, he automatically becomes wary of all the rest of us. Being a small businessman, if only one job out of every ten boomerangs on him it may well represent all of his profit for the last three months going down the drain. (In all likelihood, he has a wife and family to support, too.)

In brief, understand the contractor's problems. Have patience and give the man a little leeway. Don't tell the workers how to do their work. If you have questions, take them up with the boss. Mistakes are inevitable. A good contractor not only expects them but he can be relied on to return and make the necessary corrections.

A good contractor wants to get your work done as speedily as possible and be paid. Most operate on a small margin and delays cost them money. Their overhead expenses continue every day, rain or shine, and regardless of whether your work continues on schedule or not. Besides, the man may have half a dozen other jobs in progress at the same time and sometimes everything goes wrong at once. By understanding his problems you can go a long way toward getting good work and a satisfactory job done as quickly as possible.

Avoiding Damage and Delays

To prevent unnecessary damage, get your good carpeting and good furniture out of the way before workmen arrive. Remove your favorite shrubs and plants outside so that they are well clear of new construction work. You cannot depend on even the best workman to watch out for such things (no more than a woman can depend on the average husband). Another problem is clean-up. Your contract should state that the workmen will clean up and remove all building debris before leaving.

Clear out the space where remodeling will be done. Remove anything that is portable, including curtains and pictures; cover up anything else, such as a piano. Lay down newspaper for workmen's routes in and out of the house. Put down shoe-wiping mats between the part of the house being remodeled and the rest of the house. Close the windows to keep wind from blowing dust and dirt around; there will be plenty of it.

As for delays, even the best men in the business cannot guarantee a job being done by a given date. The best they do is give you "an approximate completion date" because of the nature of work on houses. Union problems may arise. A key worker may disappear for a week without warning (especially when the hunting season opens). Or sudden trouble arises when your house walls are opened up, requiring much re-routing of wiring and pipes.

Allow at least two to three weeks before work starts on the average job. It takes that long at least to draw up plans, order materials, and arrange for myriad other details. Any salesman who promises that work will start tomorrow is out of his mind. Allow a couple of weeks to several months, depending on the size of the job, for completion, regardless of what you may be told.

On the other hand, some men will keep you waiting for weeks and months before they show up. After everything else had been completed on a new bathroom, a neighbor of mine waited for nearly six months for the tile man to return and complete a new shower stall—a maddening delay. The only way to avoid such delays is to check in advance on the man's dependability. Of course, if you have emergency work you deserve immediate attention. This calls for finding good repairmen and sticking with them over the years.

Another solution is joining one of the home service clubs (at a $10 to $20 annual fee), such as Allied Homeowner's Association. The membership fee entitles you to fast service for anything at any time day or night. The club not only will steer you to a reputable repairman and contractor when a big job is required, but its men also will see that you get good work and are charged a fair price. To be sure, not all clubs are as responsible and responsive to their members as others. Their dependability varies from town to town according to the men who run each one. For the small annual fee required, they are certainly worth a year's trial; you lose little if one does not pan out.

A Final Word

Unfortunately, the best advice on home remodeling and repair can be wasted because many of us freeze up when a man sits down in the living room to sell us his services. It seems that he knows so much and we so little that we are intimidated. We nod silently and ask few questions because of natural human timidity about something we know little about, other than that it will cost us good money.

This should not be. There are two essential things you know; what you can spend and what you want to accomplish. If you stick to your objectives, your chances of success are increased. In addition, arm yourself with plenty of information beforehand. Start talking with friends, relatives, and contractors long before you are ready to begin work. Get books and magazines on the subject from your library. Visit showrooms.

You will be confused at first, because contractors and repairmen constantly offer conflicting advice in answer to the same questions. This is disconcerting, but after awhile the pieces begin to fall into place, and you'll be surprised at how much you're learning. You also will begin to spot the fourflusher salesman who talks persuasively but doesn't know beans about his subject.

So speak up. Don't be cowed. Simply ask your questions and settle the sticky points before you sign up. That's the only way you can be sure of getting a successful job and the most satisfaction.

Chapter 31

Saving Money by Off-Season Buying

There is a busy time and a slow time for nearly every kind of home-improvement and repair work—a definite pattern for each, according to Arthur Yeckes, president of Allied Homeowner's Association, headquarters in Roslyn, N.Y., the nation's largest homeowners' "club." It has branches in over 70 cities.

Thus by having work done during its particular off-season, a lower price often can be had. Savings result in the same way savings are made by taking advantage of seasonal clothing and furniture sales.

Yeckes points out, for example, that painters often cut their prices for inside painting during winter when bad weather rules out outside painting. To keep key employees busy on inside jobs, they tend to give more competitive estimates. They also get done faster and may even render more satisfactory service.

Pay More or Wait

He adds that, "During the spring, summer, and fall, painters with an abundance of work have been known to submit discouragingly high estimates, with the knowledge that they cannot handle the job anyway. If a customer is impatient for the work and agrees to the high price, the contractor may then 'bump' or delay a less lucrative customer to make room for the high profit job." The same things are done by other contractors.

The best prices for heating work can be had in spring and summer, the slow season for heating. The peak season starts in the fall and extends till the end of cold weather. This also applies to chimney cleaning and fireplace work.

It does not necessarily apply to contractors who handle both heating and air conditioning; their men get loaded up on air-conditioning installation work in the late spring. This coupled with cooling-service calls keeps them busy through most of the summer. The best time to buy air conditioning is from January to March. Don't put it off until May or June when prices go up, and the odds are that the installation may not be completed until summer is half over.

Spring and fall are also difficult times to get work done by carpenters, electricians, plumbers, and others who are very busy then on new house construction. You will be competing with builders for their time, as well as with the bulk of other homeowners who remodel at these times. Prices are bid up.

Cement Work, Pools, and Roofing

Most people do not think of having patios, barbecues, and walks installed until mild weather arrives, which creates extreme peaks and valleys in the demand for concrete and masonry contractors. But this work now can be done in cold weather by the use of special chemicals in cement mixes. This is particularly true of contractors who specialize in small jobs. (The big ones keep busy the year-round on roads and highways.) But don't wait for the coldest weather when the ground is frozen hard. The best time to shop for a swimming pool is in the fall when nobody else thinks of pools.

Roofing prices may be influenced by wind and weather rather than by weather seasons. Contractors are busiest during and after heavy snows in winter and after storms and heavy rain whenever they occur. The best time to have a roof inspected for potential trouble spots or loose shingles is therefore during a prolonged dry and mild spell when contractors have no emergencies to contend with. Waterproofing of basements is subject to the same influences. The rainy seasons, usually winter and spring in most areas, are not only busy times for waterproofers but also worst for a good technical reason: A basement should be as dry as possible when it is waterproofed.

Some types of repairs do not conform to a logical pattern. More storm-door and window glass is repaired in the spring after use, than in the fall and early winter. A possible reason for this is that we want such repairs done before storing the glass away for the summer but are negligent in the winter when they really need repairs.

New work and repairs on fencing, underground sprinkler systems, lawn mowers, and screening usually can be done at low competitive prices during the winter months, before the start of the seasonal rush.

Lull Times for Getting Work Done

So if possible avoid the busiest periods. Choose a lull time for your work. Here is a chart of the lull periods—the best time to buy—for a variety of home-improvement work, based on an *American Home* magazine survey of nearly 1000 home-improvement dealers throughout the nation. The survey actually was compiled to determine their busiest periods. I have extrapolated the data so that the following months are the slowest for the particular work noted.

Best (off-season) time of the year to launch home improvements

Add a room or wing	October to February (though not always possible), sometimes May and June.
Remodel kitchen	April to October
Build garage or carport	November to March
New siding and roofing	November to March
Build patio or porch	September to February
Finish basement	March to August; sometimes September and October
Interior remodeling (walls, ceiling, etc.)	March; June to September
Add a bathroom	February, April; September to November
Convert garage to livable space	December to February; July and August
New attic dormer	February to April; July and August
Enclose a terrace	February to April; November and December

Chapter 32

How to Finance Home Improvements
and Repairs at the Best Terms
and the Lowest Interest Rates

Home-improvement loans can be had with interest rates as low as 5 per cent and as high as 20 per cent. There are no standard rates. Most people end up paying high rates by simply accepting whatever financing is offered. The lender, naturally, offers first what is best for *him*. Yet in most cases a cheaper loan can be obtained for the same purpose.

I learned about this the hard way by automatically assuming that an FHA home-improvement loan carries the cheapest credit charges of all. It *is* cheap compared with *conventional* improvement loans but that's only part of the story. I obtained one for $1600 worth of home improvements. I later discovered I could have saved nearly $150 by simply getting another kind of loan for the same amount and, of all things, from the same bank.

Basic Facts about Financing

A good many home-improvement salesmen and contractors provide "easy" financing. They have regular loan forms which you merely sign and that's that. It's best, however, not to accept such financing. You will almost always do better by going to a bank yourself and obtaining your own loan, then pay the remodeler yourself when his work is done.

Often a salesman will say that his loan carries a mere 5 or 6 per cent interest rate. This is almost never so. It is deceptive in that what the salesman calls 5 or 6 per cent is actually closer to 10 or 12 per cent because it is for what is called an *add-on* loan.

The regular FHA home-improvement loan, for example, is actually a

5 per cent add-on loan with a true, simple interest rate equal to 9.4 per cent a year. Most home-improvement financing is with add-on loans, some are with what are called *discount* loans. These are the same kind of loans widely used for financing cars, appliances, furniture, shell houses, and also for so-called personal loans.

The add-on rate is figured in this way: Say it is a 5 per cent add-on. On a $1000 loan, 5 per cent is $50 a year. If the loan is for five years, the total add-on cost is then $250 (five times $50). The credit company adds this amount to the $1000, giving $1250. This is the total money you pay back in five years for borrowing $1000. As you pay back each month, you steadily reduce the amount of money you owe. Nevertheless, your total credit charge is figured as if you always owe the full amount ($1250). This is why a 5 per cent add-on is deceptive, and also why you actually pay a lot more than 5 per cent on what you borrowed.

A 5 per cent discount charge lifts the interest even higher than a 5 per cent add-on. The 5 per cent a year ($50) is subtracted from the $1000. You get only $950 on a one-year $1000 loan, but you pay back the full $1000 in monthly payments for a year. The true interest you pay comes to over 10 per cent, more than twice the discount rate.

The point to remember is that interest charges should be stated in terms of simple annual interest. Many department stores charge "1½ per cent per month," which is actually 18 per cent a year. I have also heard salesmen *insist* that their interest charges are only 6 per cent, yet by reading the small print I knew that the loans were iron-clad 6 per cent add-on charges, thus nearly 12 per cent interest. The average salesman, in fact, doesn't know the difference.

Why Credit Charges Are High Despite State Laws

Here you may say that you cannot be charged more than 8 per cent, say, because your state has a law prohibiting higher interest charges. Some states put a 7 per cent ceiling on interest, others 8 or 9 per cent.

At the same time and in the very same states finance companies can charge the equivalent of 10, 20, and even 30 per cent interest with legal impunity. They do it by means of what is called the "time-payment" charge, or a credit fee. Legally, this is not called interest. You may be charged 6 per cent interest, say, on a loan, but then a time-payment charge is added on top of the interest.

The total credit charges you pay add up, in effect, to two or three times the stated interest charge. Or the entire credit fee may be called a time-payment charge with generally no limit on its size. This happens all the

TOTAL COST OF INTEREST AND INSURANCE PREMIUMS

Amount of Advance	5 YEAR LOAN			10 YEAR LOAN			15 YEAR LOAN			20 YEAR LOAN		
	Interest	Insurance Premium	Total Payment	Interest	Insurance Premium	Total Payment	Interest	Insurance Premium	Total Payment	Interest	Insurance Premium	Total Payment
$ 1,000	$ 160	$ 13	$ 173	$ 332	$ 28	$ 360	$ 519	$ 43	$ 562	$ 718	$ 60	$ 778
2,500	400	33	433	830	69	899	1,297	108	1,405	1,795	150	1,945
6,000	959	80	1,039	1,991	166	2,157	3,113	259	3,372	4,309	359	4,668
10,000	1,599	133	1,732	3,319	277	3,596	5,188	432	5,620	7,182	598	7,780

MONTHLY PAYMENT TO PRINCIPAL INTEREST AT 6% PER ANNUM, AND INSURANCE PREMIUM

Amount of advance	5 YEAR LOAN			10 YEAR LOAN			15 YEAR LOAN			20 YEAR LOAN		
	Principal and Interest	Insurance Premium*	Total Monthly Payment	Principal and Interest	Insurance Premium*	Total Monthly Payment	Principal and Interest	Insurance Premium*	Total Monthly Payment	Principal and Interest	Insurance Premium*	Total Monthly Payment
$ 1,000	$ 19.34	$ .38	$ 19.72	$ 11.11	$ .40	$ 11.51	$ 8.44	$ .41	$ 8.85	$ 7.17	$ .41	$ 7.58
2,500	48.35	.96	49.31	27.78	1.01	28.79	21.10	1.02	22.12	17.93	1.03	18.96
6,000	116.04	2.30	118.34	66.66	2.41	69.07	50.64	2.45	53.09	43.02	2.47	45.49
10,000	193.40	3.83	197.23	111.10	4.02	115.12	84.40	4.09	88.49	71.70	4.12	75.82

* Monthly premium during first year of loan at the rate of 1/2% per annum on average outstanding balance during the year.

TITLE 1 PROPERTY IMPROVEMENT LOANS WITH EQUAL MONTHLY PAYMENTS TO PRINCIPAL AND INTEREST

Amount of Advance	Maximum Discount per Year per $100	12 MONTH LOAN		24 MONTH LOAN		36 MONTH LOAN		48 MONTH LOAN		60 MONTH LOAN	
		Monthly Payment	Equivalent Interest Rate	Monthly Payment	Equivalent Interest Rate	Monthly Payment	Equivalent Interest Rate	Monthly Payment	Equivalent Interest Rate	Monthly Payment	Equivalent Interest Rate
$ 500	$5	$ 43.86	9.58%	$ 22.95	9.43%	$ 15.97	9.43%	$12.49	9.30%	$10.40	9.05%
1,000	5	87.72	9.58	45.89	9.43	31.94	9.43	24.97	9.30	20.79	9.05
2,500	5	219.30	9.58	114.71	9.43	79.85	9.43	62.42	9.30	51.96	9.05
3,500	5 & 4	306.11	9.01	159.72	8.89	110.93	8.89	86.53	8.77	71.89	8.54

TOTAL COST OF INTEREST

12 MONTH LOAN	24 MONTH LOAN	36 MONTH LOAN	48 MONTH LOAN	60 MONTH LOAN
$ 26	$ 51	$ 75	$ 99	$123
53	101	150	198	247
132	253	374	496	617
173	333	493	653	813

Chart shows monthly payments and dollar interest for FHA 203 (k) home-improvement loans at 6 per cent simple interest per year. "Amount of advance" is the money you get. Insurance premium is the small charge paid to FHA for obtaining an FHA loan. This is one of the kinds of loans for large jobs. Monthly payments and interest for FHA Title-1 loans, the usual FHA home-improvement loan offered by banks. It is basically a 5 per cent discount loan.

time and is perfectly legal because of loopholes in states' credit laws.*
Such facts should be remembered when you obtain financing.

The Eight Most Common Kinds of Home-Improvement Loans

Here are the eight most common ways to finance home improvement
and repair work in the order of preference, from those with the lowest
credit charges up to those with the highest:

1. *The low-cost personal loan.* This is *not* the usual personal loan
widely advertised by banks and finance companies. And not all of us
can obtain one. It is simply a straight loan with a low 5 per cent simple
interest rate obtainable mainly from banks.

But getting one requires good credit. You may have to put up collateral
such as stocks and bonds, and the loan can be paid back in any of a
number of ways depending on negotiation. For example, you may elect
to pay it back in quarterly installments over a year or two. Best source for
it is your regular bank. Top amount you can borrow depends on your
credit rating.

2. *Open-end mortgage loans.* This is an excellent way to finance expensive remodeling work, but your house mortgage must have an "open-
end" clause permitting the mortgage to be opened up for refinancing
purposes. Not all mortgages contain this clause. If yours does, you can
borrow back as much money as you have already paid up on your mortgage, and the mortgage is extended, often at the same interest rate. There
are little or no new closing costs (as the case with regular mortgage refinancing), but some lenders levy a small charge for the work involved.

It works like this: Say you need $4000 to improve your house. You
have paid off $5000 of your mortgage and only $15,000 remains to be
paid. You go to the lender holding the mortgage and request a $4000
open-end loan. You get the loan and your mortgage loan is increased to
$19,000. You continue paying off the mortgage the same as before. But
it will naturally take longer to pay it off. The term of the mortgage is
lengthened by the amount of time required to pay off the additional
$4000 usually at the same monthly payments as before; sometimes the
monthly payments are boosted.

Incidentally, there are generally no restrictions on what you can do
with the money borrowed, which is good to know in a pinch. An open-end
mortgage loan can be used for any kind of improvement, or to pay an
emergency medical bill, or even for a round-the-world cruise.

* This is not necessarily to advocate a 6 per cent ceiling on all loans. Realistically,
certain kinds of loans involve greater-than-average risk and much expense on the
lenders' part; a case can be made for higher-than-normal interest rates with them.
But exorbitant rates of, say, 15 per cent or more are generally inexcusable, particularly when they masquerade as 6 or 7 per cent loans.

3. *New FHA 6 per cent home-improvement loans.* This is the widely publicized low-cost financing method created by the Kennedy administration in 1961 to spur home improvements. Chief advantages are its generous terms and low interest for loans up to $10,000 with as long as 20 years to pay. The minimum loan is $2500, unless you live in an urban renewal area—then the bottom limit is $1000. If your house is less than ten years old, the improvement must involve "major structural changes" (put in to direct the loans toward rehabilitating older houses).

You also pay a ½ per cent mortgage-insurance charge on top of the 6 per cent interest, a service charge to obtain it, and other fees for such things as a new appraisal and FHA inspection of the work done (which protects you against inferior work). Not everybody can get the top $10,000 loan. This depends on the house, the amount of work to be done, and how much of your present mortgage is still to be paid off. The amount of the loan you get plus any other mortgages and loans you have on the house may not exceed $25,000.

You ask for an FHA Section 203 (k) loan. As this is written not all banks are willing to give these loans (because of the generous terms). You may have to shop around to obtain one.

By the way, the FHA does not make direct loans to borrowers for either home improvements or buying new houses. The government doesn't put up a dime. This new FHA improvement loan plus all other FHA loans discussed in this chapter are actually made by private lenders. The FHA simply insures the lender against loss in case of default.

4. *Straight mortgage refinancing.* This is the best choice for large remodeling jobs if you do not have an open-end mortgage clause and cannot obtain an FHA 203 (k) loan. The advantages are low interest, around 6 per cent, and low monthly payments lumped in with your regular house mortgage payments. Say, for example, you need $7000 for remodeling and your present mortgage has $15,000 remaining to be paid off. A new mortgage of $22,000 is obtained ($15,000 plus $7000). This pays off the old mortgage balance as well as paying for the new remodeling expense. The new mortgage is paid off monthly like any other mortgage.

The disadvantages: New closing costs must be paid just as when you bought the house, although they should not be as high; refinancing usually takes a month or more for processing; and the interest rates on the new mortgage are likely to be higher than on the old, particularly if you bought your house back in the days when mortgage interest rates were only 4 to 5 per cent. The going rate for a refinanced mortgage is around 6 per cent in most places as this is written. If the bank that holds your mortgage makes excessive demands for refinancing it, shop around for a better deal on a new mortgage from another bank.

5. *Special refinancing of an FHA mortgage.* If you have an FHA mort-

gage, sometimes it can be refinanced with a special FHA provision, called FHA Section 203 B. It operates much the same way as regular refinancing, noted above, except that you take out an entirely new FHA mortgage up to a maximum of $25,000. The proceeds are used to pay off your present mortgage and pay for your remodeling. Your house and the new addition, however, must meet FHA construction standards, and new closing costs must be paid.

Unfortunately, many banks will not provide this financing because of the red tape allegedly involved and the low FHA interest charges. Even when they do, you should expect a delay of a month or two for processing. This is, therefore, not a hopeful method of financing. It is listed here because you may live in an area where it is available.

6. *FHA Title 1 home-improvement or fix-up loan.* This offers the lowest interest rates for what bankers term "unsecured loans." It is the grandfather of all home fix-up loans, with close to 25 million of them made by banks and other private lenders since FHA was created in 1934. And it is generally the easiest and best way to finance small jobs of up to $1000 or $2000.

Actually, the maximum loan obtainable is $3500. Interest rates are pegged at a 5 per cent add-on rate (equaling 9.4 per cent simple interest) for up to $2500 borrowed, 4 per cent add-on for any additional amount up to $3500. These interest rates make a Title 1 loan a bit expensive for amounts of more than $1500 to $2000, compared with the mortgage refinancing loans already noted.

A Title 1 loan can be obtained quickly and easily, sometimes in a few hours. It is offered by some 14,000 banks and savings and loan associations. It can be used for nearly all bonafide home improvements and repairs, including built-in appliances and air conditioning, but not for such "luxuries" as swimming pools and barbecue pits.

7. *Banks' "own loans."* This is the kind of installment loan widely advertised by banks and savings and loan associations for "quick and easy" remodeling. It is similar to the FHA Title 1 loan, except for stiffer 5½ to 7 per cent add-on or discount charges, thus from 10 to 15 per cent interest, depending on the lender.

Amounts of up to $5000, sometimes more, usually can be borrowed with as long as seven years to pay. The money can be used for any kind of improvement including swimming pools and barbecue pits, its chief advantage over the FHA Title 1 loan. Sometimes the lender requires a life insurance policy for which you pay. This is so that a suddenly widowed wife will not be left with an unpaid installment loan (and the bank will not be left holding the bag if she cannot pay it).

8. *Finance company loans.* These are the same kind of installment loans made for cars, appliances, and other consumer goods. Practically

anybody can get one. But they carry the highest credit charges—usually a 7 per cent add-on charge, or nearly 14 per cent interest. You don't necessarily go to a finance company to get the loan. Most home-improvement salesmen have the necessary forms in their brief case and you merely sign them. In other words, this is the usual installment loan offered by home-improvement dealers. The dealer, in turn, takes the signed papers to the finance company for approval and payment.

You should also know that finance companies are not famous for limiting their loans only to reputable dealers. Some companies, by and large, will accept loans, with their eyes shut, from nearly any home-improvement dealer. As a result, this kind of loan is used by many of the worst fly-by-night dealers in the business. So just because a dealer says he can get you an easy loan is no guarantee that he is a reputable dealer.

For that matter, not all banks check on the dealers whose loans they finance. A dealer may say that he has a tie with a local bank, but this, too, is no real proof that the dealer is reputable or that the loan is a good and fair one.

Two Other Kinds of Loans

You could also borrow money from a credit union if you are a member or obtain a savings account loan against your savings. The first is generally an excellent deal with generous terms and low credit charges, though there may be a limit on the size of the loan obtainable.

The second is simply a low-interest loan, usually about 5 per cent, borrowed against the money you may have in a savings account. The net interest you pay, however, is lower, since the money in your savings account continues to earn interest.

Say you have $2000 in a savings account and don't want to use it up but wish to obtain the lowest possible interest on a home-improvement loan. You borrow $2000 at 5 per cent from the savings bank, putting up your savings-account book as collateral. Since your savings-account money continues to pay interest at, say 3½ per cent, your net cost for the loan is 1½ per cent (5 minus 3½ per cent).

You cannot draw money from the savings account until the loan is repaid, but in an emergency you could obtain another loan to pay off the balance due on the home-improvement loan and release your savings to use. The chief advantage of this loan is psychological. You tend to pay up the money borrowed as quickly as possible, thus at the lowest total interest charge, and you remain secure in the knowledge of having money in the bank.

Where to Get Financing

First try your own bank, particularly if a large loan is needed. Then shop around. Don't take the first offer. The terms offered can vary greatly from bank to bank and simply trying the next bank down the street can sometimes save you hundreds of dollars.

Savings banks and savings and loan associations are generally best for mortgage financing and refinancing. Some of them are also getting deeper and deeper into straight remodeling loans. Interest rates with savings and loan associations may be slightly higher than with regular banks.

Other sources for mortgage refinancing are life insurance companies and mortgage broker firms. The life insurance companies formerly showed little interest in financing home improvements but some of them now invite this business. Some mortgage brokers specialize in refinancing mortgages. You find them in the classified phone book under "mortgage brokers."

A commercial bank, as opposed to a savings bank, is generally your best bet for a conventional home-improvement loan. Some of them also deal in mortgage refinancing, as well as with FHA loans, though not always. Nearly all have their "own loan" plans. (A savings bank has the word "savings" in its name. All others are commercial banks.)

Summary

The best kind of loan will depend, first of all, on the amount of money you need. If you need no more than $1000 or $2000, try first for a low, 5 per cent simple-interest personal loan, not an installment loan. If you have a mortgage with an open-end clause, use it for small or large amounts, up to the permissible limit.

Try for a low-interest mortgage loan when you need more than $2000 to $3000. Mortgage refinancing generally does not pay for smaller loans because of the service charges and closing costs involved (except with an open-end loan, which usually works out economically).

A regular installment loan should be used only as a last resort because of its higher interest rate. This goes for the FHA Title 1 loan, a bank's "own loan," or a finance company loan. One more word about installment loans: Avoid getting one for a long term. Keep the length of the loan down to a year or two at most, if possible. For one thing, their credit charges rise steeply over the years. For another, you are heavily penalized if you have a long-term, a four-year loan say, and pay it off ahead of time.

The "privilege" of paying it off in advance is highly expensive. You are charged a stiff pay-off penalty and this goes for an FHA Title 1 loan as well as for the highest-interest finance company installment loan. This is unlike conventional mortgage loans which can be paid off ahead of time with little or no prepayment penalty—another reason for avoiding installment loans.

Chapter 33

The Ten Biggest Home-Improvement Rackets

Not long ago a story on the woman's page of the New York *Times* reported one of the most common tragedies that can befall us when work is done on our houses. A woman whose home was in the midst of remodeling was asked by her contractor to sign the completion slip. His bank was withholding money, he said, until he produced this signed certificate and he needed the cash urgently to finish her job.

Eager to see the job finished and sympathetic with his plight, the woman signed, though she vaguely realized that she probably should not until the work was finished. The contractor got his money and disappeared, leaving the family with a half-finished remodeling job on its hands.

According to the Better Business Bureaus, this happens all the time. It is one of the worst home-improvement rackets. It puts emphasis on an important rule: *Never* sign a completion certificate until the job is completed and completed satisfactorily. A completion slip is required when your work is financed. The bank requires it before it will pay off the contractor.

If you pay cash, don't let your payments get ahead of the work in progress. When the work is completed it is a good idea to withhold about 10 to 20 per cent of the money due the contractor for a few weeks. This gives you a breathing spell in which to determine for sure that everything is properly done. If corrective work is required, it is remarkable how quickly a man will return to remedy it (with *his* money at stake).

This is not to paint all contractors as black scoundrels. Some are highly reliable, others just so-so, and still others are indeed downright gyps. In addition, there are also the pathetic men who are not dishonest and in many cases quite conscientious but their glaring shortcoming is stupidity or ignorance. They make mistakes because they don't know better.

This chapter is to familiarize you with the most common gyp schemes and how they work. According to people who are supposed to know such things, the home-improvement business accounts for the largest number of consumer frauds in the United States every year (followed by such things as the used-car racket and phony mail-order schemes).

Who Are the Victims?

What's more, you may think that you are much too smart to fall for any of the blatant schemes perpetrated every day. Don't be too sure. You may already have been taken, for example, by point 7, following list.

Many gyps prey on housewives home alone during the day, on elderly couples, and on low-income and small-town homeowners who tend to be unsophisticated in the ways of the smooth-talking gyp artist. But records show that a good many men, young couples, middle-income, and city people are also mulcted by slick home-improvement con men, and the woods are full of them. We are particular targets when we are honest ourselves. We assume other people are honest, too, and never suspect that the sincere young man with the clean-cut features could be out to mulct us. He may well be absolutely upright and dependable. The trouble is that his ranks have been infiltrated by equally clean-cut con men.

How to Protect Yourself

In addition to obtaining a signed completion slip in advance, leaving the homeowner with incomplete work, our number-one racket, here are the nine other most common home-improvement rackets and schemes, based on Better Business Bureau records, FHA experiences, and state investigations, along with advice on avoiding them:

1. *The "model home" scheme.* A salesman tells you that he can give you a big break on the price of new aluminum siding—or a new roof, or almost any other major home improvement—because your house would make an ideal "model" for his firm's product. What's more, it won't cost you a cent because they will pay you $100 for every person who buys a similar job as a result of seeing your house. "Surely you know at least half a dozen people who need new siding. That's $600 right there. You'll have your money back in no time," he says. All you do is sign up for this $3500 job—normally it's $4500, he says—and your money starts coming back as soon as we're finished.

The owner, of course, will seldom get a nickel back. In fact, the sales price quoted is inflated as much as 400 per cent (yes, that much) over the average cost of the same work by a legitimate dealer. The gyp salesman farms out the work to a cheap local contractor for half the price, pockets the difference, and is never seen again.

Moral: *Never* deal with anybody who offers a special deal in order to use your house as a model. If a salesman mentions it, show him firmly to the door, regardless of how persuasive he may sound and regardless of how big a carrot it seems. Some salesmen, to be sure, will offer you $25, say, for every lead you later send to him that he converts into a sale. This is another matter, but don't depend much on such bonus money.

2. *Furnace-dismantling racket.* The operator rings the doorbell and offers a free inspection of your furnace. Sometimes he poses as an official inspector for the city or fire department. He insists on seeing your furnace, perhaps because dangerous-looking smoke is pouring from the chimney. One woman let such men in and on going down to the basement a half hour later she found her furnace and oil burner completely dismantled, the parts broken up and strewn over the basement floor.

"We had to do it," the men said, "to safeguard your family. You'd be asphyxiated." She was forced to buy a new furnace for $850 even though the old one was perfectly good. Sometimes the operators offer a free furnace cleaning job, but then "discover" that the furnace is in such dangerous condition that they had to dismantle it and carry it off.

Moral: Do not allow "inspectors" into the house, regardless of how impressive their credentials may look at first. In the rare case of a legitimate inspection, scrutinize the man's identification card and make sure he really works for an official agency. If he cannot produce identification, or if in doubt, call the local police department for confirmation. Official inspections, by the way, do occur during and after remodeling work, not before you order such work ordinarily (unless you have applied for a building "variance"). And avoid special offers for furnace cleaning.

3. *"Bait and switch" advertisements.* The Federal Trade Commission (FTC) defines this racket as "An alluring [bargain price] but insincere offer to sell a product the advertiser does not intend to sell. Its purpose is to switch consumers from buying the advertised merchandise, in order to sell something else, at a higher price."

A typical "bait" ad often seen in newspapers offers a complete new stone front for a 30-foot house for only $79—quite a bargain, it seems. The charming little house pictured in the papers is dressed up with one of the new stone fronts. What you actually get, however, for $79 is a cheap asphalt paper, with a stone design, that is nailed on. The genuine stone shown in the ad costs at least $500 to $600. The idea is to hook you into answering the ad, and then switch you to a more expensive job.

The same scheme is used for selling a variety of other products, including "aluminum" patios and awnings (offered for $79.50 but actually costing several hundred dollars); finished basements (for only $2.50 a week but all you would really get is a 12×12-foot cubicle, far from finished); "complete" new kitchens for $695 (for a few cabinets only, as noted in Chapter 11); and low-cost combination storm window bargains (as noted in Chapter 14).

Moral: Beware of tempting low-price bargains offered in ads. Better still, avoid wild bargains. The best bargain is a good job.

4. *Debt-consolidation schemes.* This scheme is used on families in debt who need repairs on their houses. You may owe $2000 say, on one or more loans you've taken out, and also need $1000 worth of work on your house. The operator says he will consolidate your $2000 worth of debts and the $1000 worth of new work in one new loan with attractively low monthly payments.

But you pay dearly for the privilege. There will be penalty fees of several hundred dollars just for paying off your existing loans, plus another $500 charge, more or less, for arranging the new loan, plus stiff new credit and interest charges for the new loan.

In one such case, the homeowner found out, too late, that the new loan indeed came with low monthly payments (which added up steeply over the years) but it turned out that it cost him over $4500, plus interest, to pay for the $3000 worth of loans consolidated. In a rash of such cases in Cleveland, the home-improvement dealer was found to be pocketing all the money and not even paying off the old loans that he had promised to consolidate for his customers.

Moral: Don't consolidate existing loans unless it is absolutely necessary. If you do, never do it through a home-improvement contractor. Talk with several banks and deal directly with the one with the best terms.

5. *Chimney-repair racket.* A particularly vicious example is what happened to a 75-year-old Bowling Green, Kentucky, woman. She was told that her chimney would topple in the first strong wind unless it was repaired at once. She was pressured into buying a $3600 repair job. A crew of four men, posing as experts, dabbed cement on a few cracks and vanished, she tearfully told police. She had been swindled by a band of crooks.

Such swindlers will claim that they just happen to be working down the street and noticed that your chimney may collapse any minute. It's going to topple. But they can fix it immediately at low cost because they are working nearby. Warmed up, they will paint dreadful pictures of the damage done to houses by toppled chimneys. The owner is frightened into signing up for an expensive repair job. It is completed in a few hours and the men vanish.

Moral: Don't be frightened into buying immediate repairs for a chimney condition (or for any other kind of emergency repairs). Many chimneys indeed require repairs, but take your time and hire a reputable repairman with an established local business.

6. *Fake termites.* The quick-buck operator examines your house and

emerges with a piece of wood crawling with termites. (They are from a small bottle carried in his pocket.) He warns that you face an immediate house collapse unless repairs are done at once. Pressure is exerted on you to sign up so he can go to work without a moment wasted.

Moral: Don't be frightened by a termite scare and don't be pressured into buying. Investigate the condition yourself, and before buying call in other dealers for alternate bids.

7. *Two-for-one paint bargains.* Paint stores offer the "best-quality" paint for $8.98 a gallon, every second gallon free. It's done all over the country. Sometimes the second gallon costs a penny more. Actually, it's the old two-for-one gimmick, two gallons of poor $4.50 paint masquerading as top-quality paint.

The low quality of an actual sample of such paint was determined by actual test. The paint sold for $8.98 plus a second gallon free. A federal paint standard requires paint to withstand 500 cycles of a special brush test. The $8.98 paint began to disintegrate after only 25 brush cycles and was worn away at the end of 50 cycles. Two ordinary low-price paints tested at the same time showed no visible wear after 50 cycles.

Moral: Don't expect good paint free any more than you would expect a $2500 second car given free when you buy a new car.

8. *"Low-balling."* A Chicago couple signed up for a low $1500 offer to add a new room to their house. Two legitimate contractors had said the same work would cost $2500. *After* signing up, the couple were told certain extras were needed: finished flooring, wallboard, finished ceiling, painting, insulation, and the installation of each; none of which was included in the original $1500 price. They had to pay another $1500, thus $3000 in all, for the complete job they thought they were buying in the first place.

Called low-balling in the trade, this practice has flourished for years as a way to elbow legitimate contractors out of the job. Once you sign up you are hooked, and the dishonest contractor blithely says he never claimed he was furnishing all those "extras." ("Where did you ever get that idea? It's impossible at the price.")

Moral: Be wary of very low bids way under the competition. Determine exactly how much work will be done, what materials you get, and if the price also includes installation of all materials. Get an itemized, signed list.

9. *Fraudulent fire-alarm salesmen.* A phony salesman gains entry to your house by claiming he is from the Fire Safety Council, a nonexistent organization. Other equally impressive but fictitious names are also mentioned. He claims he is educating homeowners with fire-prevention demonstrations. Once inside, he displays a series of horror pictures and terrifying newspaper stories reporting the disasters and lost lives caused

by house fires. His object is to scare you into buying a fire-alarm system for $500 to $1000. After the order is signed, a couple of men string a few wires around the house and disappear.

Moral: Again, don't be pressured and don't be frightened into buying. If you are concerned about fire, a complete alarm system can be had for a few hundred dollars at most. Individual alarm mechanisms for specific rooms are available for $25 to $50 apiece, depending on the type and method of operation.

Another common racket, the aluminum storm-window racket, is described in Chapter 14.

In summary, it can be seen that a few common threads are characteristic of fraudulant home-improvement deals. Many appeal to our instinct for a bargain, offering items at a special low price that we can't afford to pass up. In point of fact, they are far from bargains.

Many other schemes can be operated only when you finance the work and finance it through the fraudulent dealer. Once you have signed the credit papers he is virtually assured of getting his money regardless of how poorly the work has been done. And many rely on high-pressure sales scare tactics. These are the hallmarks of the phony deal.

Chapter 34

Avoiding High Repair Bills:
A Maintenance Program for Your House

Like an automobile, a house should be checked periodically, certain equipment oiled or adjusted, and vital parts of the structure inspected before a small crack left unnoticed grows into a major repair job.

One home repair expert says that, "Over 50 per cent of all the emergency service calls and troubles I have seen could have been avoided by preventative maintenance."

Human nature being what it is, we naturally tend to put off until tomorrow what should be done today, particularly the chores about a house. Actually, the few periodic checks and repairs required take little time and can pay off in handsome dividends on the stitch-in-time principle.

Here is a summary of common causes of damage and repair bills in houses and what to do about them before they cause trouble. Many are simple tasks which almost anyone can do with a screwdriver, pliers, or swab of paint. Others may require an expert, but by being familiar with them you will know what to request and also know if it is done properly.

1. Warm-air heating. Inspect the air filter at least once a month, since dirt-clogged filters are the biggest single cause of constricted heat supply and false-alarm service calls. If the filter looks dirty, remove it from the furnace and shake it outdoors or vacuum it. It is clean when you hold it up to the sun or a bright light and can see clearly through it. Some filters should be hosed with water, depending on the type. Follow the instructions in the furnace manufacturer's service booklet.

Oil the blower motor and its pulley once a year, but don't overdo it, since too much oil is as bad as none at all. Not all motors, however, require oil. Some have sealed bearings, lubricated for life. This should be noted either on the blower, or in the manufacturer's instructions. Obtain a copy of the manual in any case and refer to it for other service that may be required.

The blower pulley belt (like an automobile fan belt) should be checked for proper tension. It normally should have about an inch of slack. If it is badly worn, have it replaced.

Remove the air-outlet registers and return-air grilles, located in your rooms, about once a month and clean out the dust and dirt inside of the duct throats, preferably with a vacuum cleaner nozzle. This is simply dirt and dust from the house air.

2. Hot-water and steam heat. "Bleed" the radiators every fall, especially balky ones that do not heat up. You open the water valve at the end of the radiator and drain off a bucket or two of water. Use a bucket or pail, of course, to catch the water. This releases trapped air which prevents hot-water or steam circulation inside the radiator. If a radiator still does not heat properly, drain off more water. Don't be afraid of releasing too much water, since it is automatically made up by a water-supply valve at the boiler.

There are three kinds of bleed vents for radiators: the manual, disk, and automatic float type. Most radiators have the manual kind, which sticks out near the top of one end of the radiator, is circular in shape and about a half inch-long. It has a slot which you open with a radiator "key" (sold in hardware stores) or merely with a dime. Turn it open until water comes out, then close it.

The disk kind looks like the manual kind except it contains a series of fiber disks. It is semiautomatic in operation in that it automatically lets air out when necessary. The disks swell up when wet, which is when there is water in the radiator and not air, as it should be. If air gets in, the disks contract, which opens the vent to let out the air. Sometimes the disks get worn or dirty and drip water on the floor. Replacement disks are sold (in hardware stores and by heating dealers) for replacing worn or dirty ones. The disk vent costs a little more than the manual vent.

The automatic float vent is highest in price and uses a small tank and float device much like a toilet tank float but on a smaller scale. Water in the radiator keeps the float up and the vent closed. Air instead of water in the radiator will lower the float and open the vent, which lets the air escape. The automatic vent seldom needs attention and does away with the periodic need to bleed radiators. Of course it can go bad after a number of years and then you must replace it.

It is also a good idea to drain and flush all the water in a hot-water or steam system, particularly if you have hard water, every two to three years. This will prevent rust and corrosion from building up in the pipes and heating unit.

The water circulating pump may require a drop of oil occasionally, unless it is a sealed, permanently lubricated pump. Refer to the manufacturer's manual about this.

With oil heat, the oil burner should be checked, cleaned, and readjusted every fall before cold weather sets in. The $5 to $10 service charge will come back with interest. While the serviceman is at it, have him drop an anticorrosion capsule into your oil tank. Oil-heat men report they are encountering more and more cases of tank leaks caused by corrosion. With gas heat, cleaning and adjustment is recommended every three to four years.

3. *Semiannual termite inspection* (or at least once a year). It's best to use an expert, though any moderately conscientious person can learn to do it once you see how it is done. A step-by-step check is made all around the interior and exterior walls of the house, including the foundation, the cellar, under porches, steps, and inside crawl-spaces. Look for suspicious "veins" of dirt and termite "mud tunnels," which may be anywhere from a quarter-inch to as much as a foot wide in places. Wood at or near ground level should be jabbed with a knife to detect infested sections under the surface. Wood window frames near the ground and floor beams and posts, particularly near the exterior walls, also should get the knife test.

Don't leave wood piled up near the house since dead wood is a magnet for termites. Fireplace logs should not be stored in the basement or near the house. Keep at least 4 to 8 inches of clearance between the ground level and the lowest exposed wood of the house.

Cracks and crevices in foundation walls should be plastered with cement. If your house has a concrete floor directly on the ground, inspect the plumbing access hole regularly. This is the floor opening for pipes, usually located behind a panel in the bathroom. It is a point of entry for termites from the ground.

4. *Wood rot.* Infected wood can be searched out during a termite inspection. Rotted wood is soft and decayed and breaks easily when knifed. If caught in time, replacement may not be necessary, providing the cause of the rot—moisture—is eliminated.

A certain amount of moisture and water is usually inevitable in houses. It can be controlled by providing constant ventilation where it occurs. This means plenty of natural air flow for crawl-spaces, under porches and steps, and in attics. If necessary, install large vents in such spaces for air flow in and out. Inspect the spaces periodically to be sure they are not damp.

Two of the biggest causes of wood rot, as well as wet basements, are clogged roof drains and poor water drainage away from the house. Nine times out of ten one of these is the cause of the trouble.

The vertical downspout pipes from the roof should be inspected to make sure they are not leaking and that they are dumping their water away from the house or into a dry well. If downspouts drain into ground pipes or a dry well, disconnect them periodically to be sure the ground drain pipe is not clogged. Squirt water from a hose into each one to be sure it is carried away. If the water backs up, the drainage system is clogged and must be freed. It further means that the water from the roof is backing up in the ground and very likely into the house substructure, thus a wet basement.

Keep your roof gutters free of leaves and other debris. Gutters require checking and cleaning quite frequently, especially with trees around. You can save yourself this periodic chore by putting screening across the top of all roof gutters. Special gutter screening, usually in 6-inch widths, can be bought at hardware stores or from Sears, Roebuck. It is easily attached to keep out leaves.

5. Drainage away from the house. Don't allow water to pool up next to the house. The earth around your walls should slope gently away and shed rain water. Look for depressions and fill them in with dirt, and regrade where necessary. Incidentally, it is best not to put flower beds up against the house walls, because when you water them, the same water, sinking into the ground, can cause a wet basement.

6. Plumbing. Check faucets and water outlets for drip leaks. A hidden cause of leakage and high water bills is the toilet flush tank. To test for a leak here, deposit a dye—obtainable in a hardware store—in the tank. If the dye appears in the toilet bowl without the water being flushed, you have a leak. Often it can be corrected by a new rubber ball. If not, call a plumber.

Other periodic plumbing checks: Remove bathroom shower heads and flush them out in the sink; remove and clean kitchen sink drains, especially the pop-up kind; and every fall make sure that outside water faucets and pipes are drained and shut off from the inside to prevent freezing and broken pipes.

7. Septic tanks. A properly sized tank normally does not require cleaning any more than every two to three years. It may be a good idea to have the tank inspected, though, every year. An inspection will determine if the tank is filling up to the point where it should be cleaned out. The cleaning should be done by a professional septic-tank cleaner.

He checks the level of the three layers of waste in the tank—a top layer of what is called scum on the surface, then several feet of liquid "effluent," and the settled "sludge" on the bottom. In general, a tank should be cleaned when the distance between the sludge surface at the bottom and the scum on the top is one half or less than the total depth of the tank. This is determined with a special stick.

Have the tank cleaned in spring or summer. If done during cold weather, the cold slows down the essential decomposition action of the bacteria within the tank and there may be trouble getting the tank to function properly again.

A variety of septic-tank-cleaning chemicals are on the market but experts say that none do any real good. They may help a bit but they decidedly do not take the place of regular cleaning and of proper care. In other words, don't drain foreign matter into a tank, such as paper towels, wrapping paper, old rags, coffee grounds, cooking oils and fats, the contents of ash trays, or anything other than regular food and waste.

To avoid damage to the septic tank and its tile-pipe network just under the ground, don't allow trucks or other heavy equipment in this area. Don't plant shrubs and trees here either, as their roots can damage or clog the pipes. Check the area once in a while to see that it remains well drained of rain since storm water can flood the system and make it inoperative.

8. Outside walls, windows, and doors. It's a good idea to inspect the outside of your house every spring and fall, and after bad storms. Worn and damaged spots should be repaired or painted. Cracks around windows and doors should be caulked. Exterior painting should not be put off too long or it will cost twice as much, as badly worn or peeled paint has to be burned off and a new prime coat applied. Most houses require a fresh paint job every three to five years.

Brick, stone, or masonry walls should be checked for cracks, breaks, or holes. If they are not repaired immediately, rain can get inside the house and cause damage to walls and ceilings. The hinges and roto-operators of metal casement windows should be oiled at least once a year. The channels of sliding windows and wood windows should be cleaned periodically with steel wool.

9. Chimney. Cleaning is needed every three or four years, normally, particularly if you have oil heat. Once a chimney becomes clogged with soot, blow-back is a dangerous possibility; so much soot accumulates that under certain conditions the filth may suddenly be blown back into the house.

A chimney also should be checked for cracks and loose or broken masonry. Holes or breaks in the protective screen on top should be repaired at once. Otherwise birds or small animals can nest inside and even get into the house.

10. Wiring. Since faulty wiring is a major cause of household fires, you should check all exposed wiring regularly, including appliance and lamp cords. Worn or frayed cords should be replaced. If possible, check the wiring cables leading from your main electric switch box (usually located next to the meter). If they are hot to the touch, call an electrician at once. Be careful. Use gloves and don't touch exposed wires, and allow no one but an electrician to touch anything inside the box.

11. Roof and attic. The roof should be inspected at the same time that the walls and windows are checked, and broken or loose shingles should be repaired. As already noted, roof gutters should be kept clean of leaves and dirt.

Check the attic for good ventilation all year-round. Attic vents should *not* be shut in the winter because of the year-round ventilation needed to prevent condensation. If the attic floor is properly insulated, you need not worry about excessive heat leakage from the house. Holes in attic vent screens should be repaired to keep out birds and bees.

12. Door locks. Exterior door locks need to be lubricated every four or five years to prevent sticking. The best lubricant is powdered graphite, available at hardware stores. Squirt it into the lock opening. A little graphite is also good for balky inside locks—especially the bathroom door lock, which has a way of getting stuck behind children. (Graphite also can do wonders for sticky car locks.)

13. The water heater (for hot water to spigots). Once every month or two open the valve at the bottom of the water-heater tank and drain out a bucketful of hot water. This will get rid of accumulated scale and sediment.

14. Air conditioning. As with heating furnaces, dirt-clogged air-conditioner filters often cause inadequate cooling and unnecessary service calls. Filters should be cleaned at least once a month, more often if you live in a smoggy city. If you have a central air conditioner, an annual check and adjustment is recommended, but this is not necessary for window units.

15. Appliances. Run-down appliances are the most frequent cause of service calls. Since the maintenance required varies according to type and brand of appliance, you should consult the manufacturer's instruction booklet and carry out the checks recommended. If you have lost your copy, write for another.

A few specific tips: Neglecting to clean out the clothes-drier lint trap is a widespread cause of operating trouble and fires. It should be emptied at least once a week, preferably after each load. Washers and driers should not be overloaded. And sometimes hot- and cold-water pipe valves to the washer should be shut except when washing, depending on the kind of washer. The manufacturer's instructions will mention this.

Chapter 35

A Check List for Home Remodeling, Improvements, and Repairs

Here for quick reference is a summary of the main points of this book. It can be cut out for handy use when you talk to contractors or salesman. If in doubt about any point, refer to the appropriate chapter for elaboration.

Should You Remodel or Buy Another House?

1. Do you like your present house and neighborhood and really not want to move?

2. Is your house fundamentally satisfactory and suitable for your family, even though you may need additional space?

3. Does the house lend itself to the changes desired? Can new rooms or a new addition be easily added? Is your lot big enough for expansion?

4. After all of your proposed improvements and additions are made, will the results add up to what you want in a house, with no major compromises? Remember, however, that there is no perfect house. Small drawbacks and limitations are to be expected in every house. But there is no need to tolerate glaring defects that make living in a house difficult and inconvenient.

5. Can you afford the cost of remodeling? Or would you be better off to start fresh with a more suitable new house?

6. Are you and your family temperamentally suited to the exigencies of remodeling—the construction delays, living with workmen (for months perhaps), structural chaos, and unfinished business—while the work is being done?

If your answers are mostly yes to the above questions and mostly no to the following four questions, you should probably stay with your present house and remodel rather than buy another house.

Basement wall exposed on the downside slope of your lot can be opened up beautifully with glass. Sometimes excavation may be needed.   *Courtesy Aluminium Ltd.*

Diagram illustrates excellent relationship between house and outdoor patio, both on same level, and each being highly convenient to the other.   *Aluminium Ltd.*

7. Are you unhappy with your present location and neighborhood because of poor schools, inconvenient shopping, too much traffic or commerce, time-consuming commuting, etc?

8. Is your neighborhood going downhill? Are stores, shopping centers, business offices, factories, or highways getting too close for comfort?

9. Will the cost of remodeling your house exceed the extra cost of a new house? The money required to buy a new house, on top of the price you would get for your present house, normally should be no more than the estimated total cost of remodeling your present house. If you move, don't forget to figure the expenses for financing, closing costs, furnishing a new house, landscaping, etc.

10. Do you really want to move? What are your bedrock feelings about buying another house? The honest answer to this question more than any other—how you and your family *feel* about remodeling versus moving—is usually the best indication of what to do.

Buying and Remodeling a Large, Old House

11. Is the house sufficiently spacious and attractive? Do you really want it?

12. Is it well designed with a good floor plan and room layout?

13. Can you buy it at a reasonable price?

14. What is the true cost—its selling price plus the cost of all essential remodeling and repairs? This should not exceed the price of a comparable new house and generally should be less, considering the time and trouble you will expend putting it into good shape.

15. Is it in an established neighborhood that is unlikely to go downhill? This is quite important.

16. Does it have good remodeling potential? Can new rooms be easily added? Are the kitchen and bathrooms large enough for modernization, if necessary?

17. Will you enjoy remodeling it?

18. Is it basically in good structural condition? Have you had it checked for the most likely flaws in old houses:

Termite damage and wood rot	Poor plumbing
Inadequate wiring	Worn roof and roof gutters
Run-down heating system	Little or no insulation
Sagging structure	Run-down faucet water heater

19. Is the exterior paint in good condition? What about the chimney, fireplace, bathroom and kitchen, interior paint, windows and doors?

Adding New Rooms to a House

20. Before you remodel, does the house have an efficient plan and good room layout? Is there good circulation from room to room? Good zoning?

21. If not, how can the plan be improved? Does this fit in with your remodeling plans?

22. Are new rooms properly located?

23. Is each new room large enough?

24. Does it lend itself to good furniture placement?

25. Is new space properly oriented in relation to the sun and prevailing winds? Will it receive a maximum of bright sunshine in winter, but a minimum of cold winter winds and hot summer sun?

26. Is there adequate storage? Can you build-in good storage space? (See Chapter 3 for standards.)

27. Should you hire an architect? The bigger the job, the more an architect can help.

28. Has a complete plan been prepared in advance?

29. Does a new addition to the house conform in style and character with the rest of the house?

30. Do your plans conform with your building and zoning codes?

31. Are good-quality materials specified for walls, floors, ceiling, and so on, not just the materials that are cheapest in first cost?

32. Have you made advance provisions for heating, wiring, lighting, insulation, and termite controls?

Kitchen Remodeling

33. Is the kitchen centrally located? If not, can you move it to a better location?

34. Will it have a bright and sunny exposure?

35. Is it large enough for successful remodeling?

36. Does the plan conform to the all-important work triangle?

37. Do you have enough countertop space, ample storage cabinets?

38. Are you getting a good-quality sink, faucet, countertop material, storage cabinets, flooring, and good-quality appliances?

39. Is the lighting well-designed?

40. Is there a range hood or exhaust fan?

41. Will your decoration and painting scheme make the kitchen warm, pleasant, and cheerful?

Bathrooms

42. Is a new bathroom well-located in relation to nearby rooms, and also for minimum piping costs?

43. Is it large enough for two people at one time?

44. Are the fixtures well located for easy and convenient use (good interior planning)?

45. Is the washbowl large enough for washing your face or an infant, if necessary?

46. Does it look good, with a rugged finish? Is it easy to keep clean?

47. Is the bathtub large enough for tub baths, and deep enough for minimum floor splashing? Does it have a permanent finish?

48. Is the toilet of good quality (siphon jet kind, preferably) quiet in operation, and easy to clean? Have you considered a wall-hung or quiet-flush model?

49. Are faucets and shower nozzles of good quality?

50. Are rugged, waterproof materials used for floor and walls?

51. Is there good lighting for the washbowl, bathtub, and shower?

52. Are colors chosen to make the room bright, large, and pleasant?

53. Have you included all special accessories and features you will want—ample medicine cabinet, built-in towel bars, laundry hamper, linen closet, exhaust fan, electric heater, safety grab bars for the shower, drip-proof toilet tank, and provisions for instant hot water at the faucets?

Windows, Insulating Glass, Storm Windows, and Skylights

54. Can a large new window or two improve your house?

55. If so, is it properly located in relation to the sun for sunshine in winter but minimum sun heat in summer (by means of outside shading, if necessary)?

56. Will it provide privacy inside the room as well as providing a good view outside?

57. Does the window conform in style and appearance with other windows?

58. Have you considered the merits of wood versus aluminum versus steel windows?

59. Is it a top national-brand window?

60. Will the window contain sealed double glass or will you need storm windows?

61. Does the window incorporate built-in weather stripping?

62. Combination storm windows and screens: Are you getting well-made units that will endure?

63. Skylights: Can a ceiling skylight improve rooms by letting over-head light and air flood in?

64. Is the skylight location planned for a minimum of hot sun heat in summer?

65. Are there provisions for ventilation?

66. Provisions for preventing condensation on the inside of the sky-light, especially in a cold climate?

Flooring, Wall, and Ceiling Materials

67. Are the materials appropriate for the room in which they are used? Are they chosen for rugged duty, low upkeep, and good looks?

68. Are you avoiding the cheapest, lowest-cost materials (usually lowest in quality)? Have you chosen, instead, materials that offer greater quality and durability at a small increase in first cost?

69. Exterior walls: Does a new exterior wall material conform in style and appearance with the rest of the house?

70. Is it tough, durable, and not likely to require frequent painting?

71. Aluminum siding: Have you obtained two or three bids? Have you compared the quantity and quality of siding proposed in each bid, one against the other?

72. Is the siding made by a leading manufacturer?

73. Have you checked the reputation and experience of the con-tractor? Are you absolutely sure he is reliable?

74. Exterior paint and painting: Have you chosen the best color for the house?

75. Are you getting a top-quality paint? Are its ingredients noted on the label?

76. Is the paint specifically recommended for your kind of walls (wood, masonry, etc.)?

77. Can you use a latex emulsion paint (usually the best of all)?

78. Has the surface been properly prepared before painting?

79. Is the paint being applied strictly as recommended?

New Roofing

80. Will the color and texture of new roofing enhance the house appearance? Does it contrast nicely and not clash with the wall color?

81. Are you getting a good grade of roofing?

82. Is wind- and storm-proof roofing specified (like seal-down shingles), if necessary where you live?

83. Will the roofing be installed properly?

Heating

84. Is a new heating unit sized properly for the house? Has this been determined by a heat-loss computation?

85. Warm-air heat: Is the furnace guaranteed for ten years?

86. Does the furnace have a belt-driven blower?

87. Can the air filter be removed easily for cleaning?

88. If new ducts are required, is it a well-designed perimeter duct system?

89. Is the furnace adjusted for continuous air circulation?

90. Are provisions made, if desired, for future air conditioning?

91. Hot-water and steam heat: Is the heating boiler cast iron or steel?

92. If it is a steel boiler, does it have a Steel Boiler Institute (SBI) seal?

93. Are modern baseboard radiators used? What kind: cast iron or nonferrous?

94. If baseboard radiators are used, do they have an IBR (Institute of Boiler and Radiator Mfrs.) seal (noted in manufacturer's literature)?

95. Which is cheaper locally, gas or oil heat?

96. If oil heat is used, is the equipment one of the new high-efficiency "forced-draft" brands?

97. Electric heat: What will it cost to operate?

98. Is the house well enough insulated for electric heat?

99. Are good-quality electric heaters chosen? Do you know exactly how they will work? Have you seen them in operation?

100. Heat for new rooms: Can such space be heated by your present house-heating system? Is the house system large enough to handle the new rooms, as well as the rest of the house?

101. What is your choice for an individual room heater—electric, gas, or oil? This hinges on total cost of installation and operating cost, as well as personal preference.

102. Will you need a chimney, flue vent, air intake?

103. Heating miscellaneous: Will zone control of the heating system give you better, more uniform house heating?

104. Is the thermostat located in a representative location? Is it free from outside air drafts and extraneous heat influences?

Insulation

105. Are all parts of the house or a new addition insulated properly—walls, ceilings, concrete floor, crawl-space, walls between garage and house, etc.?

106. What kind of insulation is being used? Is it rotproof, bugproof, and fire resistant?

107. Is enough insulation being used? Does it conform with the recommended minimum R values?

108. Does the insulation come with an integral vapor barrier?

109. Is the insulation being properly installed (according to the manufacturer's instructions)?

Wiring

110. Rewiring: Is a new, main electric board large enough for the house? Does it have extra capacity for major appliances or air conditioning you may buy later? Is its capacity at least 220 volts and 100 amperes —more for large houses or with special electrical equipment?

111. Are you getting at least 10 to 12 individual circuits (circuit breakers or fuses)? Are there spare circuits for future equipment needs?

112. Will outlets and switches be installed everywhere you need them?

113. Have you made a wiring plan and noted the location of all outlets, switches, special lights, and other features desired?

114. Have you thought of such features as silent switches, multiple-switch control, closet lights, and strip outlets for kitchen appliances?

Termites and Wood Rot

115. Does your house require termite safeguards?

116. If safeguards are required, as in most states, are they being provided when you add new rooms to your house? What kind of protection—soil poisoning (usually best), treated lumber, capped foundation walls, termite shields?

117. If you discover termite damage: Have you called in a reputable termite man, and preferably two or three of them for advice and bids?

118. Is the damage really caused by termites, or by wood rot, carpenter ants, or other bugs?

119. Have you taken proper measures to prevent recurrence of the damage? Do you have a termite service contract?

Buying a New Water Heater

120. Is the heater tank capacity 40 gallons or more and large enough for your house and family?

121. What kind of tank: galvanized iron, ordinary glass, good glass, aluminum, copper? Is it the best kind for your type of water?

122. How long is the water heater guaranteed?

123. If the water heater is part of the regular heating boiler, does it have adequate capacity?

124. Does it have an IWH (Indirect Water Heater) stamp?

Ventilating Fans for Attic, Kitchen, and Bathroom

125. Attic fan: Does it have adequate capacity for your house, based on a one-minute air change in the South, up to two minutes in the North?

126. Is the fan's cfm capacity based on a *ventilating* rating? It should not be a free-air or circulating rating.

127. Does the fan design and construction conform to Commercial Standard GS 178–51?

128. Is the fan located for plenty of air flow through all rooms?

129. Is the installation designed for quiet and efficient operation?

130. Are inlet and outlet openings large enough?

131. Does the fan motor have a thermal safety cut-off switch?

132. Are provisions made for automatic closing of the attic floor opening in case of fire?

133. Does the fan have a two-speed control?

134. Kitchen and bathroom fans: Is the fan large enough for the room?

135. Is it properly located?

136. Will it operate quietly?

137. With a combination fan-heater-light in the bathroom, can each feature work independently of the others and independently of the main light switch?

Central Air Conditioning and the Heat Pump

138. Central air conditioning (including a heat pump): Have you obtained two or three bids from top-flight experienced dealers? Does the dealer chosen handle a well-known national brand?

139. Is the equipment properly sized for your house, neither too large nor too small? Will it maintain your house at 75 degrees and 50 per cent relative humidity on the hottest days experienced in your climate?

140. Is the house adequately insulated for low-cost air conditioning? Will more insulation reduce the size, as well as the operating cost, of the air-conditioning system?

141. Will the system operate quietly? Is the compressor located outdoors? Have you seen and heard the same equipment operate in another house, or inquired about its noise level? Is it located where its operating noise will not bother neighbors?

142. Does the equipment carry the approval seal of the Air-Conditioning and Refrigeration Institute (ARI)?

143. Is the ductwork designed for quiet and efficient air distribution?

144. Is the ductwork insulated where it travels through un-air-conditioned spaces, such as the attic, garage, or crawl-space?

145. Does your house require thermostatic zoning? The answer is generally yes in two-story, split-level, and large, spread-out one-story houses.

146. The heat pump: In addition to the above, does the equipment have adequate winter heating capacity for the house?

147. What will winter heating cost? (This is highly important because it is electric heat.)

148. Have you asked other owners of similar equipment about their experiences with it? Are they satisfied? What are their operating bills, particularly for winter heating?

Room Air Conditioners

149. Is the unit certified by NEMA (National Electrical Manufacturers Assn.)?

150. Does it have enough Btu capacity for the room?

151. Does it operate quietly? Have you heard it run, and also listened to other makes?

152. What kind of service and guarantee will you get?

153. Will the unit require new wiring, or will it operate from an existing electrical outlet?

154. Does the unit incorporate automatic thermostatic control, adjustable air distribution, convenient controls, provisions for ventilation, accessible filters, rustproof construction?

Quieting a Noisy House

155. Specifically, what kinds of noise do you wish to quell—radio or TV, appliances, children indoors or out, street traffic?

156. If it is indoor noise, is it particularly bad because of few rugs, little upholstered furniture, and many hard surfaces around? If so, can it be softened by the addition of rugs, drapes, and acoustical tile?

157. Is it noise transmitted from one part of the house to another?

158. Can it be reduced in transit by rugs, acoustical tile, or a heavy barrier, such as book shelves to block it?

159. If the noise is created by equipment or appliances, can you quiet the mechanism?

160. If you need acoustical tile: Is it chiefly to reduce noise originating within the room where it will be installed?

161. Have you chosen a type that is rugged as well as attractive?

162. If moisture and water are present, is it a kind that is moisture resistant?

163. Have you considered soundproof construction for reducing noise in a new room or new addition?

164. Are new rooms located so that noisy activities will be isolated from rooms in which quiet surroundings are desired?

165. Do you choose new equipment and new appliances that are quiet in operation?

166. Is new equipment or a new appliance installed properly for quiet operation?

Dry Air and Humidifiers

167. Do you really have an excessive dry-air condition in winter?

168. How low is your relative humidity, as determined by a good hygrometer?

169. If so and you need a humidifier, should it be for the whole house, or merely for one or two rooms (a bedroom, for example)?

170. If needed for the whole house, are you getting the proper size for your house? See chart in Chapter 27.

171. Is it centrally located for good moisture distribution?

172. Does it have a water connection and a humidistat control for automatic operation?

173. Is it a well-made humidifier that will not clog up, due to minerals in your water, and not require frequent service?

174. If the humidifier is to be connected to your furnace, has it been oversized to compensate for intermittent furnace operation?

175. Portable humidifiers for single rooms: Is it well-made equipment?

176. Does it have humidistat control for automatic operation?

177. Is there any possibility that the moisture generated will endanger the house structure?

178. Does the house have vapor barriers? Or will you need them?

Choosing a Reputable Contractor or Repairman

179. Is he a specialist in the kind of work you require?

180. How do you know? Have you checked his references?

181. Have you talked with other families he has done work for and seen examples of his work?

182. How long has he been established in your area?

183. Does he have an office, or does he work out of a telephone booth?

184. Have you checked his bank references, not only his bank for deposits but the banks that handle his finance papers?

185. Have you checked on him with the Better Business Bureau, the Chamber of Commerce, or other similar groups?

186. Does he carry liability and workmen's compensation insurance?

187. Have you obtained bids from two or three contractors?

188. Does your contract spell out precisely all material and work to be provided, with exact dimensions and specifications?

189. Does the contract specify the exact kind of products to be furnished with brand name, size, type, and model?

190. Does it also specify work and materials *not* included, those things which you are to furnish?

191. Does it provide for cleanup and removal of debris?

192. Will the contractor provide complete working plans?

193. How long will the job take? Don't expect work to begin tomorrow and be completed a day later. On the other hand, an approximate completion date should be given and adhered to, give or take a few days.

Saving Money by Off-Season Buying

194. When is the best time of the year for the work you plan?

195. Have you planned, accordingly, to have your work done when contractors are plentiful and their prices lowest?

196. Or can you save money and get a better job by timing your work sooner or later than originally planned to avoid the rush season for that particular work? Have you discussed this with contractors?

Financing Home Improvements and Repairs

197. If your work is to be financed: What is the best kind of loan for the amount of money involved?

198. Have you weighed the pros and cons of the different loans available?

199. Can you do better by obtaining your own financing?

200. Is mortgage financing better for you than a higher-interest, conventional home-improvement loan?

201. Exactly how much interest is being charged?

202. Are you sure it is the total actual interest (not the add-on or discount rate)?

203. Besides interest, are any other credit or finance charges buried in the contract?

204. Have you shopped several banks for the best terms available, at least by phone?

205. Have you tried a credit union?

206. On a comparatively small job, can you obtain a low 5 per cent interest personal loan?

207. On a large job, can you finance it with an open-end provision in your present mortgage?

208. Or can you obtain a 6 per cent FHA 203 (k) home-improvement mortgage?

Avoiding the Outright Gyp Firm

209. Are you being high-pressured into buying on a salesman's first call? If so, don't buy.

210. Does the offer sound like a glittering bargain that you can't pass up and should buy instantly? If so, beware.

211. Are you being offered a "special low price?" If so watch out. Price the same work with other firms so you know approximately what it should cost.

212. Does the salesman glowingly say that he will use your house as a "model house" and promise you $50 to $100 or more for every customer obtained as a result of seeing your job? If so, show him out promptly, regardless of how persuasive he sounds. This is the oldest con game in the business.

213. Are you being pressured into signing by a salesman who says immediate repairs are urgent or your furnace may explode, your chimney topple, or collapse? Don't do it. Put him off and call in an expert, or a reliable person who can advise you.

214. Have you forced yourself to read every word of the contract? This may be a chore but it can save you hundreds of dollars, as well as saving yourself great trouble and anguish later. And be sure you do *not* sign the completion certificate at the same time you sign the sales order —that waits until the job is done.

Avoiding Home Repair Bills

215. Are you beset by frequent equipment breakdowns and home repair needs? Why? What kind of troubles seem to recur?

216. Have you discussed such troubles with service people for advice on preventative maintenance and what to do to minimize such troubles?

217. Have you referred to the manufacturers' instructions for your equipment and appliances? What do they say about operating procedure, periodic adjustments, and lubrication?

218. Do you make regular inspections of your house and its structure for incipient damage—termites, wood rot, suspicious cracks, broken shingles, and so on?

INDEX

Acoustical tile, 79, 289, 290–93
Acrylic paints, 174–76
Advertisements, "bait," for kitchen cabinets, 120; for storm windows, 152; "bait and switch," 321–22
Agriculture, Department of, exterior stain of, 179–80
Air conditioners, attic, 274
Air conditioning, use of storm windows with, 152; with new warm-air heating systems, 198; central systems, 263–77; health advantages of, 263–64; air-cooled, 266, 274; cost of, 267–71, chart, 270; room coolers, 271, 278–80; chilled water, 273–74; water cooled, 274–75; maintenance of, 330
Air-Conditioning and Refrigeration Institute, seal of, 276; heat gain computation form of, 278
Air ducts, for heating, 191, 196, diagrams, 213; for air conditioning, 265, 272–74
Alkyd paints, 176
Allied Homeowner's Association, 306, 307
Aluminum, as window frames, 149–50; as storm window frames, 152; as roofing, 184–87
Aluminum foil. *See* Insulation
American Gas Association, emblem of, 196, 199
American Institute of Architects, as source of names of architects interested in remodeling, 53
American Society of Mechanical Engineers, *h* insignia of, 199; fan capacity certified by, 257
Ants, flying, 239; carpenter, 243
Appliances, kitchen, 114–18
Architects, discussed, 52–54; fees charged by, 53; how to choose, 53
Asbestos-cement, as interior wall material, 167; as exterior wall material, 169
Asphalt shingles, as roofing, 181–82
Asphalt tile, as flooring, 162–63
Attics, how to check, 35; conversion of into living space, 65–68; how to plan stairs to, 67; heating and cooling in, 67–68; maintenance of, 330
Attic vents, importance of with foil insulation, 221, 267; diagrams of types of, 246
Awning windows, 147–48

Banks, as sources of loans, 315, 316–17
Basements, water problems in, 33, 72–74; conversion into living space, 69–71
Bath-O-Lett, 127–28
Bathroom fixtures, best placement of, 129; importance of choosing good quality, 129–30, bathtubs, 130; washbowls, 130–32; toilets, 132–33; faucets, 133–34; shower nozzles, 134–35; showers, 135–36
Bathrooms, discussed, 97, 122–41; inadequacy of in old houses, 35; Ann David on, 123–26; half baths, 127–28; best locations for, 128–29; costs of new, 128; minimum size for, 129; interior planning of, 129; importance of quality in fixtures for, 129–30; bathtubs, 130; washbowls, 130–32; lavatory cabinets, 131; toilets, 132–33; faucets, 133–34; shower heads, 134; safety features for showers, 134–35; shower stall units, 135–36; walls, 136–37; floors, 137–38; compartmented, 138; garden plan, 138–39; decorating, 139; special features for, 139–40; lighting for, 139–40; auxiliary heating for, 140; preventing toilet tank dripping in, 140; hot water circulating lines for, 141; booklets on, 141
Bathtubs, 130
Bedrooms, 83–84
Beech, as flooring, 161
Better Business Bureaus, 303, 319, 320
Birch, as flooring, 161
Blowers, belt-driven furnace, 195; direct-drive furnace, 195
Boilers, hot-water, how to buy, 198–99
Borer, Old House, 243–44
Brand names, importance of, in windows, 149; in heating, 195, 199; in insulation, 226; in air conditioning, 275
Brick, for exterior walls, 169–70

chart, 178; cleaner, 175; primers, 175, 176; importance of using proper type of, 180; importance of following directions in using, 180, list of pamphlets on, 180; rackets in sale of, 323
Paneling, used on basement walls, 71
Panelite. *See* Plastic laminate
Panels, prefabricated exterior wall, 169
Patios, best locations for, 46–47
Peninsula cabinets, in kitchens, 108
Perimeter duct systems, 196–97, diagrams, 213
Perlite. *See* Insulation
Permits, building, necessity for, 58–59
Pine, as flooring, 161
Plans, original house, importance of checking before remodeling, 59
Plaster, as wall material, 166
Plastic laminate, used on kitchen countertops, 110
Plastic panels, as interior wall material, 167
Plastic tile, as interior wall material, 167
Plumbers, how to find good, 122
Plumbing, poor, in old houses, 32; how to check quality of, 32; fixtures, 129–35; problems with, 135; maintenance of 328
Plumbing vent stacks, 67, 128
Plywood, in basements, 71; as exterior wall material, 168
Polystyrene, expanded. *See* Insulation
Porcelain enamel, in bathroom bowls, 131; used as prefabricated panels for exterior walls, 169
Porches, best locations for, 46–47; privacy on, 89–90; specifications for, 91–92; heating converted, 93–94; cost of remodeling, 94
Powder rooms, 127–28
Prefabrication, in bathrooms, 136; of exterior wall panels, 169
Privacy, importance of considering when building new porches or patios, 89–90
Private zone, 44
Public health department, as source of information on septic tank problems, 32
Public zone, 44
Pump, circulator, 208
PVC paints, 174–76

Rackets, kitchen remodeling, 120; paint, 180; furnace dismantling, 321; "model" home, 320–21; "bait and switch," 321–22; chimney repair, 322; loan, 322;

"low-balling," 323; termite exterminating, 322–23; fire alarm, 323–24
Radiant heat, 31, 201–2
Radiators, 199–200
Range center, in kitchens, 104, 106
Ranges, 115–16
Recovery rate, of water heaters, 249
Redwood, as exterior wall material, 168
Refrigerators, 116–17
Refrigerator work center, in kitchens, 104, 106
Remodeling, when you should consider, 17; cost of *vs.* buying new house, 18–19; disadvantages of, 21; how much to spend on, 21; costs of, 23–24
Remote control lighting, 236
Repairs, frequency of various types of, 35–36
Resale value, 23
Resistane, 120
Roof drains, 73
Roof gutters, how to check, 32, importance of for dry basement, 73; maintenance of, 328
Roofing, built-up, 183; roll, 183
Roofing materials, 181–87
Roofs, how to check, 32; problems with, caused by climatic conditions, 33–34; in new additions, 57; overhangs, as shading devices, 147; significance of leaky, 181; low-slope, 183; flat, 183; colors, 187; maintenance of, 329–30
Room coolers. *See* Air conditioning
Room heaters, 201, 204, 207
Rubber paints, 174–76
Rubber tile, as flooring, 161
"R" value, in insulation, 222–24

Sacrificial rod, in water heaters, 251
Safety, in bathrooms, 134–35, 140, 262
Savings account loans, 316
Scoreboard, 220
Septic tanks, troubles with, 32, 33; importance of knowing location of, 57; maintenance of, 328–29
Service zone, 44
Serving center, in kitchens, 104, 106
Setbacks, 58
Shading devices, 147
Shakes, as siding, 169; as roofing, 183–84
Shingles, asbestos-cement, as siding, 169, as roofing, 184–85; wood, as siding, 169, as roofing, 183–84; asphalt, as roofing, 181–83; self-sealing, 182, interlocking, 182; aluminum, as roofing, 186–87